AF615625

ZEPPELIN!

The Schütte-Lanz SL 1, which made very many flights in civilian hands before being handed over to the Imperial German Army in 1914.

ZEPPELIN!

The German Airship Story

Manfred Griehl and Joachim Dressel

ARMS AND
ARMOUR

First published in Great Britain in 1990 by Arms & Armour Press, Villiers House, 41/47 Strand, London WC2N 5JE

Distributed in the USA by Sterling Publishing Co. Inc., 387 Park Avenue South, New York, NY 10016-8810.

Distributed in Australia by Capricorn Link (Australia) Pty Ltd, P.O. Box 665, Lane Cove, New South Wales 2066

British Library Cataloguing in Publication data:
Griehl, Manfred
Zeppelin: the German airship story
1. Germany, Kriegsmarine. Naval airships, history
I. Title II. Dressel, Joachim
940.44943

ISBN 1-85409-045-3

Typeset by Typesetters (Birmingham) Ltd.
Reproduction by M&E Reproductions, North Fambridge, Essex
Printed and bound in Great Britain by The Bath Press, Avon

CONTENTS

Preface 7

Early German Airships 8
- The first step: balloons 8
- The observation balloon in action 9
- Hänlein 17
- Wölfert 18
- Schwarz 21

The Constructors and their Ships 24
- Parseval 24
- Clouth 35
- Siemens-Schuckert 37
- Transatlantische Fluggesellschaft München 'Suchard' 39
- Gross-Basenach 39
- Erbslöh 45
- Ruthenberg 48
- Veeh 49
- Steffen 50
- Zorn & Hense 50
- Schütte-Lanz 51
- *Graf* Zeppelin 60

German Airships in Combat 76
- A new kind of air war 76
- A short history of the *Heeresluftschiffe* 78
- Airships of the *Reichskriegsmarine* 92
- The Leader and his crews 104
- The end 113

German Civil Airships 118
- From DELAG to DZR 118
- ZR III 119
- The Zeppelin abroad 122
- LZ 127 *Graf Zeppelin* 123
- LZ 129 Hindenberg 128
- LZ 130 *Graf Zeppelin* (II) 132
- LZ 131 135
- The transworld airship projects 136
- German airships after 1945 137

Conclusion 140
- Military airships 140
- Civil airships 141

Appendices 142
- I. Career details of Zeppelin airships 142
- II. Career details of Schütte-Lanz airships 154
- III. Specifications of Zeppelin airships 156
- IV. Specifications of Schütte-Lanz airships 158

Select Bibliography 159

Glossary 159

Index 159

The cradle of the dirigible airship was the city of Mainz and its ingenious inventor was Paul Hänlein.

Professor Hergesell, 1909

The airship, developed thanks to Graf Zeppelin's ingenious mind and persistence, has been honed into a sharp weapon by *Fregattenkapitän* Peter Strasser, the Leader of Airships (FdL), despite all the setbacks suffered along the way . . . Graf Zeppelin's name will live on as that of a famous inventor, while Peter Strasser will be remembered as the most important leader of the German Zeppelin Force.

Admiral Scheer, 1918

PREFACE

The region around Frankfurt, Mainz and Mannheim was one of the early and important centres of airship activity and of aviation in general. It is reported that the French armed forces first used fixed balloons during the siege of Mainz by German and Austrian troops in 1793. About eighty years later a young inventor from Mainz, Paul Hänlein, proposed a modern airship which was then built and flown on several occasions in Austria. Professor Schütte, born in 1873, produced most of his twenty ships at Rheinau near Mannheim, and von Parseval was born nearby at Frankenthal in 1861. The *Internationale Luftfahrt Ausstellung* (ILA) at Frankfurt in 1909 inspired not just the spectators; all the exhibitors and flyers – Clouth, Ruthenberg, von Parseval and von Zeppelin – found it a new experience and could compare notes extensively

From that time onwards, airship aviation leapt forward, and dirigibles became more and more familiar. During 1909 the airship PL III appeared at Mainz–Gonsenheim, and in 1914 one of the first von Parseval/von Sigsfeld *Drachenballone* was based at the birthplace of one of the authors, where, furthermore, the legendary Jakob Goedecker worked on his aircraft just before the First World War. Some momentous events took place only a few hundred yards from this author's home and these ignited his interest in aviation and, in particular, German airships. His collection of all kinds of authentic material on the subject began in 1965, and this book, drawing on information compiled these past twenty-five years, looks at the development of German manned airship aviation, including the observation balloons used by the German Army until the end of the First World War.

We tender our grateful thanks to *Frau* Rangnick and *Herr* Wagner of AEG, Frankfurt; Clouth AG, Cologne; *Herr* H. P. Dabrowski; *Herr* J. Meier, for access to the archives of the Deutsche Aero Club eV, at Frankfurt, *Dr* Wustrack of Flughafen Frankfurt AG; *Frau* M. Emmerling; *Herr* F. Güstrow; the Landesarchiv, Berlin, together with the Museum für Verkehr and Technik in Berlin; *Herr* P. Petrick; *Herr* H. Riediger; *Herr* H. Schliephake; *Herr* F. Selinger; *Frau* Glaser of Siemens AG; *Dr* Illner of the Historisches Archiv der Stadt Köln; *Herr* Brumby of the Stadtarchiv in Mainz; and *Frau* Aurandt of the Stadtarchiv in Frankenthal. All these people generously allowed us to utilize photographs or information they had been compiling for many years. We would further like to express our sincere thanks to those friends and archivists in England and Germany who kindly offered their assistance while this book was being prepared. As well as *Herr* D. Herwig of the Deutsches Studienbüro für Luftfahrt, and especially *Herr* B. Lange, we wish to thank *Herren* D. and P. Schreiber and also Mr C. E. Charles, *Herr* J. Menke, *Herr* H. J. Nowarra, Mr F. Marshall, *Herr* H. J. Meier, *Herr* H. H. Stapfer and *Herr* F. Trenkle. We are especially indebted to *Dr* Heinrichs, *Dipl-Ing*. Pölitsch and *Herr* Limmer of the Deutsches Museum, München, Mr R. Forsyth, *Frau* Beck of the Stadtarchiv in Friedrichschafen, *Frau* Benz of the Stadtarchiv in Mannheim, *Herr* Geier of the Stadtarchiv in Worms, *Frau* Spiegel of the Stadtarchiv in Wiesbaden, *Professor* Klötzel and *Frau* Reich of the Stadtarchiv in Frankfurt, the Wehrbereichsbibliothek IV, *Frau* Knebel, and Zentralbibliothek of the Bundeswehr in Düsseldorf and our good friend John Provan, together with *Dr* Balmer of MTU Friedrichshafen and *Herr* Saute of the Zeppelin-Werke, for their considerable help concerning all kinds of airship aviation. We also have to thank the people who could have reported the true facts of their own eventful lives but who have, sadly, died during the last few years – *Dr* O. Dieckerhoff and *Dipl-Ing*. Zucker, who rendered much assistance to the authors.

Finally, we would be very grateful for any further information concerning the development of airships and the correction of any errors that may occur in the following pages.

Manfred Griehl and Joachim Dressel
Mainz, December 1989

EARLY GERMAN AIRSHIPS

The first step: balloons

During a cold winter's day in 1782 Joseph Montgolfier was sitting in front of his fireplace when he noticed that small particles were being raised by the hot gases going up the chimney. Intrigued, he constructed a cube-shaped body, filled it with hot air and watched it float through his living room. Then, that December, he and his brother Etienne repeated the experiment using a fabric cube with an inner diameter of about one metre and on 14 December another, larger one followed. The brothers needed some months to construct a huge 900m^3 balloon, which they displayed at Annonay on 4 June 1783 in the presence of a host of local officials.

Some weeks later, near Paris, Professor César Charles and the Robert brothers succeeded in getting their own unmanned balloon to lift off when filled with hydrogen gas. One further experiment failed on 12 September 1783, but later three animals were the first passengers to fly, in a balloon named *Martial* – an event witnessed at Versailles by Louis XVI and many other important people. The balloon landed safely near Paris. Meanwhile a real competition between the Montgolfiers and Professor Charles had got under way, and the contrasting uses of hydrogen and hot air enabled the development of each kind of balloon to be compared.

Although Professor Charles had his men worked day and night, the Montgolfiers were still able to achieve the first manned flight in the history of aviation when Pilatre de Rozier rose in a *Montgolfier*, held by a thin rope, up to an altitude of 25m. The first untethered flight took place a short time later, on 21 November 1783, when de Rozier and the Marquis d'Arlandes rose from the gardens of La Muette near Paris, crossed the River Seine and landed 25 minutes later near Croule-Barbe.

Only a few days after this, Count Francesco Zambeccari released an unmanned hot air balloon into the sky from the Artillery Ground near London; on 25 November a second followed. The Count was to lose both his money and his life trying to realize his dream of a dirigible balloon. Meanwhile Professor Charles was ready for the first manned balloon flight. He flew to Nesle, where his companion Nöel Robert left the balloon, and Charles climbed again, reaching an altitude of almost 3,000m. More flights were undertaken by balloon systems similar to those built by both pioneers.

In 1785 Meusnier was the first to record some theories about a practicable dirigible balloon but he could find no suitable means of propulsion other than the wind, whose strength and direction were unreliable. Nevertheless many other engineers and wealthy citizens were now beginning to take a keen interest in aviation, even though the dangers resulting from the quality of early balloons were considerable. Despite the disaster which befell Pilatre de Rozier and Pierre Romain on 15 June 1785, it was impossible to stem the tremendous euphoria associated with all kinds of ballooning.

The first unmanned balloon activities in Germany were announced at Nuremberg on 18 February 1786: after experiencing some problems at Hamburg, Blancard made a number of successful flights at Hamburg and Aachen throughout that year. By the end of the century the balloon had become more reliable, using fabrics and equipment of higher quality. After more than two dozen flights by different airmen, the balloon saw military action during the siege of Mainz-on-Rhine by German forces. The French *Général* d'Oye surrendered on 23 July 1794, but by then the military potential of the 'secret weapon' was established and in August Guyton de Morveau proposed that the 'Mosel Army' be equipped with balloons for reconnaissance purposes. The first German to take off in such a balloon was Wilhelm Jungius, who reached the incredible altitude of 6,500m over Berlin on 16 September 1805. His feat was followed by that of Bittdorf at Leipzig, who unfortunately lost his life during his thirtieth flight on 16 July 1812.

Four years later, in 1816, Pauly and Egg

proposed their own dirigible airship, but, just as Meusniers had discovered 32 years earlier, no reliable propulsion system was available. A period of 36 years was to pass before Henry Giffard was ready to demonstrate such a vehicle, on 24 September 1852. His airship was 44m long and had a diameter of 12m. It was propelled by a small steam engine producing about 3hp. On the completion of his first series of tests, Giffard built a second ship, but the output from its engine was still too low to enable the ship to make any headway against the wind. He conducted some trials using a new hydrogen system, but these failed, and although Giffard continued thereafter to construct balloons, his interest in dirigible airships waned.

The observation balloon in action

Balloons were used on a larger scale during the Franco-Prussian War. The French established their first military balloon unit in 1877 at Meudon, and this was expanded in 1901 to become the first fully fledged French airship battalion, comprising four companies; five years later a development unit, together with a training formation, was raised. In the United Kingdom the first military balloon unit was established in 1879 at Chatham; it became a balloon company, consisting of five sections, in about 1908.

In Prussia an airship unit was officially created on 9 May 1884, the establishment being installed three years later in the barracks near the Tempelhofer parade ground outside Berlin. In 1894 the *Luftschiffer-Lehranstalt*, a training division, was set up. In 1901 one *Luftschifferbataillon*, comprising two *Luftschiffer-Kompanien* and a *Bespannungs-Abteilung*, was based at Reinikendorf, west of the German capital. The oft-mentioned *Luftschiffer-Bataillons* Nos 2 to 5 were concerned only with genuine airships. Besides the Prussian unit, the Bavarian HQ raised its own unit, the *Bayrische Luftschiffertruppe*, which was the successor to the former *Luftschiffer-Lehrabteilung* constituted in 1890 and was staffed only by a captain, two lieutenants, four NCOs and 26 men.

The common balloon was eventually phased out in favour of the well-known *Drachenballon*, the invention of von Parseval and von Sigsfeld. *Major* Richard von Koehler has described the main advantages of the *Drachenballon*:

> Normally the fixed *Kugel-Ballon* could be used only in wind speeds of between 8 and 10m/sec. The observation gondola could be operated in speeds up to double this, with great success, but not on days when the wind blew at more than 20m/sec. On the other hand, the *Drachenballon* could be flown at a greater altitude than the early German military balloons. In an exercise

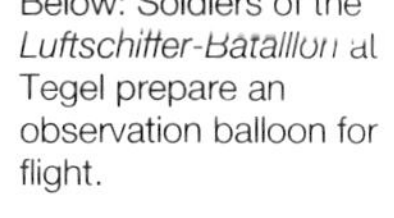

Below: Soldiers of the *Luftschiffer-Bataillon* at Tegel prepare an observation balloon for flight.

Left: Inflating a *Kugelballon* at Berlin.

on the Kniebis Mountain in 1897, two men ascended in a ball balloon near Oppenau. After leaving the calm valley at an altitude of about 800m, the fixed balloon was spun around and was thrown downwards, finally hitting the ground. In another test the balloon was blown back again, and it was therefore taken in and deflated. Then the *Drachenballon* was readied for action. Neither the anabatic winds nor the higher wind speeds affected the ascent of the balloon. The fixed *Drachenballon* gained sufficient height, 1,100m, but there was too much fog to continue the reconnaissance.

After the exercise most of the officers believed that the ball balloon did not have any great future and could be used only for training purposes or as a *Festungs-Ballon*. Domestic gas was produced in military factories and was available nearly everywhere in Germany, but the large gasometers were vulnerable to enemy artillery fire and therefore hydrogen was stockpiled at military bases, while factories were built for producing hydrogen exclusively for military purposes. There was enough canvas in reserve for the construction of new observation balloons.

The so-called *Drachenballon* constructed by von Parseval made some tethered flights with the Bavarian Princes Arnulf, Alfons and Georg (and, occasionally, Princess Clara) aboard. An involuntary balloon trip was taken in 1906 when Görgen and Plep, two newly trained *Luftschiffer*, ascended at Reinikendorf near Berlin. The wind veered to the south, and they soon found themselves over the Baltic Sea! They jettisoned all superfluous ballast, and finally their own gondola, and just managed to reach Sweden. After returning to Germany the two soldiers had to continue their ascent under supervision at Berlin, it being considered necessary that all men trained for tethered ballooning knew what to do in the event of their own balloon losing its mooring rope and flying away.

Although the Prussian Army lost one of its best officers, von Sigsfeld, in a balloon accident near Antwerp on 1 February 1902, the progress made with both fixed and mobile balloons accelerated. *Hauptmann* Hans Bartsch von Sigsfeld, for example, a good friend of von Parseval, belonged to a small group of inspired inventors and enthusiastic promoters of ballooning, and at the time of his sudden death some hundreds of ascents were taking place every year. Berson and

Below: Two balloons, based at the Tempelhofer Feld near Berlin, photographed in 1896 just prior to an ascent.

Above: The equipment of *Luftschiffer-Bataillon Nr 1* at Berlin-Tegel. The carriages were used for transporting the balloon, the baskets and the gas containers.

Süring, two Germans, were decorated for ascending to 10,800m and setting a world altitude record. Between 13 and 17 December 1913 von Kaulen spent 87 hours in the air and achieved the record for the longest time spent in the basket of a balloon, while on 18 February 1914 von Berliner covered a distance of 3,052km in his balloon – the third world record held by a German *Luftschiffer*.

By this time the old ball balloon was used for training purposes only. The *Drachenballon* was more manoeuvrable and showed a much superior general performance, and therefore the German military authorities demanded that all *Feld-Luftschiffer-Abteilungen* (FLA) be equipped with the type; moreover, such units should be independent, carrying all the necessary equipment for operations in the event of action in the field. Thus a *Feld-Luftschiffer-Abteilung* was provided with the following horse-drawn carriages, supporting the use of two *Drachenballone*:

- twelve carriages each with 20 gas canisters (6 horses);
- two carriages to transport the balloon material (6 horses);
- one carriage with a fixed winch (6 horses);
- one carriage with the men's personal baggage (2 horses);
- one carriage with all necessary provisions (2 horses); and
- one carriage with forage for the horses (4 horses)

A total of 89 men belonged to each *Abteilung* – one sergeant, two further NCOs, 72 men sitting on the horses and the carriages and seven officers with their own horses, together with the *Abteilungsführer*, two lieutenants and four observation officers. When the First World War broke out in August 1914, eight Prussians together with two Bavarian *Feld-Luftschiffer-Abteilungen* were in existence. Each of them was enlarged to comprise ten officers and sergeants, 270 men, 194 horses and 35 carriages, and in addition there were seventeen *Feld-Luftschiffer-Trupps*, each equipped with one balloon.

Because many commanding officers believed that the employment of tethered balloons would bring appropriate enemy

Far right: A *Drachenballon* of the first *Luftschiffer* unit at Berlin.

Left: A *Drachenballon* being prepared for action under field conditions in central Germany about 1910.
Below left: A balloon being transported from its field base.
Right: An observation balloon of *Feld-Luftschiffer-Abteilung Nr 12* behind the Eastern Front, 1915–16.
Below: A *Drachenballon* being used under field conditions behind the front line near Swilowka.

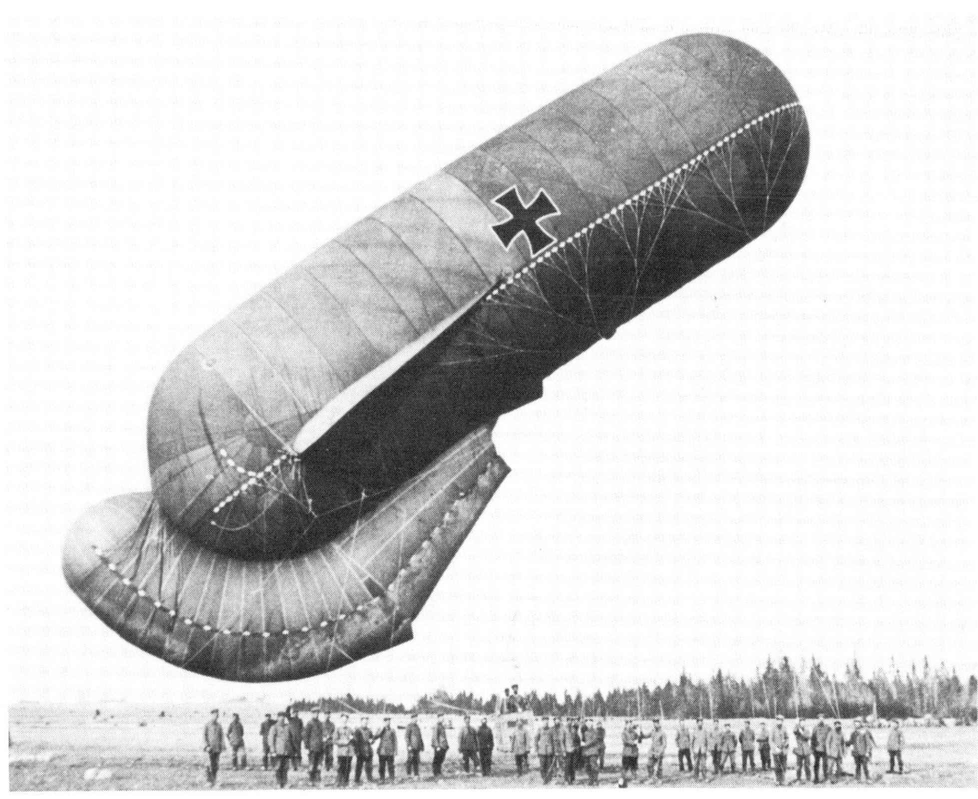

conditions for manned ballooning seemed to be far better, but because of the long lines of communication the necessary supplies took a great deal of time to arrive. However, the losses in the east were fewer in number than those affecting the *Luftschiffer* in Western Europe.

From May 1916 the FLA became the target of enemy fighters using incendiary ammunition, and one of the first balloons to be hit was No. 3 of *Abteilung 3*, shot down by a Nieuport on the 22nd of the month. During the summer a series of concentrated attacks was carried out which destroyed many of the observation balloons. The reserves were also badly hit, and for some months the balloons saw very limited service until enough 3.7mm anti-aircraft guns were provided and 08/15 machine guns issued to protect the balloon sites, which were also allocated their own fighter aircraft.

The next step was the introduction of a parachute to save the lives of the experienced officers and NCOs standing in the observation basket. The battle at the Somme had further influenced the development of the *Heeresluftschiffer* formations. With the creation of a uniform structure for all FLAs in the west, von Gallwitz became the first of the staff officers (*Stoluft*) responsible for the tactical observation of strongpoints on the regional

Left: A close-up view of an observation basket. Two soldiers equipped with binoculars stand inside.
Below: This *AE-ballon* operated over the central sector of the Eastern Front during the winter of 1916–17.
Right: Another *AE-ballon,* this one undergoing envelope tests early in 1917.

countermeasures, limited action was reported during the early stages of the war. Moreover, the 600m^3 balloon could reach altitudes of only about 600m, although with new gas and no wind this might increase to 800m. The flying observation post could identify targets for friendly artillerymen to a maximum distance of about 5,000 to 7,000yds behind the enemy lines. Some of the *Feld-Luftschiffer-Abteilungen* got rid of the heavy balloon baskets and achieved greater altitudes with one man flying on a saddle.

From 1915 large, 1,000m^3 balloons arrived at the *Feldluftschiffer*, permitting ascents up to 1,000m and a broader view of the landscape, but they had one great disadvantage: about an hour was needed to bring the balloon back to earth by hand. Until the *Abteilungen* were equipped with a motor-driven winch, the units had to use a turning reel, aided by horses, to bring the observer down. As co-operation between the artillerymen and the *Luftschiffer* grew, allowing heavy guns to be ranged accurately, the balloon was given greater priority. Every *Feld-Luftschiffer-Abteilung* was enlarged from two to three balloons, and at the same time the *Festungs-Luftschiffer-Trupps* were themselves reorganized into *Feld-Luftschiffer-Abteilungen*, thereby raising the number of balloons operated on the Western Front from only nine in August 1914 to more than 80 in November 1915. On the Eastern Front the operational

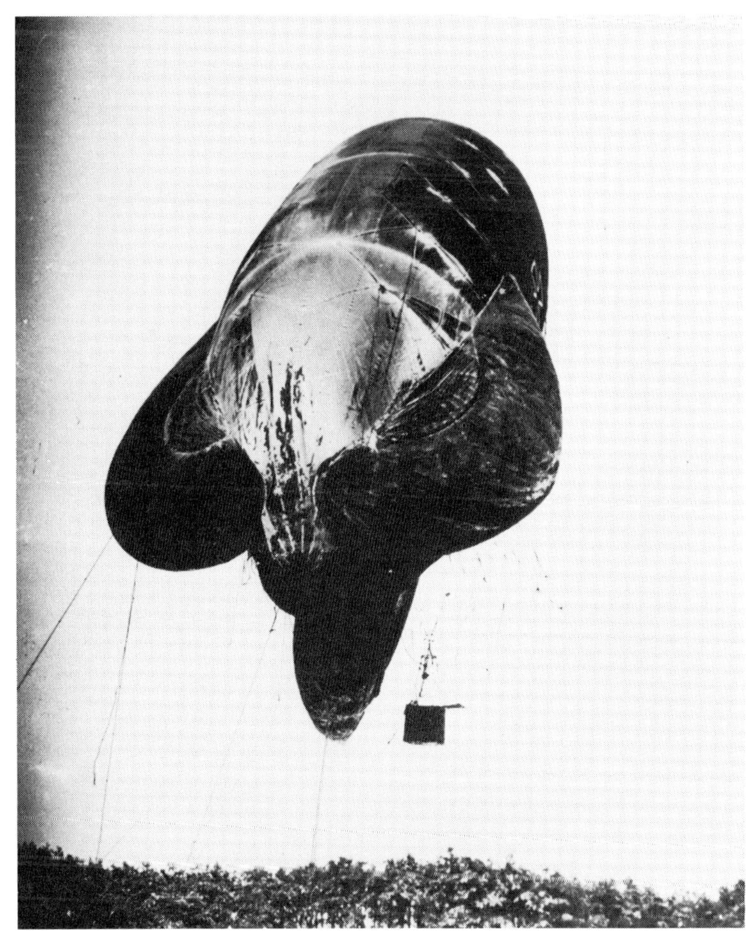

battlefields. At Verdun another *Stoluft* finally established a *Ballonzentrale*, and this example was followed by all the other *Armeeoberkommandos*. The flood of reports arriving for compilation could not be handled, however, and therefore *Gruppenkommandos*, called *Gruppennachrichtenstellen*, were formed and a huge communication network, together with individual signal sections, was immediately set up. During the winter of 1916–17 another reorganization took place: *Abteilungsstäbe* and *Ballonzüge* were formed, the *Ballonzug* becoming the tactical unit, using only one observation balloon. Two to five of these small units were assigned under the command of the *Abteilungsstab*, which was situated at the *General-* or *Gruppenkommando*. Normally each field division had one or two *Ballonzüge*.

Some improvements were noticed by *Hauptmann* Friedrich Stahl, who in 1930 reported many details about the *Fesselballone* used by the German Army during the First World War:

> Concerning equipment, some progress had been made by the beginning of the war. The English type of balloon (850m^3) was smaller than its German counterpart but its performance looked very good. Therefore a captured example was copied as quickly as possible. This *Ae-Ballon* differed from the English one only in minor

Right: A descent from a balloon by parachute, October 1918.
Far right: Defence of balloon bases against enemy aircraft was provided by fixed machine guns.

Left: One of the late *AE* type balloons during trials with a 240hp Maybach piston engine at Munich in November 1918.

detail of quality, brought about by the shortage of high-grade rubber; the German manufacturers were ultimately forced to do without rubber entirely, whenceforth all the *Ae-Ballone* utilized an envelope made from a combination of canvas and Zellon, a synthetic substance. The disadvantage of this was its susceptibility to the influence of the weather and the difficulties of handling it for the ground crew. The first problem was solved when canvas hangars were produced and sent to the front-line units. The *Ballonzüge* were then equipped with a new motor-driven 80hp winch together with stronger cable which enabled the balloons to be flown in higher wind speeds. The new winch carriages were very heavy, requiring a tractor to move them in the field.

Most of the front-line units were issued with this new equipment, and they also received extra personnel, trained by the newly established *Luftschifferschule* at Jüterbog (the school later moved to Namur). In order to preserve intact active balloon formations, officers and men received their instruction in full-scale *Ballontrupps* based behind the Western Front and associated with training divisions and shooting ranges around important French strongholds. Twenty-three *Abteilungsstäbe*, together with 128 *Ballonzüge* and twelve independent *Ballontrupps*, were active at different places by early 1917. During the defensive operations in the West which followed, the observation balloons were used mainly for ranging friendly artillery or for tactical observation. Light signalling was introduced to relay local information to the infantry, but the latter were unable to interpret the signals and this kind of communication was discontinued.

In the summer of 1917 the organization of the balloon units was revised again. The *Oberste Heeresleitung* introduced a *Kommandeur der Luftschiffertruppe (Koluft)*, a commanding officer who was responsible for integrating the balloon forces of his *Ballonzentrale*. Each *Koluft* assumed command over a *Feldluftschifferpark* which was responsible for providing all the supplies from its own pool of *matériel*, the latter being delivered by the home *Inspection der Luftschiffertruppen*. The *Koluft* also commanded the repair shop for the winches and a field production site able to generate about 1,500m^3 of hydrogen gas, sufficient for the regular replenishment of the balloons based nearby and for inflating some of the reserve balloons. Some specialist operators took aloft the new 700mm and 1,200mm cameras which superseded the old 300mm equipment used by the *Luftschiffer*, supplementing observation both by the naked eye and by means of binoculars.

Apart from surveillance in the West, the *Luftschiffer* were also engaged in the struggle raging on the Eastern Front, especially in Serbia and Romania. Here, however, the balloon formations found it very difficult to move their carriages along the muddy roads during wet weather and as a result the units remained far behind the front-line divisions. Later, when the ground froze, the balloon became an important asset both in the Balkans and in Russia. The mountain war in Italy required a different approach. During that campaign six *Ballonzüge* were employed, although here again it was sometimes impossible for the detachments to follow their own units because the heavy equipment could not be transported through the rugged terrain of the Dolomites. A small number of balloons, however, were seconded to the combat divisions.

On 9 November 1918 an *Ae* type balloon (or *K-ballon*) was fitted with a 240hp Maybach engine and tested at Munich, its small gondola containing the motor and the crewmen. Small rudders were added to each side of the hull. However, nothing further became of this vehicle by the end of the war.

By the time hostilities ceased, 56 *Luftschiffer-Abteilungsstäbe*, together with 184 *Ballonzüge*, had seen active service, and by 11 November 1918, the day of the Armistice, a total of 470 observation balloons had been produced and used operationally, plus a number of captured examples. In addition to balloons and airships on the fronts, from 1916 the German Army employed barrage balloons over the Saar to protect important industrial regions against attacking enemy aircraft, especially at Neunkirchen but later also at Diedenhofen, Schleebusch and Leverkusen. Many such 160m^3 balloons were moored, at altitudes of between 2,000 and 3,000m; larger balloons were of course used for the same purpose in the Second World War.

Hänlein

In Germany, one of the first people to direct their thoughts towards a practicable dirigible balloon or airship was Paul Hänlein. He knew of the odd theories of the Austrian Jakob Kaiser, who had suggested that tame eagles could be used to propel his balloon, and the proposals of Jakob Degen, who envisaged a small balloon moved forward by his own muscle power, but neither of these ideas seemed to Hänlein to be the best way to progress.

Paul Hänlein, who seems also to have been well aware of Dupuy de Lôme's dirigible airship design, was born at Mainz. During the siege of the French capital by the Germans in 1870 he first had the idea that balloons could be useful for wide-ranging reconnaissance tasks, able to deliver important information to friendly ground forces, and he displayed his first model airship, in a large market hall near the Rhine, in December that year. The construction of Hänlein's airship differed from that of all others developed by his contemporaries and also introduced entirely new techniques. Hänlein himself stated, on 1 December 1870, that

> 1. The drive unit for my balloon should also be a gas generator, because the engine would use gas taken from the balloon, and it should carry substances other than water for cooling the propulsion plant.
> 2. The archimedean screw [airscrew] should be fitted as close as possible to the bottom of the balloon, but on the front so as to be more effective than the French designs.

After organizing his ideas, he built a scale model of his balloon, 11.8m long and 3.5m in diameter. It was of 'grid' construction instead

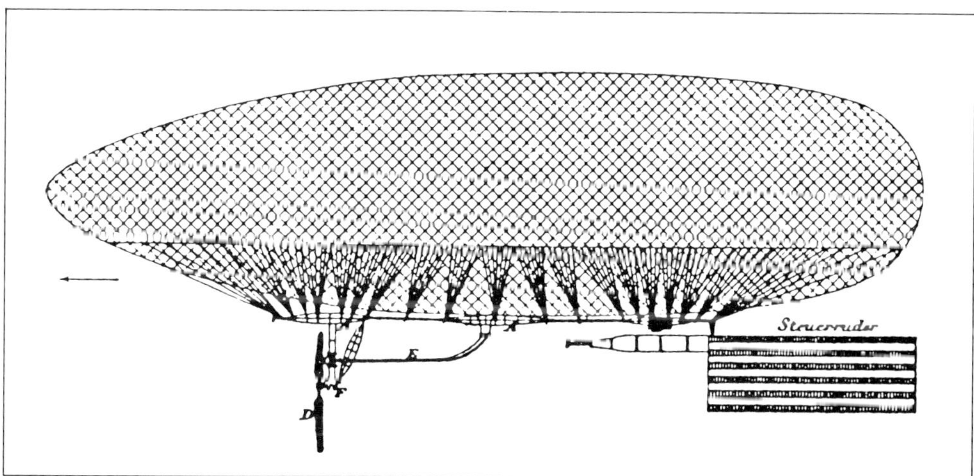

Right: A drawing of Hänlein's first airship model of 1871.

Left: Paul Hänlein's airship at Brünn.

of having a ventral gondola, in order both to strengthen the entire vehicle and to provide a firm structure to support the gas turbine and the rudders. The model was displayed at Mainz Fruit Hall in 1871, but Hänlein failed in his efforts to enlist the financial support he needed to build a full-scale dirigible. He therefore moved to Vienna, where he exhibited a model in the Sophien-Saal, another large hall, and attracted the interest – and backing – of a number of enthusiasts. Thus Hänlein was able to build a large airship, which differed from his small scale models in being cylindrical in shape with conical ends and in having a pusher airscrew. The ship took until November 1872 to build. Meanwhile a large hangar to house it was under construction near the Vienna gas works, but it proved impossible to supply enough gas to fill the ship and so it was transported to Brünn, where it was inflated with coal gas at the Military Riding School. The first trials were carried out on 13 December 1872, both 4–7hp engines driving a two-bladed airscrew of 4.6m diameter. The enlarged rudder system functioned without serious problems.

Hänlein's airship had a diameter of 9.2m and a length of about 50m. The expected altitude could not be reached since the gas that was used proved denser than calculated, although in late December 1872 the ship succeeded in carrying out a second short flight, demonstrating a speed of 5.2m/sec (about 10kt). Hänlein next proposed substituting hydrogen gas, but he was unable to find new sponsors to support the necessary conversion and was finally forced to stop working. All his subsequent attempts to design improved airships failed, and his ship was ultimately scrapped and the equipment sold.

Paul Hänlein died in 1905 without having enjoyed any major success, owing to financial constraints. Nevertheless he had shown the way to an effective, well-designed airship. In 1876 Nicolaus August Otto constructed and successfully tested a four-stroke engine at Cologne-Deutz. Some seven years later, from this beginning, Gottlieb Daimler succeeded in producing a fast-running engine.

Wölfert

While most of the French balloon engineers pursued different courses from that of Hänlein, the German forester Georg Baumgarten built his first model airship during 1880 and showed it at Leipzig some months later. During 1881 he met the bookseller *Dr* Hermann Wölfert and the two men agreed to work together on a small airship propelled by the new 2hp Daimler piston engine. Baumgarten died in 1883, but not before the pair had conducted some preliminary trials, on 10 February 1882, at the Tempelhofer Feld, the large military range near Berlin-Charlottenburg, and had introduced their small experimental airship to officials of the German War Ministry and officers of the General Staff.

The first full-size ship was also shown near the German capital, at the Hasenheide. The envelope was of pure silk and was inflated using domestic gas. Wölfert had also tried to propel the small airship by using muscle

Right: The proposed Hänlein ship of 1874.

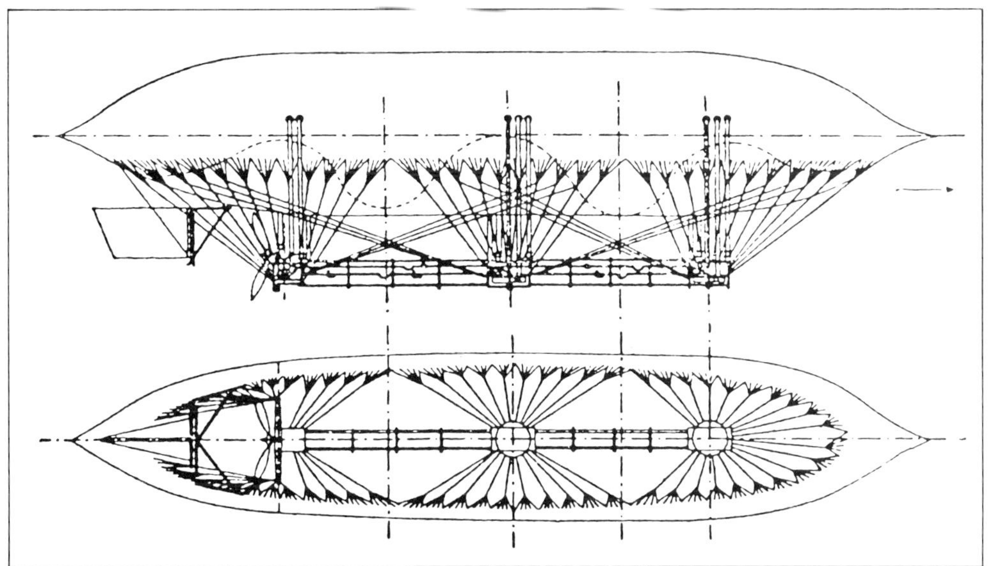

Right: *Dr* Hermann Wölfert sitting in the early experimental basket of his airship, about 1895.

power but it proved impossible to steer the vehicle in this way; the larger ship, named *Wölfert I*, was equipped with a Daimler engine and it made a tethered ascent in August 1888 from Daimler's factory near Stuttgart.

The next airship to be constructed by *Dr* Wölfert was called *Deutschland*; this took off for the first time on 6 May 1896 at Berlin. During the summer of that year six more flights were made, revealing an average speed of about 28kph (15kt) thanks to its 7hp Daimler motor. Wölfert's dirigible was what came to be described as a 'non-rigid airship', using a fabric hull with a gondola slung beneath, the latter made of metal and fitted with a large rudder aft.

During its eighth flight, on 12 June 1897, *Deutschland*'s rudder broke off as the ship was flying over the parade ground at Tempelhofer

Above: Wölfert's *Deutschland* was presented during an exhibition in Berlin in August 1888.
Left: *Deutschland* was flown in late 1896 at Tegel after a new engine had been installed.
Right: On 12 June 1897 the improved airship was destroyed in an explosion over the Tempelhofer Feld near Berlin.

Right: The *Schwarz-Luftschiff* photographed during final assembly in the hangar at Tegel, 1896.

Feld. Both passengers, Wölfert himself and Knabe, the mechanic, considered switching off the engine but suddenly flying sparks ignited the gas. Wölfert had been warned

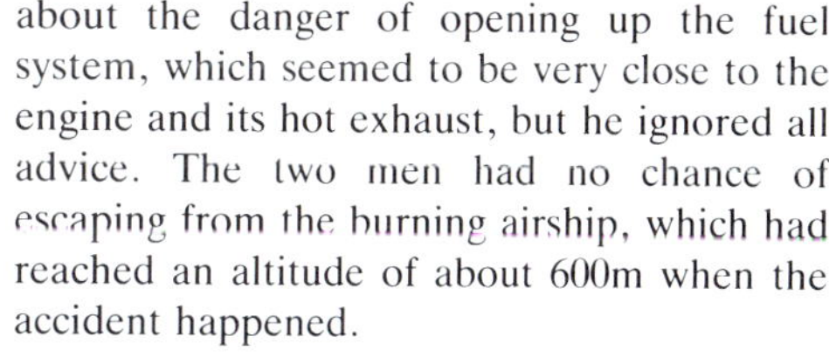

about the danger of opening up the fuel system, which seemed to be very close to the engine and its hot exhaust, but he ignored all advice. The two men had no chance of escaping from the burning airship, which had reached an altitude of about 600m when the accident happened.

Schwarz

David Schwarz, a timber merchant, was another important German airship pioneer. Since 1880 he had been working on ambitious plans for an all-metal airship powered by a Daimler-Benz piston engine, and at the time Wölfert and his friend died, his experimental ship was under construction. The design differed significantly from that of Wölfert's ship: it was larger, and the entire covering was aluminium. The military authorities considered Schwarz's ideas interesting, and his project received official support. However, it encountered many technical difficulties.

The ship, which was constructed by Weisspfennig, von Watzesch-Waldbach and *Oberingenieur* Tenzer, had a gas capacity of about 3,500m³. It had a length of 38.32m and a diameter of 24.32m and was powered by a puny 16hp piston engine. A large hangar was built at Tempelhof in 1895 and the ship was manufactured here using aluminium components some 0.18 to 0.20mm in thickness.

Left: Preparations for the Schwarz airship's only ascent, 3 November 1897, at Berlin-Tegel.
Below left: The Berg/ Schwarz ship over Schöneberg near Berlin.
Below: The remains of the Schwarz airship on 4 November 1897 after its emergency landing near the German capital.

An attempt was made to fill the ship for the first time in August 1886 but the gas was of very poor quality; moreover, the construction standards of the ship fell short of the constructor's requirements. On 13 January 1887 David Schwarz died in Vienna. However, two weeks later Melanie Schwarz, his widow, concluded a contract with Carl Berg to enable the airship to be modified and completed, the metal envelope now incorporating internal hydrogen bags. On 3 November 1897 it was inflated with the help of von Sigsfeld of the *Luftschiffer-Bataillon* at Tempelhof. In the middle of the preparations the *Kaiser* appeared together with some officers and demanded to be taken aloft on this first, experimental flight. Everyone present tried to dissuade Wilhelm II from embarking on this risky venture but nobody seemed able to change his mind. When the ship was weighed it was, fortunately, discovered that only one man could be transported in the small passenger basket.

Shortly after being inflated, the envelope began to leak in several places, so Ernst Jagels, the 'Airship Leader', promptly cranked up the small engine and the ascent began. Then one airscrew gave up, and a few minutes later another one stopped when the driving belt suddenly snapped. Nevertheless the ship continued to climb, eventually disappearing in the dense cloud cover over Berlin. Jagels opened one of the valves and the ship immediately began to descend rapidly, its course tracked by a German officer named Georg von Tschudi. It hit the ground hard near Wilmersdorf, the aluminium hull crumpling and the command gondola badly damaged. It looked as though the pilot had been killed, but Jagels crawled out of the remains unscathed. Wilhelm II was doubtless glad that he had stayed on the ground.

Despite the mishap, the German authorities were fascinated by this new form of travel through the *Luftmeer*, the ocean of the air, and improved airships quickly followed.

THE CONSTRUCTORS AND THEIR SHIPS

Parseval

August von Parseval was born in Frankenthal, near Ludwigshafen, on 5 February 1861; he died on 22 February 1942 in Berlin. In 1880 he was promoted to the rank of *Leutnant* while serving with the Bavarian Army at Augsburg together with his comrade von Sigsfeld, at which time both men began to consider the potential of aviation. Von Parseval designed a hydrogen-propelled aircraft with a wing span of 8m and a weight of 80kg, but it made only a few 'hops' – none longer than 100m. Up until 1883 he worked on proposals for balloons of various shapes and then began to design a full-size observation balloon. He was given leave between 1889 and 1891 to allow him more time to crystallize his ideas and in 1907 he left the Army altogether, having reached the rank of *Major z.D. (zur Disposition)*. In 1911 he was appointed emiritus professor at the *Technische Hochschule* at Berlin-Charlottenburg and within a few years had designed a small-scale model of the proposed *P*-type airship.

Von Parseval's first non-rigid experimental ship had a gas capacity of 2,300m^3. Its envelope was held taut by two inflated *Ballonetts*, each operated by a small 15hp Daimler-Benz piston engine, and the craft became known as a *Ballonett-Airship*. Its construction did not differ greatly from subsequent designs. After working with *Hauptmann* H. Bartsch von Sigsfeld for a period, *Major* von Parseval was engaged to build a *Drachenballon*. Von Sigsfeld died in 1902, after which von Parseval turned his mind to the design of a motor-powered non-rigid airship. The first experimental craft was constructed that same year by the well-known Riedinger Works at Augsburg, and the first take-off was made at Berlin-Tegel on 26 May 1906, four more flights following soon afterwards. Funded with one million Reichsmarks by Emperor Wilhelm II, the *Motorluftschiff-*

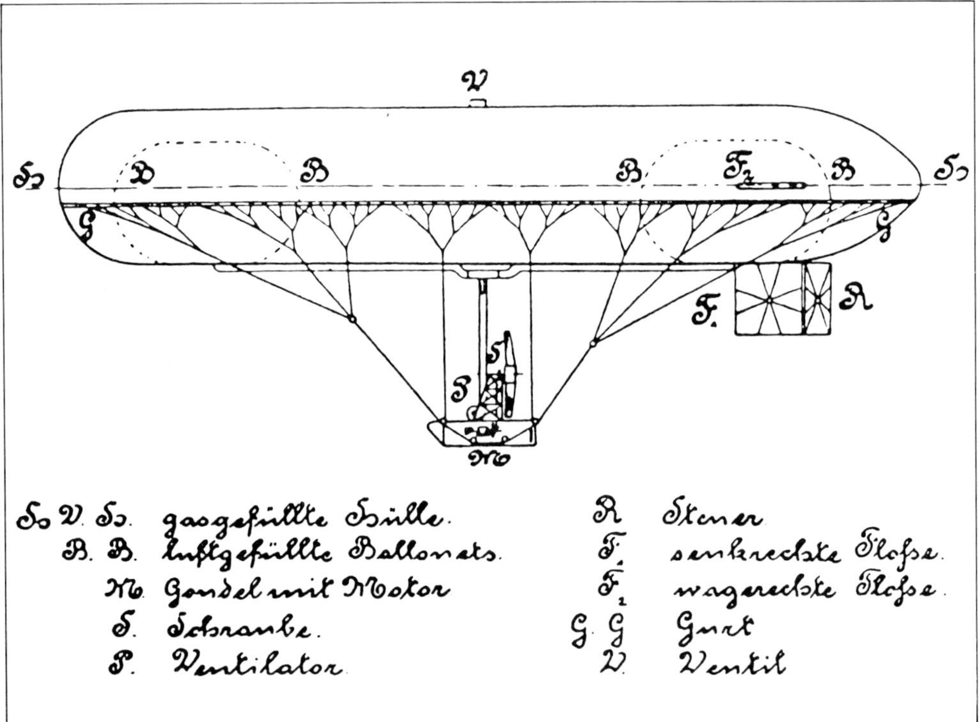

Left: A drawing of the first Parseval experimental airship.

Right: The first experimental Parseval ship, which flew for the first time on 26 May 1906.

Studiengesellschaft was established to develop the suggestions made by the *Major*, who became its first technical director after he had left the Army.

A small hangar was built in late 1906 at Reinikendorf to enable improvements to be made to the *P*-type airship, whose trials were resumed the following year. The experimental *P Versuch-ship* was the successor to the *A Nr 1* type and had a length of 50m, a diameter of 8.9m and a volume of about 2,800m^3. Gas was carried in two *Ballonetts* so designed to give the envelope symmetrical shape. Provided a pressure of 10kg/m^2 were maintained within the envelope, the structure could support a gondola fitted with an engine and carrying all necessary equipment; with a constant pressure of 20kg/m^2 a speed of more than 15m/sec (about 30kt) could easily be achieved.

The first Parseval airship was propelled by an 86hp engine driving 4.2m-diameter propellers which turned at 250rpm. Each airscrew was made of canvas into which metal strips had been sewn; later, wooden airscrews were fitted for greater efficiency. Another problem was that the gondola was situated too far away from the bottom of the airship envelope, with the result that it tipped violently. Von Parseval suggested fixing larger fins to the aft of his ship.

After some difficulties with the elevator controls had been corrected, the first eighteen flights ended with a seven-hour mission from Tegel to Brandenburg and back. Further important modifications were made, and the ship received the new designation PL 1. During the morning of 28 October 1907 the ship, crewed by *Hauptleute* von Kehler and von Krogh and two others, covered the distance between Tegel and Brandenburg in about 2hr 15min. It attained a maximum speed of 40kph (about 21½kt) but when the engine failed the crew was forced to descend. About two hours later the Parseval lifted off again and reached the Tegel hangar at about 6 o'clock in the morning. These test flights were so successful that the German High Command ordered its first production ship before the year was out.

After analyzing his early experiences in 1907, von Parseval himself stated that the non-rigid airship had notable advantages over the rigid variety:

1. The cost of building one of his non-rigid ships would amount to only one-fifth that of one of von Zeppelin's rigid ships;
2. The Parseval ships could be transported very easily;
3. No special field facilities were required

Left: *Major* von Parseval with his improved first ship.

– any flat meadow could be used to prepare the ship for flight;

4. It was not necessary to erect expensive hangars, and in an emergency the airship could quickly be deflated;
5. The Parseval ship seemed to be much more stable during flight;
6. Because there was no internal structure, the payload was much larger than that of a comparable rigid airship;
7. The chances of a non-rigid ship becoming damaged seemed remote.

The new production airship was designated *A Nr 2* and differed little from *Nr 1* except that it was larger, had a more tapered aft section and was fitted with stronger rudders, the ventral rudder being increased in area. It had a length of 58m, a diameter of 9.4m and a volume of 3,200m^3. The engine was now a 150hp unit and the fuel capacity was sufficient to enable the ship to stay aloft for more than sixteen hours.

Between 13 and 22 August 1908 A-2 was busily engaged in evaluation trials. The first long-distance flight took place on 14 August when it toured Berlin for two hours, covering a distance of 90km. During one of the landing manoeuvres during this period the gondola touched down hard and *Hauptmann* von Krogh's left forearm was broken, but there was no serious damage to the craft. The following day, 22 August, it was announced that the head of the German High Command, *Generalleutnant* von Moltke, was to be present during the next trials. However, because of the strong winds the airship could not be steered when its single engine failed, but the crew carried out a successful emergency landing in a field, albeit damaging the craft, which, three hours later, was dismantled and transported back to base. Nevertheless, these events showed that forced landings would probably be harmless and that the Parseval ships had advantages in that they could be set up and flown with the minimum of fuss.

In September 1908 A-2 was inflated again and prepared for a demonstration in front of an official commission from the War Ministry. *Dr* Hugo Eckener made a report concerning the initial evaluation of von Parseval's ship in 1909:

> First, the officials had stated that the airship had to show that it could spend ten hours in the air. It had to climb to an altitude of 1,500m above ground level and had to be capable of being operated in limited field conditions. The endurance flight was carried out on 15 September 1908 without any problems. The ship left Tegel with a crew of five, went to the Magdeburg area, from there to Potsdam and finally back to Tegel again, taking eleven hours. It covered a distance of 290km. When it descended, there was enough fuel on board for a further four hours in the air. A short while later Wilhelm II arrived at the military range at Berlin-Tegel for an inspection. There he saw both the new Army balloon and the Parseval airship. It proved to be impossible to fly the balloon, however, because the weather was very bad, but the airship rose from the ground although during a subsequent flight one

Below: The Parseval PL 3, used by the German Army as P II, took part in a parade on 22 April 1910.

of the rudders broke away and damaged the gas cell. The gas escaped and the crew were forced to land in a garden. The hull was damaged in several places by trees, but nobody was injured or killed. It took until October for the ship to be repaired. During that time PL 2 received a new, substantially modified intake valve. After that the crew had little difficulty reaching the required 1,500m, at which altitude the ship would loiter for about an hour. Then *Nr 2* was handed over to the Imperial German Army.

From 1909, all Parseval ships were built by the recently founded Luftfahrzeug GmbH at Bitterfeld, near Berlin. The next one, PL 3, of *B Nr 1* type, was the first Parseval to be proposed for carrying passengers, but later it too was assigned to the Army. The new ship had a gas volume of 5,600m^3 but this was ultimately increased to 6,600m^3 because the gondola was too heavy. It was the first airship to be equipped with a gondola big enough to accommodate two of the new NAG engines, each with an output of 100hp. Enough fuel could be carried for lengthy journeys, with an endurance of between 20 and 24hr at a reduced speed. The range was estimated to be between 450km (maximum performance) and 1,000km (medium performance) and the maximum speed would be more than 50.5kph (27.2kt).

The Parseval *B Nr 1* took part in the ILA international aviation exhibition at Frankfurt and in the autumn of 1909 it was transferred to southern Germany, passing over Nuremberg and Augsburg and landing at Munich in October; it later moved to Stuttgart, returning to Frankfurt a few days later. Many passenger-carrying flights were made by the Parseval airship from the end of September 1910, including one, with Graf Zeppelin on board, to the Eibsee near the Zugspitze. During the next two months a total of 36 such flights were made all over Bavaria, and especially over the Bavarian Alps. On 10 October 1910 the ship was flown back to take part in the exhibition at Berlin-Johannistal and after some more circuits of the city Wilhelm II honoured the crew and von Parseval.

Meanwhile the gondola was modified again and the propeller replaced by a wooden-bladed unit. Confusingly, PL 2 was given the military designation P I, and PL 3 became P II when taken over by the *Heeres-Luftschiffer* after 61 successful flights. On 16 May 1911 P II was damaged and was immediately struck off charge. The next airship, PL 4, was smaller and had a maximum speed of only about 40kph. It was built by personnel from the Austrian *Heeresverwaltung*. The principal specifications for the Parseval ships were published on 14 August 1909 during the ILA and are shown in Table 1.

PL 6 was purchased by the *Deutsche Luftverkehrsgesellschaft* and was seen all over Germany. The 6,800m^3 ship was used for civilian flights. In 1910 the ship was trans-

ferred from Bitterfeld to Dresden, later moving to Munich. Between June 1910 and December 1911 it made a total of 240 accident-free flights, covering 15,000km and transporting more than 2,200 passengers. The ship was later lengthened and handed over to the Imperial German Army.

The next ship was sold to Russia, while others served as small training craft. The larger PL 11 was the heaviest ship built before 1909, equipped with two engines each of 150hp which permitted a continuous service speed of more than 60kph (over 32kt). Further airships for export followed, and the few which remained in Germany were turned over to the armed forces.

Left and below: Two views of PL II on exercise in western Germany in 1910.
Right: PL 3 made many commercial flights all over Germany. Here the ship had landed at Mainz-Gonsenheim.
Below right: The Parseval PL 3 at Zürich.

TABLE 1: PRINCIPAL SPECIFICATIONS OF PARSEVAL AIRSHIPS

Type	Gas capacity (m^3)	Max. speed (m/sec)	Endurance (hr)	Service ceiling (m)	Crew	Passengers
A	4,000	13	15	2,000	3	3
B	6,600	14	20	2,500	3–4	7–8
C	2,000	11	8	1,000	2	2
D	1,200	9	5	600	1–2	1–2
E	3,200	10	6	1,500	2–3	3–5
F	1,600	8	5	600	1–2	1–2

TABLE 2: SUMMARY OF PARSEVAL NON-RIGID AIRSHIPS

Designation	First take-off	Operator	Gas capacity (m^3)	Remarks
P 1	26/05/06	Experimental	2,300[1]	
PL 1	21/09/09	Kaiserlicher Aeroclub	3,200	Rebuilt P 1
PL 2	13/08/08	German Army	4,000	Army P I
PL 3	18/02/09	German Army	6,600	Army P II; w/o16/05/11
PL 4	25/07/09	Austrian Army	2,300	
PL 5	08/12/09	Luftverkehrs GmbH	1,450	*'Sportluftschiff'*
PL 6	30/06/10	Luftfahrzeug GmbH, German Navy	6,800, 8,000	*'Verkehrsluftschiff'*
PL 7	30/10/10	Russian Army	7,600	
PL 8	07/02/13	German Army	8,000	Army P II (*Ers.*)
PL 9	10/10/10	Turkish Army	1,700[2]	
PL 10	17/04/11	Luftfahrzeug GmbH	1,700	
PL 11	13/12/11	German Army	9,500[3]	Army P III
PL 12	11/05/12	Rhein.–Westf. Flug GmbH	8,000	Named *Charlotte*
PL 13	03/04/12	Japanese Army	8,000	
PL 14	27/02/13	Russian Army	9,600	
PL 15	15/04/13	Italian Army	10,000	
PL 16	02/10/13	German Army	9,600	Army P IV
PL 17	30/09/12	Italian Army	9,600	
PL 18	23/04/13	Royal Navy	8,500	No. 4; named *The Lady of the Air*
PL 19	20/04/14	German Navy	10,300	
PL 20	–	Royal Navy	–	Not delivered
PL 21	–	Royal Navy	–	Not delivered
PL 22	–	Royal Navy	–	Not delivered
PL 23	–	Export airship	–	Not delivered
PL 24	–	Export airship	–	Not delivered
PL 25	08/08/15	German Navy/Army	13,600	
PL 26	26/10/15	German Navy	13,600	
PL 27	08/03/17	German Navy	31,100	Not accepted by Navy
PN 28	1929	Trumpf (Germany)	2,600	
PN 29	1930	Sidenhuset (Sweden)	2,600	
PN 30	1930	Civil airship	2,600	

[1]Later 2,800m^3. [2]Later 2,200m^3. [3]Later 11,000m^3

A summary of the non-rigid airships built by the Parseval works, comprising 30 different craft (of which three were constructed between 1929 and 1930), is given in Table 2. Of the airships listed, six were used by the Imperial German Army – PL 2, 3, 8, 11, 16 and 25, the last originally assigned to the Navy and flown only for a short time. The first non-rigid ships transferred to the Army were P I and II, which took part in the 1909 manoeuvres at Cologne. A year later, on 23 April 1910, P II joined forces with the Gross-Basenach M II and the Zeppelin Z II at Bad Homburg near Frankfurt for aerial manoeuvres, rehearsing operating procedures applicable to large airships in the field. PL 11, powered by two 250hp Körting engines, was one of the fastest Parseval ships and saw service with the Army before the First World War. PL 16 was used for training.

The Navy operated four ships, PL 6, 19, 25 and 27. The first to be flown under military command during the war was the former demonstrator PL 6, which was handed over to the Navy on 1 September 1914 to enhance the latter's reconnaissance capability. Only four

Right: PL 8 was operated by the German Army as P II (*Ersatz*) and flew for the first time on 24 December 1912.

Right: PL 16 was handed over to the German Army and by 1913 had been modified.

Left: PL 16's gondola received a glazed front and a modified engine arrangement.
Below left: Tests with the Siemens glider were undertaken by Parseval airships in 1916.

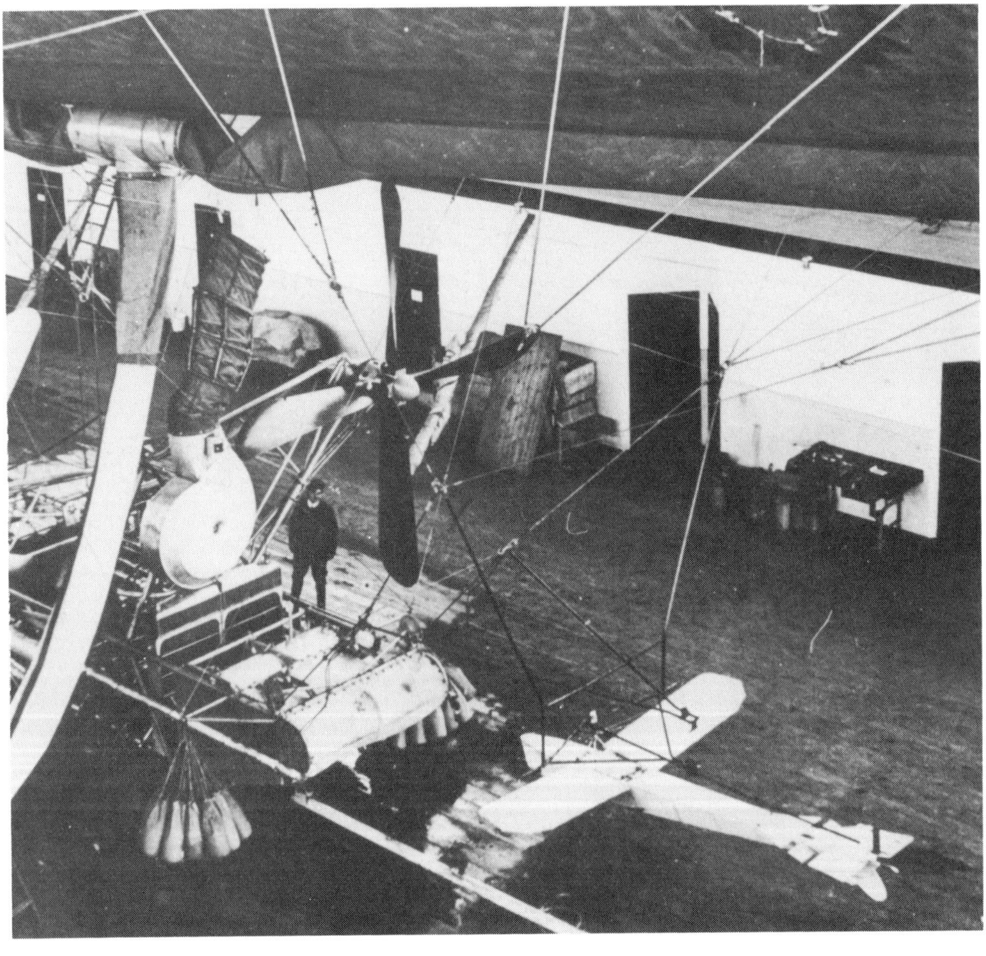

Above right: PL 25 first rose on 8 August 1915. The ship had a length of 110m and featured a closed command cabin.
Right: A close-up photograph showing PL 25's modern command gondola. The ship was operated by both the Army and the Navy.

missions were completed, from Kiel by *Oberleutnant d.R.* Meier. The airship's range was not great and PL 6 was struck off charge early in 1915 after Prince Heinrich, *Grossadmiral* and *Generalinspekteur* of the Imperial Navy, declared that non-rigid airships did not have the qualities required by the service. P IV was a 9,600m^3 ship with 360hp engines and was commanded by *Oberleutnant* Meier; it was dismantled on 24 March 1916 after only two reconnaissance missions over the Baltic Sea. PL 19 served with the Navy and was commanded by *Hauptmann* Stelling during a raid against Libau on 25 January 1915. However, the engines failed and the crew was forced to land; one man was able to escape and reach his own lines but the remainder were taken prisoner.

The next Parseval ship, PL 25, represented a big step towards the goal of commissioning a really well-equipped naval reconnaissance craft: compared with the ventral gondola of PL 16, the closed compartment of PL 25 looked most impressive. The ship spotted for mines in May 1915 and was engaged in Navy operations early in 1916. It was subsequently

handed over to the Army, serving as a training ship until 2 August 1917. The next ship, PL 26, saw only limited service, being burnt out on 19 November 1915 in its hangar at Bitterfeld. The last Parseval built during the war, PL 27, was never commissioned by the German Navy because its aft section proved too heavy. It was scrapped – and a large number of raincoats were tailored from its hull!

In 1929 and 1930 Wasser- und Luftfahrzeug GmbH built three small advertising ships, PN 28, 29 and 30. They were constructed by *Dipl-Ing.* Naatz. A Siemens-Halske Sh 14A radial engine of 160hp gave each a speed of about 80kph (43kt) and an endurance of 12hr, and up to six people (inclusive of the crew) could be accommodated. One of these ships, PN 29, carried out more than 200 flights until a crash-landing in the Baltic ended its career; the crew, fortunately, were saved. A number of other large Parseval airships were projected, but none was realized.

Clouth

In 1909 the Rheinische Gummiwarenfabrik of Franz Clouth at Nippes near Cologne built a small airship. It had a length of about 42m and

Above left: The last, and most advanced, Parseval design – PL 27.
Left: PN 28 under construction, showing the small cabin.

Above: Three non-rigid ships were built by Parseval-Naatz after World War One; the second of these was PN 28, *Triumph*.
Right: The last PN design was flown in Sweden by the Sidenhuset Corporation.

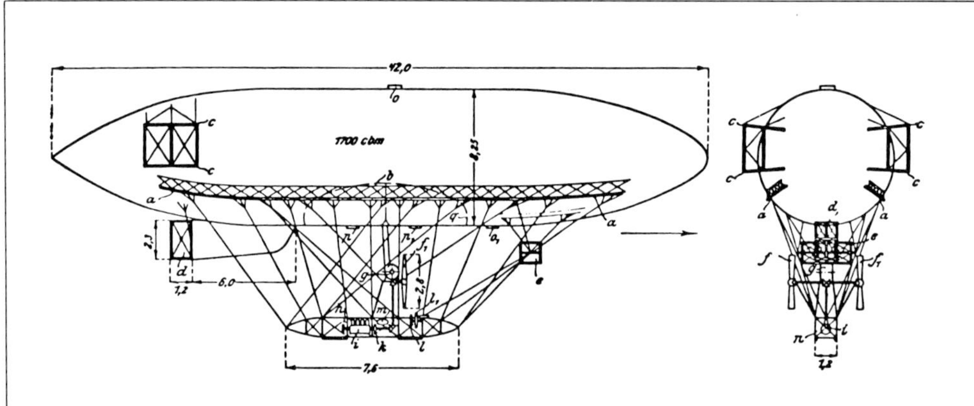

Above: The Clouth airship was first inflated in the summer of 1909.
Left: Side and front elevation drawings of the Clouth airship, October 1909.

a diameter of 8.5m and was propelled by a 42hp Adler engine driving two propellers flanking the ventral gondola. The vehicle weighed 1,490kg, with the gondola alone accounting for 850kg, and the gas capacity was only 1,700m^3.

The ship rose for the first time at 6.30 a.m. on 20 August 1909, with Richard Clouth aboard, accompanied by *Herr* Theben. Three days later the airship was shown again at the ILA at Frankfurt, where it flew more than fifteen circuits. At the end of its flight the crew tried to return to the exhibition field but the wind was too strong and so they decided to land in the city itself, which they did without damaging the craft.

Two days later *Hauptmann* von Kleist, *Oberleutnant* von Berlepsch and an engineer went up in the small gondola when suddenly the gas pressure decreased and forced the crew to descend from about 600m. The airship became entangled in trees near Frankfurt but was eventually cut free. The *Clouth I* was brought back to Cologne for repairs and subsequently flew again. Franz Clouth received the Golden Trophy of the town of Kronberg/Taunus and later the Medal of the International Exhibition at Brescia after completing more than fifty flights.

The ship was rebuilt to larger dimensions and carried out a long-distance flight on 20 June 1910, taking off at Bickendorf near

Right: *Clouth I*'s gondola, photographed during the airship's trials.

Cologne at 12.05 p.m., passing Jülich, Maastricht, St Trond and Tirelmont and descending near Brussels at 6.20 p.m. where it was put on display for several days. The ship and all patent rights were sold to the Luftfahrzeug-Gesellschaft at the end of 1910. Its ultimate fate is unknown.

Siemens-Schuckert

Willi von Siemens, the son of the famous Werner Siemens, began work on designing a tall, non-rigid airship following consultations with the German *Generalstabschef*, von Moltke; construction was carried out by *Prof. Dr-Ing.* Krell, one of the Siemens directors, together with three experienced engineers, Alexander Dietzius, Hans Dietzius and R. Haas. Originally of 13,500m^3, later enlarged to 15,000m^3, the SS 1 had three gondolas slung beneath the envelope. A canvas-covered walkway led from the main gondola to those forward and aft, each of which was fitted with two 125hp Daimler engines. The main gondola – where the commander rode – had a length of 9m and housed a new type of engine telegraph for transmitting orders to the personnel in the other gondolas. The engines drove both two and four-bladed propellers,

Below: The Siemens-Schuckert SS 1 during trials at Biersdorf in 1911.

Left: The rear gondola of the Siemens airship, which was equipped with three propellers.

the former employed for moving the ship sideways. Although non-rigid ships could be landed more easily than the Zeppelin airships, the Siemens design aroused no more interest than did the Parseval ships.

Siemens needed about two more years' work to perfect all his ideas concerning the layout of the hull and its internal compartmentation. The covering itself consisted of three layers combined with two of india rubber. The Siemens ship rose for the first time on 23 January 1911, achieving a speed of about 71kph (37.75kt). After 27 more flights the envelope was deflated in order to enlarge it. The new SS 1 flew with the same inflation pressure as the original without any noticeable loss of dynamic lift, thanks to the constant excess pressure which reduced the diffusion of the gas in the cells – one of the important advantages of the design.

During 1912, after a further ten company flights, the SS 1 was taken over by the German

Below left: SS 1's first take-off occurred on 23 January 1911.

Below: SS 1, photographed during trials near its hangar at Biersdorf.

Army, but it appears that the design was too complex for the military, even though it made 64 short flights, the longest being of seven hours' duration. On 2 February 1912 *Graf* Ferdinand von Zeppelin was by chance on board the command gondola when, during the final landing manoeuvres, the ship ran into a ditch owing to the forward gondola engine having too much speed. The envelope was momentarily bent into an arch but only a few tubular steel components were damaged and these were replaced within three days.

In general, the Siemens ship proved that a large non-rigid airship was capable of carrying three gondolas with the necessary payload. Compared with the Parseval PL 25 type, which had only one large gondola under the hull, the Siemens design was able to carry more men and equipment, but the 'Zeppelin lobby' exerted considerable influence on German commanders, who voted to build a fleet of large, rigid ships. A short time later the experimental SS 1 was dismantled. A total of 73 flights had been made in 1913, and few difficulties had been experienced.

Siemens also built a rotating hangar, 136m long, 25m high and weighing 1,200 tonnes. It was closed on the sides by canvas and turned by two 40hp engines. It contained well-equipped workshops for minor repairs, while beneath the turntable ring was a huge basement for storing 15,000m^3 of gas in steel containers. After the Siemens ship was broken up the hangar was frequently home to the Parseval P 6 and the Gross-Basenach M IV.

Transatlantische Fluggesellschaft München 'Suchard'

Prior to the First World War Josef Bruckner, a German-American journalist, suggested crossing the Atlantic Ocean by non-rigid airship from Tenerife to the northern coast of South America. Sponsored by the famous Suchard Schokoladen Fabrik and built by Riedinger at Augsburg, Bruckner's ship had a length of 60m and a capacity of 7,000m^3, subsequently increased to 10,000m^3. It was completed in 1910 and named *Suchard* at Kiel on 15 February 1911. Instead of a gondola, the airship was fitted with a motorized lifeboat developed by the Lürssen shipyard at Vegesack and equipped with all the necessary nautical instruments. Two NAG engines each of 110hp were installed in the boat. Serious doubts were raised concerning the performance and range of the ship, however, and the crossing was postponed from the spring to the autumn of 1911 to allow for flight trials.

As a result of these, the ship was immediately lengthened to 76m and had its capacity increased to about 12,500m^3. New rudders and larger fins were also fitted. Fuel for the journey was carried both in the envelope and in the boat itself, which now had a length of 10.17m. More trials brought about a further postponement of the venture, to April 1912, but in the event *Suchard* never made the crossing. Another flight possibly took place in May 1912 at Johannisthal, before the ship was transported to Tenerife, but since funds had run out the ambitious scheme was finally abandoned.

Gross-Basenach

After the successful flight of Lebaudy's airship and the interest shown in it by the French military authorities, the German War Ministry was compelled to pay greater attention to manoeuvrable, motor-propelled balloons. Aware of the designs of *Graf* von Zeppelin and *Major* von Parseval, the Prussian *Luftschiffer-Bataillon* also began to put forward its own proposals, and *Oberingenieur* Basenach and the former *Hauptmann* Sperling tried to find a way of adopting Lebaudy's concept. Their deliberations resulted in a semi-rigid airship featuring a *Ballonett Typ*, consisting of a supporting understructure to which the balloon was fixed

Left: The first ship built by the *Luftschiffer-Bataillon*, at Berlin-Tegel in 1907.

by netting. Despite Basenach's responsibility for its construction, the name of the technical leader, *Major* Gross, came to be associated with the new craft.

The first small experimental airship to this design was manufactured by Siemens-Schuckert in Berlin in the summer of 1907. The envelope was cylindrical, with a length of 40m and a diameter of about 7m and filled with 1,400m^3 of gas. Beneath the balloon superstructure a gondola was slung by means of thick ropes, a keel under the aft section of the envelope terminating in a large fabric-covered rudder. Two fins for stabilization were fitted at right angles to the keel. In the gondola a weak-fuel Gaggenau car engine of 25hp was installed, driving two small airscrews at 600rpm; the first take off occurred on 7 May 1907 using a French engine but the latter failed on several occasions. Pitch control was

Left: The first experimental ship was rebuilt in 1911, having been damaged in July 1908.

Above: The Gross-Basenach M I was evaluated at Tegel from June 1908 under field conditions.

achieved by displacement at the centre of the envelope – the same system as that used by von Parseval. The early Gross-Basenach airships were built to accommodate three or four passengers for flights of about six or seven hours' duration.

Later on the envelope was enlarged, giving a length of 42m and a diameter of 8.2m, thereby increasing its capacity to 1,800m^3, and the rebuilt craft took to the air again on 23 July 1907. The test flight revealed the desirability of enlarging the fins, and following some further brief ascents the ship was flown on a six-hour sortie in early October 1907. Some days later, on 25 October, Wilhelm II visited his *Luftschiffer-Bataillon* at Berlin-Tegel and inspected both the early Parseval and the Gross-Basenach. His demand for a larger ship was noted by the German High Command.

During the winter of 1907–08 a new ship was built, originally with a length of 65.5m but subsequently extended to 74m; it had a diameter of about 12m. Inside the envelope were two *Ballonette* which could be inflated separately in order to alter the craft's centre of gravity. The ship weighed 4,698kg and was propelled by two 75hp Körting engines. The first flight took place on 30 June 1908 and on 11 September that year it carried out a mission lasting about 13hr. The ship was later designated M I. The Gross-Basenach M II followed within a short period of time. It had a Telefunken wireless system and made a flight lasting almost 17hr on 4 August 1909. Both M I and M II took part in the *Kaiser-Manöver* with good results, although their speed of 45kph (24.3kt) seemed low; moreover their payload was deemed inadequate, even after their capacity was increased from 4,800 to 5,200m^3. In April 1909 *Oberingenieur* Basenach stated that

> . . . the number of flights increased because the ship was able to operate in unfavourable weather. In addition, stronger ships would have

Right: M I was used by the Army until 30 June 1908.

Left: M II was lengthened twice and in 1910 took part in the air parade at Bad Homburg near Frankfurt.

Below: M II was used as an experimental ship for testing new wireless equipment.

an advantage during both defensive and offensive actions. Compared with the standard French airships, the Gross-Basenach M I and M II were superior in 1909, but it was to be expected that foreign countries would be involved in building more powerful craft . . . Before the *Luftschiffer-Abteilung* started to build larger ships, however, it would be prudent to wait for the first results of the evaluation of the Siemens-Schuckert ship. Therefore a smaller 6,000m^3 non-rigid airship with a maximum speed of about 55kph was of greater interest.

After successfully completing a number of flights, M I took part in a parade on 22 April 1910. In company with the non-rigid Parseval P 1 and the rigid Zeppelin Z 2, it lifted off at Cologne and headed for Bad Homburg with the help of a strong wind. All three landed near the parade ground, the last of them the slow M I. The ship was enlarged for a second time in 1913, receiving the military designation M Ib; M II was first evaluated not earlier than 20 April 1909 and had its envelope increased to a capacity of 5,200m^3 during the winter of 1909–10. Much development work was carried out by the *Luftschiffer* unit at Tegel, Basenach wishing to improve his ships as much as possible. A setback occurred on 12 September 1911, however, when M II exploded.

M III had a capacity of 7,800m^3 and was propelled by four Körting engines, each of 75hp; the total weight of the airship, with the gondola fully equipped, was 6,596kg. The first flight took place on 31 December 1909 and the

Above: M III, the third *Luftschiffer-Bataillon* ship. It was later damaged when the hull caught fire in the hangar.
Right: M III under test at Tegel in 1910.

second was completed at an average speed of about 60kph (32.3kt), making this ship the fastest in the world, with a performance better even than that of the Zeppelins. After modifications to the engines and envelope, the latter increased in capacity to 9,000m^3, average speeds of between 68 and 70kph (about 37kt) could be achieved. Trim was varied by means of large water canisters, moved from one part of the structure to another by compressed air. The rebuilt M IIIb made its first flight during January 1910.

However, the performance of the newer Zeppelin designs was still superior, and their military payload had increased. In December 1911 Gross and Basenach announced, during a conference held under the chairmanship of the former *Oberst* Messing, that they would build a larger airship, a semi-rigid type which would take account of the results of the Siemens evaluation. The ship was manufactured by the *Luftschiffer-Bataillon* in 1909 and began its trials on 11 February. Its two Körting engines each produced 200hp, and the envelope had a capacity of 11,000m^3 and a length of 96.6m. In order to improve its payload the ship was later rebuilt by Siemens-Schuckert at Biesdorf with a volume of 13,500m^3 but the technical and tactical demands of the German High Command could still not be fulfilled so the ship was lengthened again to 120.7m, with a capacity of 19,500m^3. The gondolas were incorporated into the lower superstructure and the two Körtings were exchanged for three more powerful Maybach CX engines. The new ship was taken over by the German Army on 11 August 1913. On 7 September 1914 M IVc was handed over to the Navy at Kiel and

TABLE 3: SUMMARY OF GROSS-BASENACH NON-RIGID AIRSHIPS

Manufacturer's designation	Military designation	Operator	Gas capacity (m^3)	Service entry
M *Versuch*	M V	LS-Bataillon	1,400	07/05/07
		Berlin-Tegel	1,800	23/07/09
M I	M Ia	Army	4,800	30/06/08
			5,200	?
EM I[1]	M Ib	Army	5,500	26/02/13
M II	M IIa	Army	4,800	20/04/09
EM II	M IIb	Army	4,800	12/08/09
			5,200	?
M III	M IIIa	Army	7,800	31/12/09
EM III	M IIIb	Army	9,000	15/08/12
M IV	M IVa	Army	11,000	11/03/09
EM IV	M IVb	Army	13,500	11/08/13
EM IV (*Umbau*)	M IVc	Navy	19,500	07/09/14

[1]EM=Rebuilt ship.

Below: The Gross-Basenach M IV entered service on 11 March 1909.

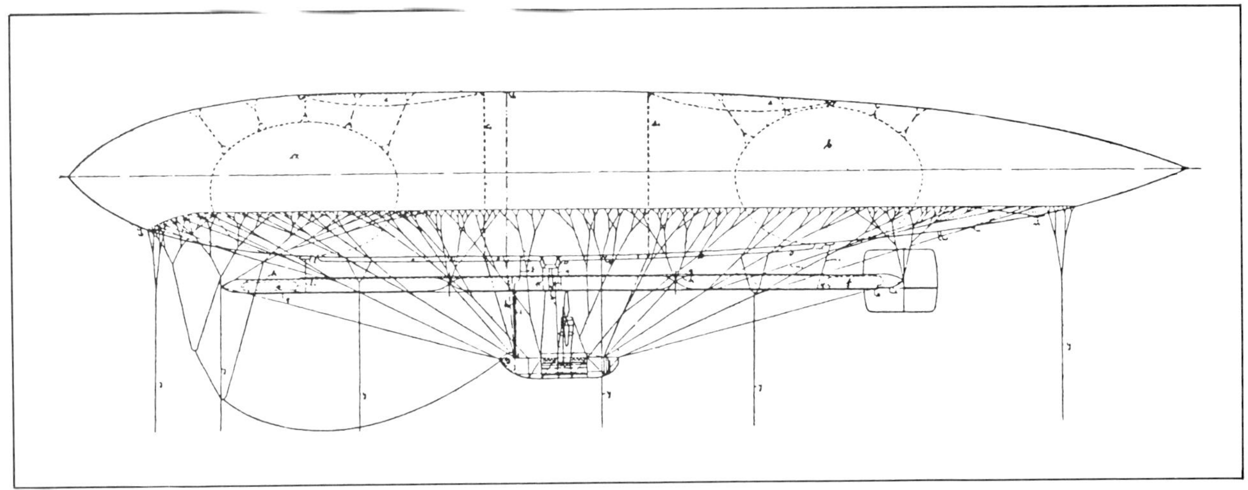

Above: The Gross-Basenach M III.

Below: A photograph of M IV taken during one of the ship's early flights

it carried out 24 reconnaissance missions between 28 December 1914 and 3 November 1915 while commanded by *Hauptmann* von Jena; on 10 September 1915 a small enemy submarine was attacked with 100kg bombs. Meanwhile the airship's envelope was beginning to deteriorate, and since official interest in semi-rigid ships was declining it was dismantled and scrapped when the *Beschaffungsamt* refused to allow the manufacture of a new hull. The engines were used for other airships operated by the German Navy.

Erbslöh

After winning several prizes taking part in balloon competitions, Oscar Erbslöh founded the Rheinisch-Westfälische Motorluftschiffahrt-Gesellschaft and became chairman of the new company. Early in 1909 a small semi-rigid airship with a diameter of 10.5m was constructed at Elbersfeld. Beneath the 53.2m-long envelope was a fixed metal gondola 26m in length which accommodated a 125hp Daimler-Benz engine, used both for driving the ship and for filling the 3,300m^3 *Ballonett*.

Left: After a rebuild, M IV became operational again on 11 August 1913.
Below left: The non-rigid airship manufactured by the Rheinisch-Westfälische Luftschiffahrts-Gesellschaft in 1909.
Right: In 1910 the Erbslöh was flown on at least four occasions.

The Erbslöh took off for the first time on 10 December 1909 and returned safely two hours later; ten days earlier, the crew had had to pull the ripcord to bring their craft down, both of the mooring ropes having broken.

Further flights took place on 12 and 13 December that year but unfortunately an engine failure forced the crew to make an emergency landing at Rensrath. Next morning the ship took off again, crossed the River Rhine near Neuss and landed between Neuwerk and Mönchen-Gladbach. The absence of any trained ground crew led to the ship being damaged, but it was repaired during the following month. It was back in action on 12 December 1910, exactly one year later, during anniversary celebrations for the Motorluftschiff-Gesellschaft, but on 13 July 1910 it crashed when the pressure relief valves failed. The log of the disaster was found in the

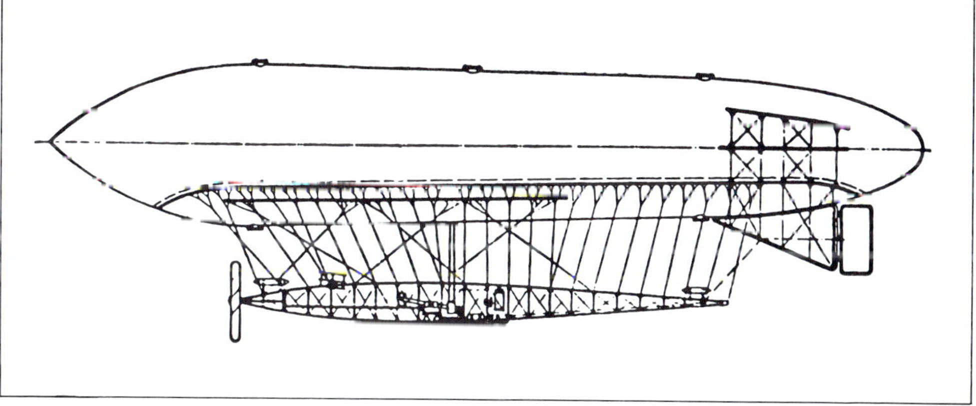

Right: The Erbslöh airship as it appeared in August 1910.

hands of the dead engineer Rudolf Kranz:

> Take-off 9hr 4min; ascending 9hr 9min, dense fog, travelling in northerly direction, no ground sight possible, the sun is coming through, elevator downwards, 280m at 9hr 11min . . .

Ruthenberg

Hermann Ruthenberg, who lived at Berlin-Weissensee, built two, and possibly three, small semi-rigid airships between 1909 and 1913. The first ship had a gas volume of 1,200m^3, a weight of 800kg (envelope 350kg, gondola 370kg) and a payload of 450kg. The keel structure, weighing 75kg, supported a small two-man gondola equipped with a 24hp four-cylinder motor-car engine.

Ruthenberg's ship took part in the 1909 ILA at Frankfurt where its builder was awarded the so-called *Zeppelin-Preis*, worth 10,000 Reichsmarks, plus an additional 2,000

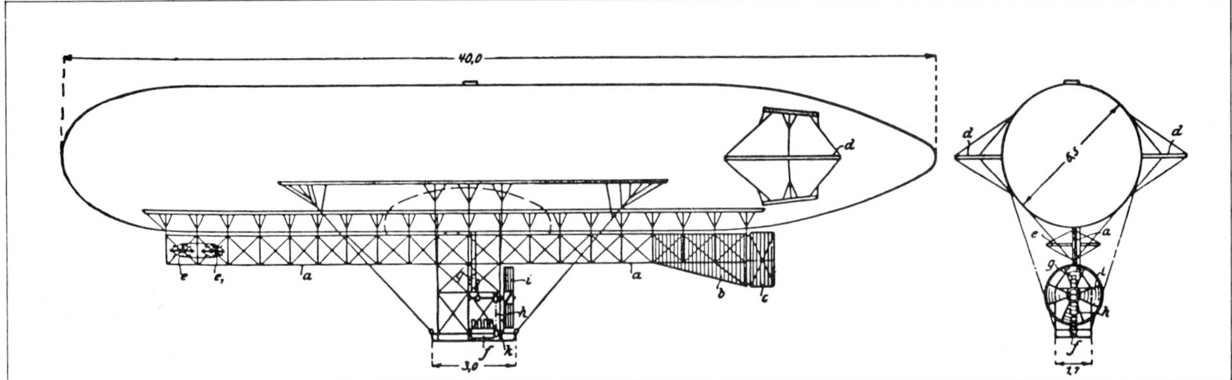

by the German War Ministry for the design of the propellers. Flying on 30 August and 25 September, *Ruthenberg I* completed twenty-five passenger circuits, at a maximum speed of about 35kph (19kt) and was the smallest ship to take part in the display. It was later sold to Hugo Hassl and stationed at Hamburg, remaining airworthy until 1912.

The second airship, *Ruthenberg II*, was built in 1911. It had a gas volume of 1,700m^3 and a length of about 46m and was propelled by a single 75hp Fiat engine. The craft was damaged during an emergency landing caused by a loss of gas but was repaired early in 1912. The third ship, under construction in 1913, was larger than either of its predecessors, with an estimated gas capacity of about 2,700m^3. There is no evidence that this ship, powered by two Fiat engines, was ever completed, although it had been purchased by the Luftfahrzeug-Gesellschaft at Krefeld.

Left: Hermann Ruthenberg built three semi-rigid ships; the first (shown) rose on several occasions at Frankfurt in 1909.
Centre left: Elevation drawings of the Ruthenberg airship showing the modifications made in late 1909.

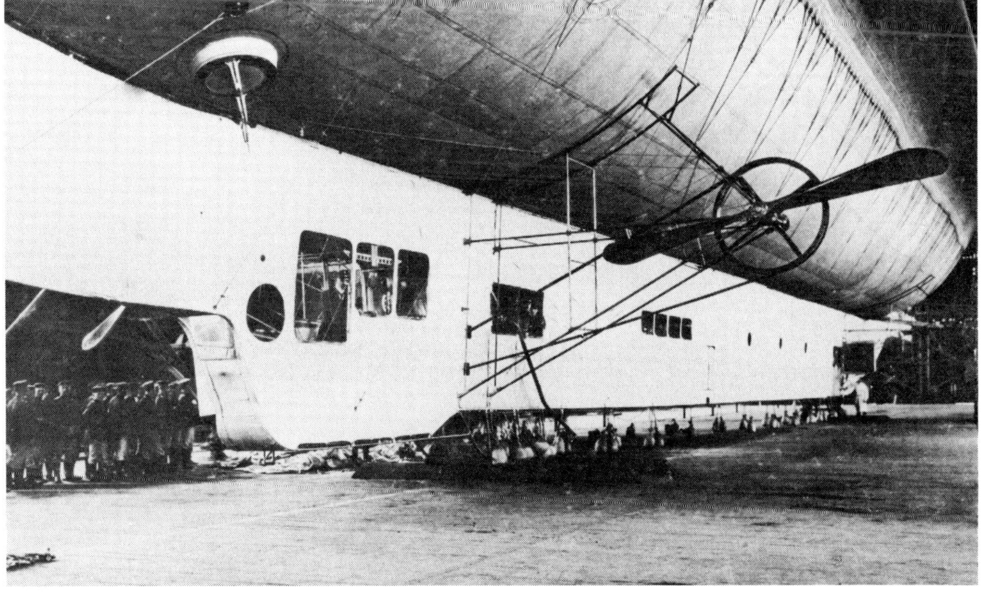

Veeh

The semi-rigid Veeh I was begun at Munich by *Ing*. Veeh but then transferred to Düsseldorf where it was completed by the Deutsche Luftschiffwerft. A large keel under the hull provided ample space for the installation of two 130hp Daimler engines together with the command post and accommodation for the crew. Each powerplant drove two propellers positioned adjacent to the canvas-covered keel (the latter was at first uncovered and differed in design from the later version), which terminated in a large fin made of tubular steel and canvas. During the early flight trials, begun on 8 July 1913, protective plates were fitted above the airscrews in order to prevent serious damage should the propellers fail. It was also discovered that the elevators were too small, and these were therefore modified. The 'cockpit' seemed very advanced for its time. Two *Ballonetts* were installed in the envelope, which was 70m long and 12.4m in diameter and had a capacity of about 9,100m^3.

During its evaluation the ship was forced to land 30km outside Cologne, possibly

Left: The Veeh airship was first flown with an uncovered keel.
Above right: In 1913 the Veeh I received a redesigned keel of more modern appearance.
Right: The modified Veeh airship rose for the first time on 8 July 1913.

Above: The Steffen ship *Kiel I*, of semi-rigid construction. Below: A drawing of the Zorn & Hense 'flying train'. Right: SL I under construction at Rheinau near Mannheim.

because of design faults in the control surfaces. No external damage was noticeable after the craft touched down but during deflation the weight of the hull deformed the keel aft. The dismantled ship was brought back to Düsseldorf in order to repair the damage, but no information concerning its subsequent career is available.

A second design was produced by 1913, reportedly involving a larger airship with a volume of 14,500m^3 and a length of 95m, but no further details are available.

Steffen

In 1909 Bruno and Franz Steffen started building a small motorized airship at Kronshagen near Kiel. It was constructed as a semi-rigid craft with a length of 32m and was called *Kiel I*. It had a gas volume of about 6,000m^3 and was propelled by a 30hp Buchet engine. The ship took off for the first time on 25 March 1910.

Zorn & Hense

The Rheinische Patent Luftschiffahrtsgesellschaft Zorn & Hense was founded in 1910 at Krefeld in order to realize the ambitions of Theodor Zorn, who wanted to build a so-called 'Flying Balloon Train' made up of three airships. The semi-rigid envelope had a wooden framework and was to be inflated with hydrogen, and in an emergency the ship could be separated into three pieces. There were plans for fitting a cabin with accommo-

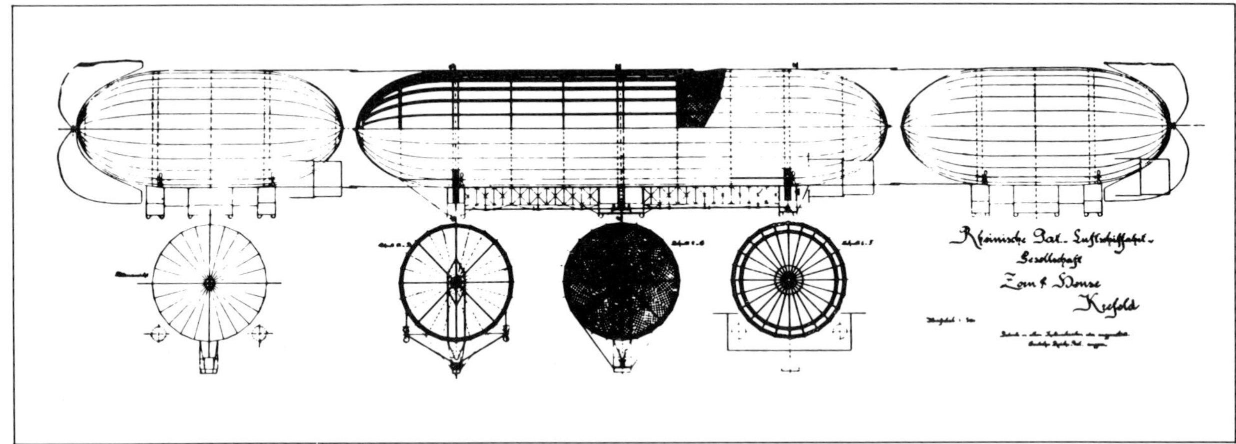

TABLE 4: AIRSHIP PERFORMANCE, 1855–1911

Year	Airship	Powerplant	hp	Speed, m/sec (kt)
1855	Giffard	Steam engine	4	3.0 (5.8)
1872	Hänlein	Gas engine	3.5	5.0 (9.7)
1884	Renard & Krebs	Electric motor	9	6.0 (11.7)
1897	Schwarz	Piston engine	12	5.0 (9.7)
1900	Santos Dumont	Piston engine	16	8.0 (15.5)
1902	Lebaudy	Piston engine	50	11.0 (21.4)
1905	Zeppelin LZ 2	2 × piston engines	170	11.0 (21.4)
1906	Parseval PL 1	Piston engine	90	10.0 (19.4)
1911	Schütte-Lanz SL 1	2 × piston engines	480	19.7 (38.3)

Far right: The interior of the first SL ship in the huge Rheinau hangar in 1911.

dation for 33 passengers, and Zorn envisaged airship services all over Germany. The weight of the proposed craft was 10,793kg, the main vehicle accounting for 4,931kg and each outer ship 2,931kg. The total gas volume would be 13,615m^3 (7,015m^3 for the main envelope and 3,300m^3 for each of the others), and payloads of up to 6,565kg were expected. However, despite the sterling efforts of both partners, the ship remained only a dream.

Schütte-Lanz

The Schütte-Lanz SL 1 was the first of twenty ships completed by *Professor* Johann Schütte, who was born at Osterburg on 26 February 1873 and died on 29 March 1940 at Dresden. It was built in the large hangar at Rheinau near Mannheim, the construction work undertaken by Schütte himself, with financial backing provided by *Dr* Karl Lanz. The ship was powered by four 125hp Daimler-Benz piston engines installed in two ventral gondolas. Nearly all the structural parts of the airship consisted of special veneers which were waterproof and protected from frost, although this did not prevent a certain amount of deformation when wet. SL 1's speed was greater than that of any other airship built thus far (a summary of airship performance since 1855 is presented in Table 4). Within 56 years the designs had advanced greatly, and it had become possible to fly against the wind and to set a course to predetermined destinations.

When LZ 4 met with an accident, *Geheimrat* Johann Schütte started to consider modifications that could usefully be applied to all airships, and at the end of 1908 decided that it would be necessary for him, with the co-operation of his students, to develop his own scientifically designed, high-performance airship. In partnership with *Dr* Karl Lanz, *Professor* Schütte founded the Schütte-Lanz Luftschiffbau on 22 April 1909. The first experimental craft, SL 1, was a rigid design

Left: SL II descending at Rheinau early in 1915.
Right: A close-up view of SL II's second gondola showing the engine and machine gun installation.
Far right: SL 10's starboard motor gondola, which was armed with one heavy gun. The photograph was taken on 15 January 1917.

TABLE 5: EXTRACT FROM LOG OF SL 1

Flight no	Date	Endurance (min)	Remarks
1	17/10/11	50	First flight, Rheinau–Waldsee/Mannheim
2	18/10/11	60	Return to Rheinau (accident)
3	31/10/11	50	Test flight over Rheinau
4	01/11/11	90	First circuit over Mannheim; new engines and envelope fitted
5	13/04/12	15	Accident at Brühl near Rheinau
6	19/05/12	70	Flight tests with new rudders
7	29/05/12	120	Further tests and circuit flying
8	31/05/12	195	First long-range flight to Karlsruhe
9	01/06/12	120	Rheinau–Speyer–Heidelberg–Neustadt
10	07/06/12	160	Neustadt–Grünstadt–Worms
11	09/06/12	300	Worms–Mainz–Wiesbaden–Darmstadt–Heidelberg–Rheinau
12	12/06/12	180	Rheinau–Darmstadt; meeting with Z III
13	19/06/12	180	Darmstadt–Speyer–Heidelberg–Mannheim
14	23/06/12	90	First trials after modifications
15	28/06/12	210	Second trial at Rheinau
16	04/07/12	330	Rheinau–Koblenz–Bonn–Cologne
17	06/07/12	180	Circuit around Bonn
18	09/07/12	270	Flight back Cologne–Rheinau
19	11/07/12	120	Evaluation flight; performance calibration at Rheinau
20	13/07/12	120	Long-range flight Rheinau–Frankfurt
21	15/07/12	270	Return from manoeuvres to Rheinau
22	22/07/12	180	Rheinau–Darmstadt–Rheinau
23	24/07/12	370	Rheinau–Berlin; stop at Gotha owing to bad weather
24	27/07/12	330	Gotha–Berlin–Johannisthal
25–42	27/07/12–30/08/12	Each 60–90	18 circuits; parade in honour of *Kaiser* Wilhelm II
43	04/09/12	660	Return from Berlin; forced-landing near Fulda
44	09/09/12	325	Continuation of flight to Rheinau
45	04/11/12	150	Trials and testing of new wireless equipment
46	07/11/12	145	Second wireless trials
47	09/11/12	85	Final trials before transfer to Imperial German Army
48	16/11/12	210	Performance trials; one propeller and one gas cell damaged
49	19/11/12	90	Trials with wood and steel propeller fitted
50	22/11/12	215	Rheinau–Worms–Darmstadt–Rheinau
51	03/12/12	120	Rheinau–Speyer–Schifferstadt–Speyer
52	04/12/12	270	Speyer–Neustadt–Heidelberg–Pforzheim–Heidelberg–Rheinau (high-altitude flight)
53	06/12/12	995	Long-range flight Rheinau–Biesdorf (near Berlin); inspection prior to handover to German Army

suitable for long-distance flights, built to gain practical experience of such airships. SL 1's log (see Table 5) states that 53 flights were made between 17 October 1911 and 7 December 1912. It provides a reliable record of all flights prior to the airship's handing over to the Imperial German Army on 30 December that year. It survived in Army hands for only seven months.

The next ship, SL II, surpassed the Zeppelin airships in performance. It was transferred to the Austrian allies and was used from 22 August 1914 by the regional *Oberkommando*, who reported a total of six missions over Poland and France during the next month. On 26 December 1914 the ship attacked Nancy and Compiègne. During the summer of 1915 SL II was lengthened at

Below: SL 9 under construction at Leipzig.

TABLE 6: CAREER DETAILS OF SCHÜTTE-LANZ RIGID AIRSHIPS

Manufacturer's designation	Built	Operator	No of missions	Remarks
SL 1	01/05/09–13/04/12	Army	–	Destroyed by thunderstorm 17/07/13; decommissioned
SL 2	01/01/14–21/05/14	Army	6	Stranded 10/01/16; decommissioned
SL 3	01/09/14–06/02/14	Navy	32	Ditched near Steinort; crew saved
SL 4	30/11/14–11/05/15	Navy	23	Damaged by thunderstorm at Stolp
SL 5	08/12/14–01/06/15	Army	–	Destroyed during handing-over ceremony 01/07/15
SL 6	16/03/15–23/10/15	Navy	6	Exploded during take-off 18/11/15; crew killed
SL 7	05/04/15–28/09/15	Army	6	Training airship; decommissioned 28/02/17
SL 8	03/10/15–19/04/16	Navy	37	Flown in action; scrapped 26/11/17
SL 9	01/11/15–09/06/16	Navy	16	Hit by lightning and exploded 30/03/17; crew killed
SL 10	15/10/15–16/06/16	Army	2	Missing during reconnaissance mission over Black Sea
SL 11	10/04/16–12/08/16	Army	3	Shot down over London 03/09/16
SL 12	01/04/16–14/11/16	Navy	9	Crashed during landing; decommissioned 28/12/17
SL 13	01/06/16–29/10/16	Army	–	Not suitable for military use; burnt at Leipzig 08/02/17
SL 14	09/05/16–23/08/16	Navy	4	Decommissioned following crash 18/05/17
SL 15	20/08/16–29/11/16	Army	–	Decommissioned at Sandhofen/ Mannheim
SL 16	14/06/16–08/02/16	Army	–	Decommissioned at Spich
SL 17	01/11/16–19/04/16	Army	–	Decommissioned at Allenstein
SL 18	12/03/17–mid 1917	Army	–	Destroyed in hangar collapse at Leipzig
SL 19	15/06/17–end 1917	Army	–	Not completed
SL 20	05/11/16–10/09/17	Navy	2	Lost with other ships in Ahlhorn explosion 05/01/18
SL 21	01/03/17–10/10/17	Army	–	Decommissioned shortly after completion
SL 22	01/10/17–12/06/18	Navy	–	Decommissioned 1920
SL 23	–	–	–	Projected
SL 24	–	–	–	Projected

Rheinau, and it carried out another offensive mission on 7 September. On the return to Germany the crew escaped disaster at the last moment. A few months later *Hauptmann* von Wobeser and his crew became stranded in SL II at Luckenwalde, and then Wobeser's new ship, SL X, went missing over the Black Sea. Only one dead body and some wooden debris

Below: SL 10 during evaluation by Schütte-Lanz personnel near Mannheim.

Right: SL 11 crashed on 3 September 1916 after returning to base and was finally written off seven days later.

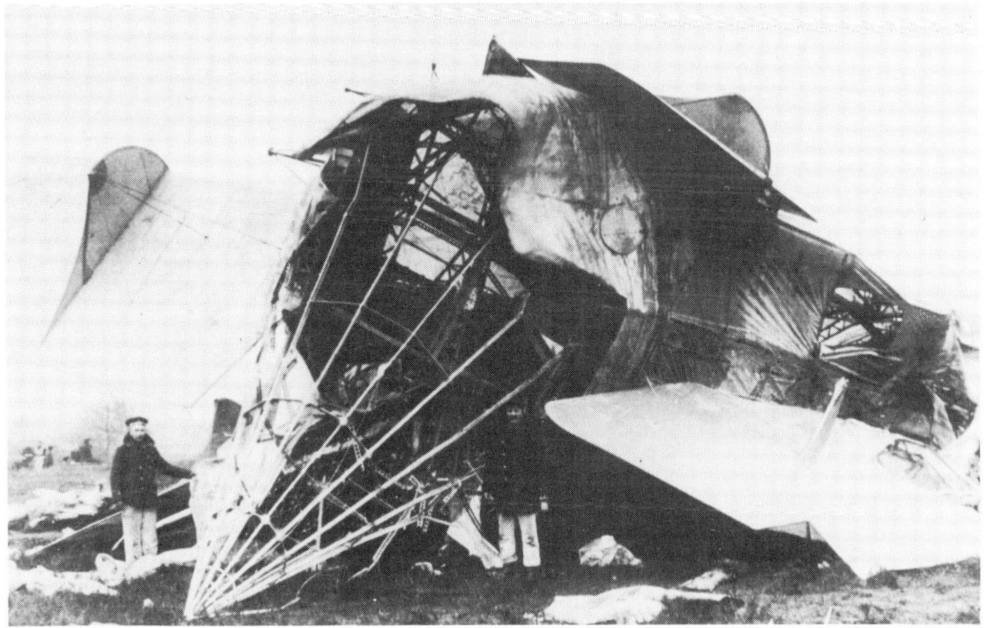

got washed ashore, and details of the accident are unknown to this day. SL VII was based at Rheinau and Königsberg and took part in six raids led by the experienced *Hauptmann* Pochhammer. The last Schütte-Lanz ship to be operated regularly by the Army was SL XI, which was sent to bomb London on 2 September 1916. The crew failed to reach their target, however, and the ship was shot down by Leefe Robinson.

Of the ten Schütte-Lanz airships operated by the Army, only four flew on combat missions over enemy territory, the rest being used for training. At least four of these had internal damage and thus could not be used offensively. The German Navy took over its first Schütte-Lanz, SL 3, after the first flight, which occurred on 20 February 1915. A highlight of its career was its attack on the British submarine *E4* on 24 September 1915 while escorting the auxiliary cruiser *Meteor*. The ship survived a total of thirty reconnaissance missions and one raid over southern England in the middle of that year. The next ship, SL 4, made 21 reconnaissance sorties over the Baltic Sea. SL 6 ended its life after only six missions owing to an explosion on take-off on 18 November 1915. *Kapitänleutnant* Wolff's SL 8 was not completed until April 1916, and the ship operated over the North and Baltic Seas until it was decommissioned at the end of 1917; it made 37 sorties,

Right: A close-up view of SL 15's control gondola taken in June 1916.

TABLE 7: SUMMARY OF SCHÜTTE-LANZ RIGID AIRSHIPS

<table>
<tr><th>Manufacturer's designation</th><th>Operator</th><th>Military designation</th><th>Type</th><th>Gas capacity (m³)</th></tr>
<tr><td>SL 1</td><td>Heinrich Lanz</td><td>–</td><td>A</td><td>20,500</td></tr>
<tr><td>SL 2</td><td>Army</td><td>SL II</td><td>B</td><td>27,500</td></tr>
<tr><td>SL 3</td><td>Navy</td><td>SL 3</td><td>C1</td><td rowspan="3">32,400</td></tr>
<tr><td>SL 4</td><td>Navy</td><td>SL 4</td><td>C2</td></tr>
<tr><td>SL 5</td><td>Army</td><td>SL V</td><td>C3</td></tr>
<tr><td>SL 6</td><td>Navy</td><td>SL 6</td><td>D1</td><td rowspan="2">35,100</td></tr>
<tr><td>SL 7</td><td>Army</td><td>SL VII</td><td>D2</td></tr>
<tr><td>SL 8</td><td>Navy</td><td>SL 8</td><td>E1</td><td rowspan="12">38,800</td></tr>
<tr><td>SL 9</td><td>Navy</td><td>SL 9</td><td>E2</td></tr>
<tr><td>SL 10</td><td>Army</td><td>SL X</td><td>E3</td></tr>
<tr><td>SL 11</td><td>Army</td><td>SL XI</td><td>E4</td></tr>
<tr><td>SL 12</td><td>Navy</td><td>SL 12</td><td>E5</td></tr>
<tr><td>SL 13</td><td>Army</td><td>SL XIII</td><td>E6</td></tr>
<tr><td>SL 14</td><td>Navy</td><td>SL 14</td><td>E7</td></tr>
<tr><td>SL 15</td><td>Army</td><td>SL XV</td><td>E8</td></tr>
<tr><td>SL 16</td><td>Army</td><td>SL XVI</td><td>E9</td></tr>
<tr><td>SL 17</td><td>Army</td><td>SL XVII</td><td>E10</td></tr>
<tr><td>SL 18</td><td>Army</td><td>–</td><td>E11</td></tr>
<tr><td>SL 19</td><td>Navy</td><td>–</td><td>E12</td></tr>
<tr><td>SL 20</td><td>Navy</td><td>–</td><td>F1</td><td rowspan="3">56,300</td></tr>
<tr><td>SL 21</td><td>Army</td><td>–</td><td>F2</td></tr>
<tr><td>SL 22</td><td>Navy</td><td>SL 22</td><td>F3</td></tr>
<tr><td>SL 23</td><td>Not allocated</td><td>–</td><td>G</td><td>68,800</td></tr>
<tr><td>SL 24</td><td>Not allocated</td><td>–</td><td>H</td><td>78,000</td></tr>
</table>

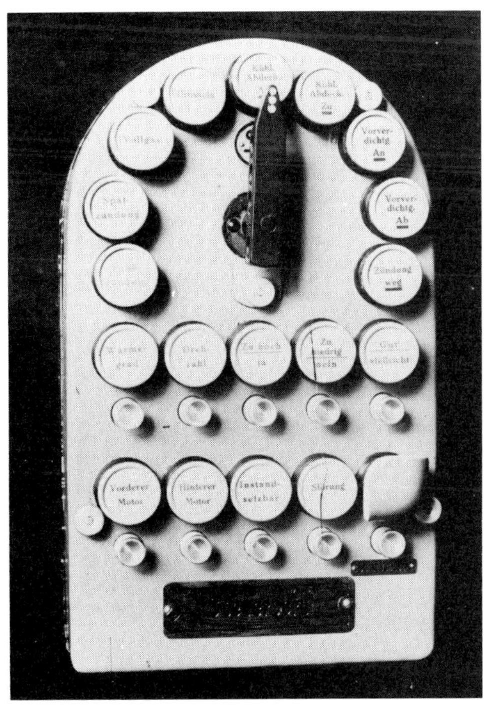

Left: The interior of the Schütte-Lanz SL 15, prepared for action, late 1916.
Above: SL 15's machine telegraph.
Above right: A general view of the *Spähkorb* ('sub-cloud car' or reconnaissance basket), used during offensive missions over Western Europe.
Right: SL 15 at Rheinau on completion.

Left: A close-up view of the gun platform on the roof.
Below: SL 20's rear gondolas.
Above right: A side view of SL 20. The ship was completed on 10 June 1918 and decommissioned in 1920.
Centre right: A drawing of the huge SL 22 combat ship.
Below right: The command gondola of SL 22.

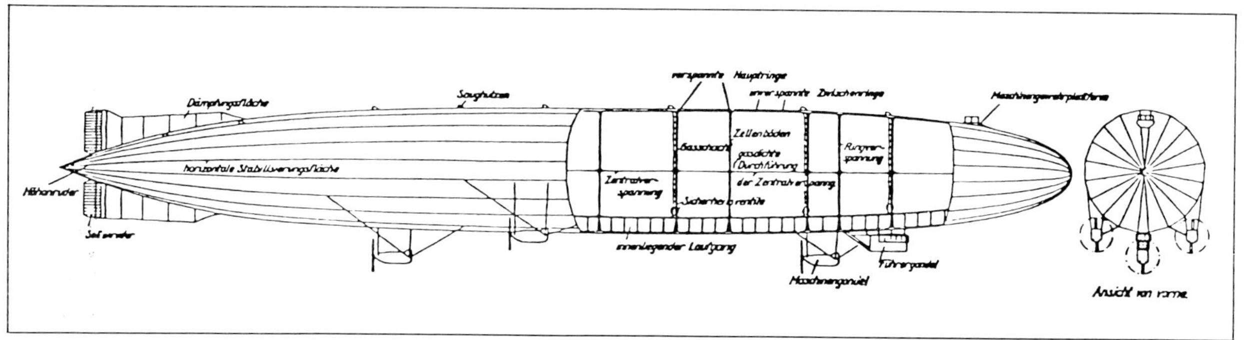
Dämpfungsfläche
Saughutzen
verspannte Hauptringe
unverspannte Zwischenringe
Höhenruder
horizontale Stabilisierungsfläche
Zentralverspannung
Zellenböden
Gasschacht
gasdichte Durchführung der Zentralverspannung
Ringverspannung
Sicherheitsventile
innenliegender Laufgang
Führergondel
Maschinengondel
Ansicht von vorne

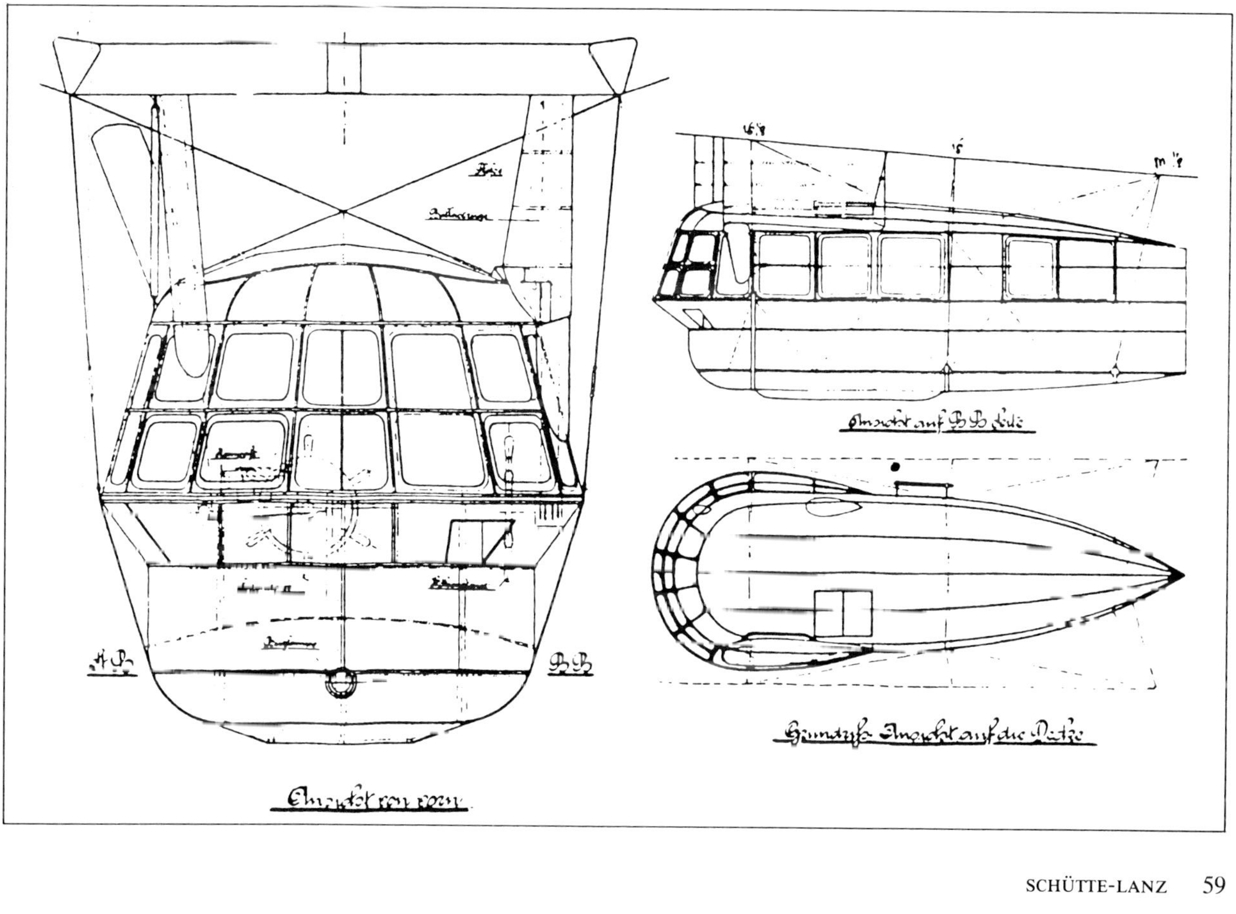

more than any other Schütte-Lanz. Both SL 9 and SL 12, completed during 1916, were also engaged in reconnaissance duties.

The last combat airships built by Schütte-Lanz and handed over to the Imperial German Navy, SL 14 and SL 20, saw only minor action before both were burnt or scrapped. SL 21 was merely evaluated, and the last ship, SL 22, was used for trials from 12 June 1918 and did not see operational service. Altogether 20 out of 24 Schütte-Lanz ships were actually completed; there were eight basic versions, as shown in Table 7.

On 18 January 1917 Peter Strasser, the experienced *Führer der Luftschiffe*, reported to the commanding officers of the Naval HQ in Berlin:

> The handing over of three new Schütte-Lanz ships of the 30,000m^3 class, together with that of the SL 13, is today still impossible because there are no more trained crews available.

Then he contended that SL 21 to 23 could be operated only if SL 8, 9 and 14 were to be decommissioned. However,

> Most of the Schütte-Lanz ships are not usable under combat conditions, especially those operated by the Navy, because their wooden construction cannot cope with the damp conditions inseparable from maritime service.

But the most telling argument against extending the operational careers of these ships was their fragile wooden construction; SL 13, for example, was severely damaged when its structure collapsed. Strasser concluded by saying that it seemed to be better to pay Schütte-Lanz compensation than continue to fly with undependable ships under combat conditions. The story of the Schütte-Lanz airships thus ended with demands from their builders for huge sums of money, but neither Johann Schütte nor Karl Lanz received anything other than a small fraction of their due – a fate which befell many others striving to build a more reliable airship. Most inventors and constructors were forced to abandon their work because public funds tended to be used to subsidise only the larger companies such as von Parseval, Schütte-Lanz and, especially, von Zeppelin.

Graf Zeppelin

The most familiar name among German airship builders is that of Ferdinand Adolf Heinrich *Graf* von Zeppelin, who was born on 8 July 1838 at Lake Constance. In 1853 he was studying at the *Politechnikum* in Stuttgart and two years later he became a member of the *Kriegsschule* at Ludwigsburg. He served as a lieutenant with the *8 (Württ.) Infantrieregiment* at Stuttgart for about two months. In October 1858 he was sent to Tübingen University, where he stayed for two years before joining the Engineering Corps. On 30 April 1863 he was awarded a grant to travel to North America, where, after meeting Abraham Lincoln, he visited the Potomac Army and accompanied one of the Union's officers in his observation balloon.

On his return to Germany, at the end of 1863, he served with the *Württembergische Armee*. In April 1865 he was appointed as a personal adjutant, and in 1866 he took part in the German campaign against Austria which ended with the victory at Königrätz. He was decorated with the *Ritterkreuz* of the military Order of Merit. In April 1868 he joined the *Grosse Generalstab*, the supreme German staff, in Berlin and was transferred to the *Garde-Dragoner-Regiment* early in November that year. From 24 to 26 July 1870, during the Franco-Prussian War, he took part in a

Below: SL 22 during a descent at Rheinau, summer 1918.

TABLE 8: GERMAN AIRSHIP PIONEERS, 1872–1913

Constructor	First ship	First flight	Construction
Hänlein	*	13/12/72	Non-rigid
Wölfert	*Deutschland*	06/05/96	Non-rigid
Schwarz	*	03/11/97	Rigid
Zeppelin	LZ 1	02/07/00	Rigid
Gross Basenach	M I	23/07/04	Semi-rigid
Parseval	P 1	26/05/06	Non-rigid
Clouth	I	20/08/09	Non-rigid
Ruthenberg	1	30/08/09	Semi-rigid
Erbslöh	1	01/12/09	Semi-rigid
Steffen	*Kiel I*	25/03/10	Semi-rigid
Siemens-Schuckert	SS 1	23/01/11	Non-rigid
Schütte-Lanz	SL I	07/10/11	Rigid
Bruckner	*Suchard*	00/05/12	Non-rigid
Veeh	I	08/07/13	Semi-rigid

*No designation

Far right: A portrait of Ferdinand Graf von Zeppelin just before the outbreak of the First World War.

Recognizierungsritt (reconnaissance mission on horseback) behind the French lines.

From 1874 von Zeppelin served as a *Major* with the *2 Württembergisches Dragoner-Regiment* at Ulm and became the commanding officer of the *Ulanenregiment* at Stuttgart. After being appointed *Oberst* he was sent as an envoy to Berlin in 1887, where he prepared an impressive memo dealing with the need for dirigible balloons. Because von Zeppelin criticized the Prussian command over his own *Württembergische* forces he was promoted to *Generalleutnant z.D.* and was retired in November 1890, and he now found himself with time available to turn his thoughts to the conduct of warfare. Produced in collaboration with Theodor Kober, von Zeppelin's first designs were sent to Berlin and studied by *Professor* Helmholtz.

On 31 August 1895 he applied for a patent for a huge manned airship and wrote a second detailed paper about dirigible balloons. He believed that his airship would be very useful for the following tasks:

1. Naval reconnaissance and air photography;
2. Army reconnaissance and air photography;
3. Intelligence-gathering and survey work;
4. Developing Germany's overseas colonies;
5. Exploring unknown regions of Africa, Antarctica and the Arctic;
6. Meteorological research over great distances; and
7. Building up a worldwide postal service.

Although the first two roles concerned the military aspects of manned aviation, von Zeppelin was convinced that his ideas about air travel would have other important applications. In 1897 he noted in his diary:

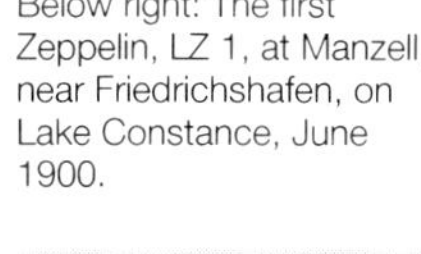

Below right: The first Zeppelin, LZ 1, at Manzell, near Friedrichshafen, on Lake Constance, June 1900.

It is my opinion, concerning new flying machines other than balloons, that none of the many types built to date has a future; Hiram Maxim's aircraft, for example, was destroyed after leaving its guide rail. But I feel sure that the dependable aircraft will be developed very soon. The experiments of Otto Lilienthal were very impressive, but without adequate propulsion there is no real possibility of safe manned flight.

In the event that men are able to construct reliable aircraft, the latter will have many advantages. Able to fly at their own speed, aircraft of the future will be very manoeuvrable, independent of temperatures and the restricted altitudes of balloons.

On 30 December 1896 the *Verein Deutscher Ingenieure* (VDI), gave its blessing to *Graf* von Zeppelin's suggestions and expressed the hope that people would support his ideas by contributing money to build an experimental airship. Four years later, in June 1899, the *Graf* initiated the construction of a large floating hangar on Lake Constance. On 18 July the hangar drifted away and had to be brought back in place by a steamer, and the next day it happened again, but at the end of the month the work was finished. On 7 July 1900 the hangar was hit by lightning, although neither it nor the huge airship taking shape inside was damaged.

The ship, designated LZ 1, was taken out for its maiden voyage that same month, hauled out on a huge pontoon by a small steamboat. After a prayer, *Graf* Ferdinand von Zeppelin together with his friend *Baron* von Baizes and three others entered the two gondolas. The ship rose, but eighteen minutes later one of the engines failed and then the elevator mechanism broke down and von Zeppelin was forced to land. New problems arose when he tried to bring the ship back to its hangar, but in spite of some minor damage the many helping hands succeeded in coaxing it back into its lair.

The next flights took place on 17 and 24 October 1900, and the ship reached a speed of 32.4kph (17.5kt). The *Graf* was well pleased, and he now travelled to Berlin in order to win further funding for his project. However, no help was forthcoming and in mid-November von Zeppelin was obliged to

Left: LZ 1's first take-off, on 2 July 1900 over Lake Constance, is watched by some children.

Left: LZ 1 during summer 1910 at Manzell after damage sustained when the ship was being returned to its hangar.
Right: LZ 1 collapsed while being rebuilt because of the weight of its structure.

Above: LZ 1 photographed while being moved out of its floating hangar near Friedrichshafen.

lay off most of his workers. In December 1900 he was forced into liquidation, one of the last employees to stay being *Dr* Ludwig Dürr (1878–1956), who was responsible for constructing all his famous airships. Despite his award from *Kaiser* Wilhelm II of the *Roter Adlerorden I. Klasse*, it seemed impossible to get any more official backing to re-establish his company again, and in 1903 von Zeppelin therefore appealed to the public for money to build a second ship, LZ 2. The response was gratifying, and two years later, on 30 November 1905, the new airship lifted off. Within a few weeks, however, on 17 January 1906, the ship was stranded at Kisselgg and totally destroyed. Nevertheless, more money flowed in, and he was able to begin the construction of a third huge ship with the designation LZ 3. It was ready for its first flight on 9 October 1906 but attempts to obtain further funding failed until the *Graf* sought permission to start a national lottery. Subsequently some 6,250,000 Reichmarks were collected, and his work was able to continue.

LZ 4 was completed in 1908 and took off for the first time on 20 June 1908. This ship was involved in many long-distance flights, and in a wide circuit over the Swiss Cantons on 3 July 1908 the royals of Württemberg accompanied *Graf* Zeppelin on a tour over Lake Constance. Shortly after his 80th birthday von Zeppelin's fourth ship rose at Friedrichshafen for a long distance journey of about 1,500km. Flying in a northerly direction, the *Graf* tried to reach Mainz as a turning point but at Geinsheim-Kornsand the

Left: *Graf* Zeppelin's second ship, LZ 2, outside its hangar.

Left: LZ 2 at Manzell just prior to its maiden flight on 17 January 1906.

Left: LZ 3 leaves its hangar at Manzell to carry out a circuit over Lake Constance.

ship was forced to interrupt its journey and land near the banks of the Rhine about 20km south of Mainz after one engine broke down. The weight of the ship prevented it from rising again and therefore ballast, equipment and some crewmen were taken off, and the ship was able to continue its journey, watched by dozens of VIPs who had been following by car, including *Grossherzog* Ludwig of Hessen, Prince Heinrich von Preussen and Prince von Battenberg. After a circuit over Nierstein and Oppenheim, LZ 4 disappeared in a southerly direction again, but a sunny day ended in disaster. At Echterdingen, near Stuttgart, the Zeppelin had to descend once more because its engines failed, and shortly after LZ 4 touched down a thunderstorm broke, tearing the huge craft from its mooring. It was tossed for half a mile and, damaged by trees, it burst into flames. Two mechanics, one of them *Obermeister* Schwarz, were trying to repair the engines at the time and they were fortunate in escaping from the ship at the very last moment.

Meanwhile Luftschiffbau Zeppelin GmbH had been founded and work had begun to design and manufacture improved airships. Thousands of Germans had supported the company with money and there was some important help from government authorities too. To gain greater publicity, LZ 3 flew again from 23 October to 10 November 1908, and for its eighth flight Prince Heinrich von Preussen and the German Crown Prince took

Right: LZ 4 at Kornsand near Geinsheim, on the Rhine, on 4 August 1908, about two months after its first flight.

Above: The large floating hangar approaches completion.

their places in the roomy gondola. By mid-November von Zeppelin was honoured by Wilhelm II for his contribution to manned aviation. Vast sums of money were still needed to realize the ambitions of, and expensive ships envisaged by, Ludwig Dürr, and so the *Zeppelin-Stiftung* (Zeppelin Foundation) was established.

Further successful flights followed, for example LZ 3's eleventh and twelfth sorties and LZ 5's long-distance journey beginning on 2 June 1909, covering Nuremberg, Leipzig and Halle and lasting 37hr in total. A short time later LZ 3 was handed over to the German Army and flown under the military designation Z I. LZ 6, another of the early ships, was flown for the first time on 25 August 1909. Two days later the ship took off again, and in 1931 the famous airship leader H. von Schiller described this and subsequent flights:

> On 27 August 1909, early in the morning, *Dr* Ludwig Dürr took off in the direction of Berlin. Two hours later the forward engine transmission broke off and the ship had to descend near Ostheim/Gunzerhausen. The crew spent more than three hours on repairs. At 16.20hrs LZ 6 reached Nuremberg-Dutzendteich, where enough gas was available to refill the envelope. At 2.12hrs in the morning LZ 6 rose and passed over Bayreuth, Hof and Plauen. In the afternoon the port engine failed once more and seconds later the propeller flew off. At 18.26hrs the ship landed at Bitterfeld, its arrival awaited by the Crown Prince and *Graf* von Zeppelin. During the night the broken engine was overhauled. On 29 August von Zeppelin took over the ship and arrived over the Tegel military base about noon. The *Graf* stayed at Berlin for a meeting with Wilhelm II to discuss the military and civil applications of his airships, and LZ 6 climbed off again and set course back to Friedrichshafen some minutes before midnight. The following day one propeller blade spun off and damaged gas cell No. 6. The gas deflated, but an emergency landing was negotiated without any problems. A replacement propeller was taken from Z II which was based at Cologne,

Left: *Direktor* Colsman, L. Dürr and *Graf* Zeppelin pose in the front gondola of their airship at the ILA in 1909.
Below left: LZ 4 landing at Frankfurt-Rebstock next to a *Drachenballon.*
Below: LZ 4 burnt out at Echterdingen near Stuttgart after a career involving many flights over Germany.

Right: LZ 5 was damaged at Göppingen following the ship's return to Manzell on 2 June 1909.
Below: LZ 5 totally destroyed at Weilburg.

Left: LZ 6 took off for the first time in 1909. It was used as an experimental airship.
Below left: An early Zeppelin airship photographed near Berlin in 1912.

while the metal strips were changed for static drive shafts and the torn cell was repaired. On 1 September 1909 the ship was ready to take off, and it arrived at the floating hangar about 23hr later.

On 4 September some *Reichstag* officials were invited to fly in von Zeppelin's LZ 6 on one of six short circuits over Lake Constance. Four days later the first wireless trials were conducted during two flights, one of which carried the King of Saxonia on board. Later, in mid-September 1909, the ship was sent to the ILA at Frankfurt. The Zeppelin was next engaged in the *Kaisermanöver* at Düsseldorf before its return to Friedrichshafen on 22 September 1909.

Subsequent trials demonstrated the exciting potential of a wireless system in an airship. From 22 September LZ 6 was tested with a third engine, which raised the maximum speed to 54kph. On 27 October the ship was moved from its floating hangar to the marquee at Friedrichshafen. After its 45th flight LZ 6 was deflated and lengthened to 144m; it now boasted eighteen gas cells, one more than previously, and its total volume had increased to 15,000m^3. The first test-flight in its new configuration took place on 19 August 1910, and two days later the ship was transferred to Baden-Oos, from where eight additional flights were made up to 10 September. On 1 September the second DELAG ship was completely destroyed at Baden-Oos when fire broke while the motor gondolas were being cleaned. There were no casualties . . .

The loss of this ship did not dismay the traditionalists among the German generals and admirals, and in an attempt to rescue the project *Direktor* Colsman contacted various townships and tried to win their support with promises of a detailed programme to build huge airships hangars all over Germany and therefore establish a network of Zeppelin routes connecting each town. To this end, the *Deutsche Luftschiffahrts-Aktiengesellschaft* (DELAG) was founded on 16 November 1909, in association with the well-known Hamburg-Amerika-Line. The first ship to be operated under this new venture was LZ 7 *Deutschland*, which was transferred to its new base near Düsseldorf on 22 June 1910. However, only five flights were made before the ship became stranded, six days later, in Teutoburger Forest as a consequence of bad weather. Nobody was hurt, and the passengers, mostly journalists, were able to disembark from the *Deutschland* by ladders, although the DELAG was forced to scrap the ship.

As mentioned above, the lengthened LZ 6 was burnt out at Baden-Oos while under maintenance by the DELAG after only 34 flights. The next ship, LZ 8, named *Deutsch-*

Below: Disasters befell the DELAG during the first years of the corporation's existence. These are the remains of LZ 6.

land II, was brought to Düsseldorf on 11 April 1910 but just over a month later, on 16 May, it was destroyed after colliding with its own hangar. Thus within a few months the DELAG had lost all three of its ships to accidents, and the prospects of securing insurance cover for a fourth did not appear good. More positively, however, *Dr* Eckener succeeded in contacting Karl Maybach (the son of Wilhelm Maybach), who had designed a new 145hp engine with a low fuel consumption, and as a result of their discussions Maybach-Motorenbau, which had moved to Friedrichshafen, received sufficient orders to warrant the erection of a new factory south of the Zeppelin works.

LZ 9 was tested intensively over southern Germany in 1911. It was proposed for operation by the DELAG but in fact was transferred to the German Army under the designation Z II (*Ersatz*), after the first Z II had been written off on 25 April 1910. *Direktor* Colsman thus had to await LZ 10, which became the famous *Schwaben*. The first

Far left: *Dr* Hugo Eckener. Left: The rather primitive gondola fitted to LZ 8. The ship was commanded by *Dr* Dürr.

Right: The seventh Zeppelin was handed over to the DELAG and named *Luftschiff Deutschland.*

flight for this ship took place on 26 June 1911 and on 20 July it completed a spectacular flight to Switzerland. There were eight crew members and passengers on board LZ 10 when course was set for Lucerne, and after making some circuits of the city the ship steered to the Rigi Mountain. After passing Zürich, Wintherthur and Frauenfeld, the airship crossed Lake Constance and returned to Friedrichshafen. Flights such as this were instrumental in making airship journeys a popular pastime for the rich, and the *Schwaben* alone was engaged in 218 'pleasure cruises', carrying a total of 4,354 passengers and covering a distance of 27,321km. Just a year later, however, the ship was destroyed by fire in Düsseldorf. Meanwhile *Dr* Eckener had managed to raise both the technical standards of airship construction and the flying experience of his men. When Eckener instituted his passenger flights using a modified cabin with enough room for 24 paying guests, a steward was provided, offering exquisite refreshments on board.

Left: The famous civil airship *Schwaben* being pulled down by military ground crew at Düsseldorf.

Right: LZ 10 *Schwaben* crossing Friedrichshafen in 1911.

SACHSEN
VIKTORIA LUISE
VIKTORIA LUISE

Left: Two DELAG ships, *Sachsen* (LZ 17) and *Viktoria Luise* (LZ 11), in the large hangar at Baden-Oos.
Below left: *Viktoria Luise* descending to a meadow near Worms.
Below: The passenger compartment of LZ 13 *Hansa*.

On 14 February 1912 LZ 11, *Viktoria Luise*, was commissioned under the command of *Dr* Eberhard Lempertz. Propelled by three 170hp Maybach engines, the 18,700m^3 ship transported a total of 2,995 paying passengers during its time with the DELAG and by 31 July 1914 had made 489 flights. Military personnel were often to be seen on board for training purposes, and on 1 August 1914 the *Viktoria Luise* was handed over to the Imperial Army, serving as a training ship based at Leipzig, Dresden and Liegnitz. Its 1,000th flight was completed at the end of June 1915, and LZ 11 had covered a total of 64,125km before it was destroyed on 8 October that year while entering its hangar. The next Zeppelin, LZ 12, became the property of the Army as Z III and was stationed at Friedrichshafen, Fulshbüttel, Frankfurt-Rebstock, Baden-Oos and Metz. It was decommissioned on 1 August after 28 months' service as it was considered to be out of date.

The DELAG ship *Hansa* (LZ 13) entered service on 30 July 1913 and made 297 flights up to the end of October 1913, including a spectacular long-distance sortie over Denmark and southern Sweden which had covered more than 700km by the time the ship landed at Hamburg-Fuhlsbüttel. With the First World War imminent, the Army took over command of LZ 13 and used it for training purposes with considerable success. After some time spent at Düsseldorf it was transferred to Johannisthal near Berlin. Most of the men trained on *Hansa* belonged to the Imperial German Navy. During the summer of 1916 the ship was declared obsolete and was decommissioned.

LZ 17 Sachsen was also built for the DELAG and was the last ship to see civilian service. Its maiden flight took place on 3 June 1913; it was commanded by the well-known *Dipl-Ing.* E. A. Lehmann and later by *Kapitän* Hacker. LZ 17 was powered by three 170hp Maybach engines and could fly at speeds of up to about 80kph (43kt). By 31 July 1914 it had covered an aggregate distance of 39,919km in 741 hours' flying, carrying 9,837

TABLE 9: AIRSHIP STRENGTH BY NATION, 1914

Country	No of ships	Total volume (m^3)
Germany	17	244,100
France	14	116,600
Russia	13	63,800
Italy	11	71,265
Great Britain	7	25,000
Austria	3	15,900
Belgium	3	12,800
United States	3	2,200
Japan	2	9,200
Turkey	1	2,200
The Netherlands	1	910

TABLE 10: IMPERIAL GERMAN ARMY ZEPPELIN AIRSHIPS, 1914

Year built	Manufacturer's designation	Military designation
1909	LZ 3	Z I
	LZ 5	Z II
1910	–	–
1911	LZ 9	*Ersatz* Z II
1912	–	–
	LZ 15	*Ersatz* Z I
	LZ 16	Z IV
1913	LZ 19	*Ersatz* Z I
	LZ 20	Z V
	LZ 21	Z VI
	LZ 22	Z VII
1914	LZ 23	Z VIII
	LZ 25	Z IX

people during its 419 flights, including one on 10 June 1913 from Baden-Oos to Vienna in nine hours. During the spring of 1914 the ship was lengthened from 140m to 148m, extending its range to 2,800km.

On 1 August 1914 the ship was transferred to military authority and was subsequently based at Leipzig, Potsdam, Posen, Königsberg and Cologne. One month after hostilities began, on 2 September, its crew were ordered to carry out a bombing raid on Antwerp; a year later *Sachsen* was handed over to the Navy in order to assist in the latter's training programme.

Right: LZ 17 *Sachsen* received camouflage and was operated by the German Army after a total of 419 flights.

Left: LZ 11 *Viktoria Luise* had become part of the training establishment of the German Army by summer 1914.

Left: LZ 13 was handed over to the Government to become a training vessel on 1 August 1914.

In 1914 Germany operated more airships than any other nation (see Table 9), but with *Sachsen*'s transfer to the Navy the passenger-carrying careers of the early Zeppelin airships ended. The DELAG had safely transported thousands of passengers in some 1,500 flights between 1910 and 1914, but none of the four craft involved – *Schwaben* (LZ 10), *Viktoria Luise* (LZ 11), *Hansa* (LZ 13) and *Sachsen* (LZ 17) – survived the war to resume civil flying.

By the time the First World War broke out the Imperial German Army had taken over eleven of the 25 Zeppelin ships built, as shown in Table 10, but despite the presence in its fleet also of the few early *Heeres-Luftschiffe* and a single Navy airship, L 3 (LZ 24), it had only a limited offensive capacity. Only 232 flights were made by Army ships up to August 1914, although they gathered much valuable data on how aerial warfare might progress in the future.

GERMAN AIRSHIPS IN COMBAT

A new kind of air war

When advanced internal combustion engines became available via the motor-car industry they brought, within a very short period of time, the prospect not just of revolutionising modes of transport on the ground but of influencing other modes of transport too. The range and performance of the dirigible airship were immediately improved, and the military potential of the non-rigid airship also looked very promising.

During 1906 and 1907 *Major* von Parseval had gained some useful experience with the non-rigid airship he had constructed. Built by the *Motorluftschiff-Studiengesellschaft*, it fulfilled the demands of the German *Heeresleitung*. The craft had to be capable of:

1. A minimum endurance of 10hr;
2. A 1hr flight at an altitude of 1,500m;
3. A minimum speed of about 12m/sec (23.3kt); and
4. Having the envelope inflated, and its mission prepared in general, outside a hangar.

Von Parseval's designs satisfied the Army and his ships were handed over to the *Luftschiffer-Detachment*. A short time later *Graf* Zeppelin's early rigid airship was able to achieve the following results, again as required by the *Oberste Heeresleitung*:

1. An uninterrupted flight lasting 24hr;
2. A minimum range of 700km;
3. The ability to reach a predetermined destination; and
4. A safe landing on solid ground.

The promising progress made by *Graf* Zeppelin led to the first *Heeresluftschiff*, called *Luftschiff Zeppelin* Z I, being accepted for service by the *Luftschiffer-Detachment*, thereby opening a new chapter in military history. However, this craft was a far cry from the well-equipped, high-performance, long-range Zeppelin and Schütte-Lanz airships that would later equip the German armed forces. A whole range of technical problems had to be addressed before effective military missions could be flown. For example, a costly ground infrastructure had to be established, involving huge hangars, gas depots, facilities for the production of hydrogen, maintenance shops and a system of wireless stations. Altogether, during the course of war some fifty airship hangars were available in Germany and the occupied territories, while further installations were taken over from the civil authorities on the outbreak of war. The most important military airship bases were Nordholz near Cuxhaven and Ahlhorn near Oldenburg, each of which could handle 22 large ships. Apart from fixed hangars there were also some which rotated (for example at Nordholz) and which could thus be turned into the wind as required.

The actual performance and range of the early ships was, however, insufficient for strategic operations over enemy countries during the first months of the war: in spite of their many virtues the new air weapons of the *Oberste Heeresleitung* were too small and vulnerable to carry out effective missions over Europe. The explosive hydrogen gas was unpredictable, and the craft's integrity was too much at the mercy of its service ceiling, air temperatures and other physical phenomena. For example, if the dynamic lift were too little, it was necessary to reduce the water ballast; too great, and gas had to be released by the crew. The limited capacity for fuel and water ballast also brought dangers, while on top of all this was the pervading influence of the weather. In practice, only a small number of ships failed to return through being hit by lightning, others possibly becoming victims of explosions similar to that which destroyed the *Hindenburg* at Lakehurst when it was being readied for landing. Most of the remaining casualties were victims of bad weather during take-off or landing manoeuvres.

The German airships were very vulnerable to incendiary ammunition and therefore had to fly at ever greater altitudes. The later types could climb to 7,000m but because engine output weakened with height, special high-altitude motors were fitted to some of the more advanced Navy ships. The major problem was the lack of oxygen at altitude. At

Right: LZ 3, designated Z I on transfer to the German Army.

Right: LZ 5 paid a visit to Weilburg on 25 April 1910. The ship was designated Z II by the Army.

first each crew member used a separate oxygen bottle, but the contaminated air was impure and, later, liquid oxygen, heated up to normal temperatures, was used. Each crew member was equipped with his own mouthpiece and was able to draw on the oxygen support system from flexible tubes available at all the main crew positions. Some missions almost failed when the crew became airsick, their ships having ascended to dangerous altitudes. On L 44's first sortie, for example, during the night of 24 May 1917, all the engines failed and the ship climbed to an altitude of nearly 6,000m. *Kapitänleutnant*

Above: LZ 5 after modification into an operational Army airship.

Stabbert, his crew and *Fregattenkapitän* Strasser, the FdL, survived their ordeal and managed to bring the airship down to 3,900m. Another incident occurred while L46 was endeavouring to attack targets in eastern England. The commander lost consciousness and most of the crew became airsick, and Strasser ordered the watch officer, *Oberleutnant* Frey, to take over command. When the commander, *Kapitänleutnant* Hollender, came round on the way back, he was astonished to discover that his First Officer was busy landing the airship. Both these problems were brought about solely on account of a lack of oxygen. Discounting these technical shortcomings, of course, enemy forces were responsible for many of the losses over Western Europe, and especially those over the British Isles.

A short history of the *Heeresluftschiffe*

On 1 October 1913 the *Luftschiffertruppe* was enlarged to comprise five battalions. The first had been set up in 1884 in Berlin and, together with *Luftschiffer-Bataillon Nr 2*, which was raised in 1911, was assigned to the *Garde-Korps* – a move which immediately increased its standing. The third unit was established in Düsseldorf and Cologne in 1911 and became part of *VIII Armee-Korps*, while *Nr 4* and *Nr 5* were founded in 1913 and stationed around Mannheim, Metz and Graudenz. During the summer of 1913 four so-called *Fliegerbataillone* were in existence, but those were dissolved on 1 October 1913 because their craft were still performing too poorly to be militarily effective. The need to train crews meant that airships would not be ready for active service until the early winter

Below: Z II (*Ersatz*) was lengthened and then used for training purposes.

Right: LZ 15, an *h*-type ship, became the second Z I, designated Z I (*Ersatz*).

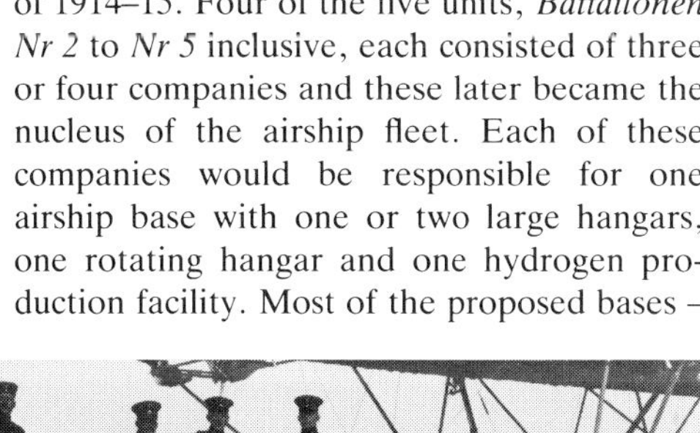

of 1914–15. Four of the five units, *Battailonen Nr 2* to *Nr 5* inclusive, each consisted of three or four companies and these later became the nucleus of the airship fleet. Each of these companies would be responsible for one airship base with one or two large hangars, one rotating hangar and one hydrogen production facility. Most of the proposed bases – Düsseldorf, Darmstadt, Mannheim, Lahr, Friedrichshafen, Graudenz and Schneidemühl – were near the borders, with only a few – Hannover, Dresden, Leipzig and Jüterbog – in central Germany. None of the airship hangars (length 180m, width 35m, height 28m) was completed until the outbreak of war, and the *Luftschiffer* was therefore allocated the military airship hangars at Königsberg, Allenstein, Thorn, Posen, Liegnitz, Cologne, Metz, Strassbourg and Trier, but because some of these were either too small or inconveniently sited, the German *Oberste Heeresleitung* directed that private hangars at Düsseldorf, Frankfurt/Main, Baden-Oos, Dresden, Leipzig and Berlin were to be requisitioned.

Below: LZ 9 was the third Army airship and was operated from Cologne, Metz and Gotha.

In August 1914 only the *Heeresluftschiffe* Z IV to Z IX, the Schütte-Lanz SL 2, the Gross-Basenach M IV, the Parseval P IV and three former civil airships of the Deutsche Luftschiffahrts-AG (DELAG), *Viktoria Luise*, *Hansa* and *Sachsen*, were ready for limited military action. Of these, four were intended for operations over on the *Westfront* and three over the *Ostfront*. The German Navy received M IV, while two other airships were in the

Above left: LZ 21 (alias Z VI) was engaged in one of the raids on Liége and was damaged in action by AA batteries.
Left: A close-up view of an early Zeppelin being manoeuvred by a civilian ground crew at Baden-Oos.
Above: Despite camouflage measures (this is either Darmstadt or Mannheim), Allied flyers still found the huge hangars.

process of being commissioned. All the others were too old for active service and were to be employed solely for training.

Because early German airships were small (18,000–25,000m^3), their military payload was very limited and their maximum ceiling still only 2,400m, and it therefore came as no surprise when four ships (Z V to Z VIII) were lost during the first month of the war. However, despite the limitations of the German airship force, the British Secret Service was worried, as was made clear on 1 January 1916:

> Information from a trustworthy source has been received that the Germans intend to make an attack on London by airships on a great scale at any early opportunity.
>
> The Air Department of the Admiralty must make it plain that they are quite powerless to prevent such an attack if it is launched with good fortune and favourable weather conditions.

In fact the airships' roles, especially that of bombing important military and civilian targets in hostile territory but also that of strategic reconnaissance, seemed incapable of being fulfilled during daylight. The first losses had provided a bitter lesson: only the crew of SL 2, engaged in reconnaissance sorties for the Austrian Army, had been able to supply much valuable information about enemy forces. Therefore the German General Staff decided in September 1914 that all airships were to be used offensively only on dark, moonless nights and only against large targets (for example, Antwerp, Ostend, Nancy or large Russian troop concentrations behind the front lines). The airship commanders were given freedom to carry out their secret orders, and since the condition of the weather was the decisive factor for a successful outcome to any mission, they were allowed to select one of a group of targets themselves. Despite all the odds two ships, one led by *Hauptmann* Masius, succeeded in attacking Paris on 26 March 1915. Compiègne (SL 2), Calais (Z X) and Ostend (Z X) were bombed in March, but only by a single Army airship on each occasion.

The advent of larger ships, of between 32,000 and 38,000m^3 volume and powered by new Maybach engines, raised top speeds from 70 to nearly 100kph (from 37.75 to 54kt) and service ceilings to 3,000m prior to the release of the bomb loads and up to 4,500m on return flights. While most of the older ships could lift a maximum of some 1,000kg, the new generation of ships could carry 2,000 to 3,000kg of fragmentation and incendiary bombs and, furthermore, could fly missions of about 30hr in duration and in inclement weather thanks to the improvements in engine technology.

Thus, despite intensive efforts, the proposed 'Zeppelin weapon' did not become viable until April 1915; it had not been possible to keep to the planned date of 1914.

Early in 1915 the position of *Chef des Feldflugwesens im Grossen Hauptquartier* was created. The leader of the airships was responsible for all active ships, together with the fighting condition of all troops belonging to the *Luftschiffertruppe* and all training units. In April some minor sorties were flown against Nancy and Poperinghe, while between 29 April and 31 May the first 32,000m^3 ship, LZ 38, operated over Harwich, Southend, Ramsgate and inner London. During the first *London-Angriff* the docks were attacked with about 1,400kg of bombs. The blasts of the explosions were visible to the crew, who now knew that the British air defences would be very quickly improved.

On the night of 6–7 June 1915 the enemy struck back. Aircraft attacked Gontrode and destroyed LZ 38 in its hangar, and LZ 37 was shot down by Lt Warneford near Ghent. Only one crew member, *Steuermann* Müller, survived the latter action, sustaining minor injuries when he fell through the roof of a house into the still-warm bed of a nun who had left it only minutes before! The third ship, LZ 39, was returning from Harwich and escaped into the dense fog just as the attack on Gontrode took place.

Because the short summer nights were not conducive to lengthy missions, a period of rest and new preparations now followed, the next series of sorties over Western Europe being proposed for late summer or autumn 1915. The raids were in fact resumed in September with LZ 77 and LZ 79. Well-known 'veteran' officers began to emerge, such as *Oberleutnant zur See* E. A. Lehmann (the most successful commander, with fourteen sorties), *Hauptmann* Alfred Horn (twelve raids), Linnarz (six) and Schramm (four). *Hauptmann* Götz was another. After bringing a difficult mission to a successful conclusion he wrote the following summary of events:

Combat Report

Concerning the war operation of the Airship LZ 74 on the night of 7–8 September 1915

1. Order of the *Chef des Feldflugwesens: Attack on the city of London*

2. Crew:

Hauptmann George	*Kommandant*
Hauptmann Sommerfeldt	*Erster Offizier*
Oberleutnant Luge	*FT-Offizier*
Feldwebelleutnant de Perthes	*Fahringenieur*
Obersteuermann Seibert	*Höhensteuermann*
Obersteuermann Strobl	*Seitensteuermann*
Obermachinist Weik	*Backbordmotor*
Maschinist Schaab	*Vorderer Motor*
Maschinist Linden	*Achtermotor*
Maschinist Döpelheuer	*Steuerbordmotor*
Vicefeldwebel Beutler	*Maschinengewehrschütze*
Gefreiter Zigan	*Maschinengewehrschütze*
Unteroffizier Kuhnke	*FT-Unteroffizier*
Unteroffizier Auer	*Hilfsmaschinist*

3. Weather conditions:
Good. Predominant wind north-north-west at an altitude over 3,000m. A little hazy.

4. Course of the mission:
Departure 19.27 in the evening. The fire at St Agathe and Evère were still visible from a distance, and the directional fire of Steenbrügge-Ostend was very helpful. Without these indicators it would be very difficult to find the right course to the British coastline. There were no noteworthy facts until now.

Fifty minutes later some British ships were noticed steaming in line ahead. One of the ships tried to locate the airship but fortunately was using too small a searchlight and a few minutes later LZ 74 was too far away.

It was very difficult to reach the required altitude because there was not enough ballast in the ship. The decrease in temperature at an altitude of 3,500m was only 15°C and the weight of the ship had therefore been increased by 600kg. In order to make the raid as effective as possible only 3,850kg of water ballast had been carried along. LZ 74 was armed with twenty 58kg general-purpose bombs, twenty 10kg bombs and an additional thirty-two incendiaries – a total weight of 2,000kg. It was necessary to drain off all the ballast together with 250 litres of fuel and half the cooling water in order to reach the service ceiling for the attack.

LZ 74 crossed the British coast north of the Thames near Foulness Island. Only a few lights were visible on the ground and only a pale glow in the direction of the city of London when approaching at an altitude of about 3,200m; all the suburbs over which the airship passed were completely blacked out. Following the direction of the wind, and bearing in mind the known positions of British defences, the order was to attack London from the north when LZ 74 reached Brentwood–Woodford. Meanwhile the first searchlights were noticed by the crew. The commander of SL 2 later mentioned that when his ship reached London only a few searchlights were in action; just ten minutes later the arrival of LZ 74, following, was anticipated by all the British anti-aircraft units.

It was impossible to avoid contact with the searchlights, so the commander did not change course. However, it was very dusty over London and thus the beams did not have a very great range: although more than ten large lights were

Above: Z IX (production number LZ 25) was completed at Friedrichshafen and first flew on 29 July 1914. It was destroyed in the raid on Düsseldorf.
Right: The 26th Zeppelin was operated by the Army and received the tactical designation Z XII.

trying to pinpoint the German airship it was only possible to hit LZ 74 for a few seconds. The German crew recognized the River Thames with its bridges and ships. All the railway stations were well camouflaged.

The first bombs were released over Leyton railway station, in order to reduce LZ 74's flying weight rather than because of the interesting nature of the target; the real attack started about an hour after midnight and the main targets were the docks near Bow in the East End of the city. *Hauptmann* George estimated that his bomb load would have hit the Surrey Commercial Docks, possibly the West India Docks too and Bethnal Green Station nearby. Large fires were visible from the sky. Between 12.54 and 01.50 the airship was engaged by several batteries, but without any success. One of many incendiary shells, recognizable by their white smoke trails, passed by LZ 74 within a few metres before exploding about 400m above the ship. Both gunners, standing on top of the hull of the Zeppelin, took cover because some of the shells were so close.

The airship left England near the River Crouch, again flying over the cloud cover. There was no possibility of the commander and his men determining the actual position of the ship.

Above: LZ 26, which made eleven raids, was one of the few ships to be equipped with a manned *Spähkorb*. Below: LZ 42 (tactical code LZ 72) was decommissioned at Jüterbog in February 1917 after being used as a training ship.

Above: LZ 47 was shot down on 22 February 1916 in spite of its improved defensive armament. Above right: In addition to the machine guns on the roof of the wartime Zeppelins, most of the ships had 20mm weapons mounted in the gondolas.

While driving on eastwards they noticed the shape of a Schütte-Lanz airship and fifteen minutes later the men realized that SL 2 was in the same situation. After the forts of Amsterdam were seen both ships climbed again and changed their direction to westward. LZ 74 landed at Namur at about 10.10 with two hits on its structure and one engine having failed on account of a mechnical defect.

[Signed] George, *Hauptmann*
and *Kommandant*

In addition to the attacks carried out by SL 2 and LZ 74 over England, raids were made over France. Especially busy was LZ 77, commanded by *Hauptmann* Alfred Horn, which was employed in attacks on the country's main armament manufacturing centres in January 1916. After one flight of some hours without finding his target, Horn dropped bombs on to the important railway junction at Epernay. On 31 January the ship made its second attempt to bomb Paris, and 2,600kg of ordnance was released.

Meanwhile the important German land offensive at Verdun was close at hand. In

Right: LZ 63 (LZ 93) at the Düsseldorf airship base early in 1916.

Left: Heavy machine guns were sited around the airship bases in order to protect the hangars.

order to disrupt communications to the French positions, the *Oberste Heeresleitung* decided to use, in addition to aircraft and heavy artillery, four airships. Two of the four were, however, shot down, one of them, LZ 77, being hit by a shell fired by an unknown motorized anti-aircraft unit while approaching the target at Revigny near Brabant-le-Roi on 21 February 1916.

LZ 79 was lost a few days later without casualties while carrying out an emergency landing near Ath. After a final mission against Margate on 26 April 1916, LZ 87 became a training ship based at Jüterbog. After the next loss, that of LZ 95, other ships were brought into serviceable condition – *Hauptmann* Barth's LZ 81, *Leutnant zur See* Lehmann's LZ 90 and 98, and *Hauptmann* Falk's LZ 88, together with *Hauptmann* Wilhelm Schramm's LZ 93 and *Hauptmann* Linnarz's LZ 97. Three of these ships were of the 32,000m^3 type, the others of the larger 35,800m^3 class. The defensive armament was increased, an additional machine gun at the tail and others on each side of the main gondola augmenting the existing weapons fitted on top of the hull. Trials were conducted to evaluate the 20mm and 37mm armament, but because of their bright muzzle flash the introduction of the heavier weapons was delayed.

In the summer of 1916 the first of the 55,000m^3 airships was ready to be handed over to the Army airship detachment but at the last moment the craft was transferred to the Navy, who had an urgent need for a powerful, high-performance airship for fleet reconnaissance work. The next offensive missions took place in August and September 1916, when London, Boulogne and Calais became the targets for Army airships. After that LZ 97 and LZ 98 were sent to the Eastern Front.

The last mission for a *Heeresluftschiff* took place early in 1917. *Vizefeldwebel* Zigan, a member of the crew of LZ 107, took part in the raid on Boulogne under the command of *Hauptmann* Sommerfeldt and his First Officer, *Leutnant* von Wrangel, on 16 February:

> At 05.47 the well-camouflaged *Heeresluftschiff* LZ 107 was sent to Boulogne where most of the *matériel* of the American Expeditionary Corps was stored; the barracks were also of great interest. There were no problems with the flight until we reached Brussels. Setting course for Ghent, however, a rain front forced the ship to climb above the cloud, but because navigation was almost impossible the commander decided to use the small *Spähkorb*, a device rather like a little wingless aeroplane suspended on a steel cable under the airship and carrying one man. With LZ 107 still flying above the clouds, von Wrangel, sitting in the *Spähkorb*, was lowered 1,000m beneath the ship. However, von Wrangel was unable to give Sommerfeldt any useful information, because a thick haze covered the landscape below. At 09.32 the machine gunners reported a glow in the estimated direc-

tion of Ghent. From there the airship set course for Ostend, which was reached about one hour later. After passing over Flanders, LZ 107 crossed Calais, where von Wrangel saw some small coasters and searchlights trying to pinpoint the German Zeppelin. West of Calais ballast was released and LZ 107 reached an altitude of about 2,700m. Dozens of huge searchlight beams now swung about the sky, trying to locate the enemy after French forces had reported the advancing airship. In the afternoon, at about 14.30, the target was found.

Obersteuermann Seibert approached the city without difficulty, thanks to his great experience. Although two out of nearly twenty searchlights succeeded in finding the ship, and ground defences tried to shoot the attacker down, course was held by the crew. This was the first mission to experience a new kind of ammunition: after each shell detonated, a hail of twenty glowing bullets flew off in all directions, although fortunately most of the explosions occurred at between 3,500 and 4,000m. Suddenly the target appeared and the bombs were released one after the other. Then the airship set course for the open sea.

The gunners now reported seeing two bright points of light. The points grew, and both materialized as enemy aircraft. One of them shot something like a flare rocket in the direction of LZ 107, but the range was too short. Because the attacker flew at a lower altitude than the airship it was impossible for the latter to open fire, both guns being mounted on the platform on top of the Zeppelin's hull. Perhaps the second fighter lost LZ 107 because of the excellent cover offered by the clouds. A few minutes later the ship disappeared in the cloud and the crew started pulling up the *Spähkorb* again. But the mechanism failed and it took the entire crew seven uncertain hours to bring von Wrangel back into the ship by hand. The problems caused by the reconnaissance gondola which still hung more than 1,000m under the Zeppelin had caused severe delays and after 19hr 33min the ship arrived over Hanover with enough fuel for only another ten minutes' flying.

Most of the *Heeresluftschiffe* were operational over south-east Europe, Italy, the Black Sea and the Mediterranean. The first Army airships to be based in the eastern part of the Reich were Z IV (*Hauptmann* von Quast), Z V (*Hauptmann* Grüner) and SL 2 (*Hauptmann* von Wobeser). The first mission was carried out on 28 August 1914 against the railway station at Mlawa but due to enemy action an emergency landing became neces-

Below: LZ 103 (production number LZ 73) was completed at Potsdam near Berlin and was decommissioned in 1917.

Above: LZ 86 (production number LZ 56) carried out raids over the Eastern Front and was lost (pilot error) on 4 September 1916.
Left: The wreckage of LZ 85 at Salonika in 1916.

sary and the crew were taken prisoner. After two reconnaissance missions Z IV attacked Warsaw on 25 September 1914. On 1 February 1915 the ship was withdrawn from service because it was out of date and was disarmed. The next two ships, Z XI and LZ 34, both of the 22,470m^3 type, were lost at the end of May 1915 having made raids on Kowno, Grodno, Bialystok and Warsaw.

Early in 1915 all six operational ships were often used for attacking the enemy's railway communications behind the front line. *Sachsen*, the old Z XII (commanding officer E. A. Lehmann), L 39 (*Hauptmann* Falk), LZ 79 (*Hauptmann* Gaissert), LZ 85 (*Hauptmann* Scherzer) and LZ 86 (*Hauptmann* Linnarz) saw a great deal of action. For example, LZ 39 dropped 500kg of bombs on Nowo-Minsk

Above: On 5 January 1918 the huge hangars at Ahlhorn were destroyed, together with LZ 87 based there.
Right: LZ 93 (production number LZ 63), scrapped after German Army airship aviation was abandoned in 1917.

and Nowo-Georgiewsk and during the last of its five missions, on 17 December 1915, was severely damaged by the Allied air defences. The rear section of the forward gondola broke off, although the crew succeeded in carrying out an emergency landing near Luck.

During the Romanian Campaign of autumn 1916 German airships were engaged in several raids against Bucharest and the area around Ploesti. *Hauptmann* Hans Barth's LZ 81 was stranded in Bulgaria after a daring raid on the enemy's defences at Tirnova. The ship

Left: A well-camouflaged LZ 107 returns to Düren.

Left: *Hauptmann* Falck commanded LZ 73 (LZ 103) and carried out a successful raid on Calais on 1 October 1916.

crashed during an emergency landing and was decommissioned soon afterwards. *Hauptmann* Wolff's ship was destroyed while landing at Szentandras on 5 September 1916 after a mission to Ploesti. After five unsuccessful sorties, including one against military installations at Valona and Kischinew, LZ 97 was withdrawn from active service in 1917. The fourth ship, LZ 101 (production number LZ 71), arrived at Jamboli in August 1916 and survived seven raids against targets in the East, including one attack on Odessa harbour. Finally LZ 101, commanded by *Oberleutnant* Koreuber, left the southern war theatre during September 1917.

One particular mission that demonstrated the difficulties experienced by German airships in the South was recalled after the war by *Hauptmann* Ernst Scherzer, who had commanded *Sachsen* for two months in the summer of 1915:

Report concerning the war mission of LZ 85 on the night of 31 January–1 February 1916

1. Order:
Attack on the shipping and harbour at Salonika

2. Payload:

Crew: 16 men	1,300kg
Fuel for 18hr	3,600kg
Water	6,000kg
Bombs	2,000kg
Machine guns and armament	400kg

3. Description of the mission:
Since 10 o'clock this morning the weather stations in southern Serbia have reported the weather clearing up and only light winds from the south to the south-east; later it reported that the brightening up was considerably better than for some time previously. Because other stations reported a cloudless sky, a clear night was anticipated, and the mission therefore got under way at 3.52 in the afternoon. *Oberleutnant* Scherzer decided to set course for Verseez and from there to the Morawa Valley. The Morawa was visible when darkness fell and later in the night too.

At 20.25 in the evening Nisch came into view from a distance and was reached at a constant altitude of 2,000m. The clouds on the tops of some of the mountains did not affect navigation, but it was discovered that the altitudes of the mountains quoted on the maps were much too low and near Leskovac the ship was forced to steer through a narrow valley with high rock faces either side: on the map the height of the mountains was stated to be 1,500m while the ship was driving on at 2,000m.

At 21.05 the landscape disappeared beneath a dense sea of clouds. While crossing the mountains between the Morawa and Wardar Valleys the ship climbed to 3,000m to try to re-orient itself in the region of Usküb and Koprülü where fewer clouds were expected. After flying for one hour SSW, course was changed to SE. At 23.50 the cloud ceiling was passed and some ten minutes later the cover became a haze, disappearing altogether when Krivalak on the Wardar was reached. By following that river the crew sighted Salonika, but south of the town, still over the sea, was a dense bank of clouds. The ship stopped south of Salonika in order to observe the harbour and the ships at the quays, and some darkened steamers and ships with lights set were discovered in the bay. LZ 85 headed for two probable transport vessels and then to the harbour moles with their ammunition storage facilities. Some 60kg bombs were aimed at the ships and there was one hit close to the starboard side of one large vessel. It was impossible to say if any of the unlit ships were damaged in the attack. Most of the GP [general-purpose] bombs were released over the harbour and railway installations. Two of them detonated at the head of a mole and a further six in the inner harbour, and others hit the stores, causing huge explosions and possibly setting ammunition ablaze. The last bomb was responsible for a fast-spreading fire. Altogether fourteen small bombs were dropped on military warehouses north-west of the town.

Only a very few guns managed to engage the airship because its appearance came as a surprise to the enemy forces. After that the ship left the Salonika area and returned the same way it had come, although, because the winds had changed, the homeward journey took longer to complete and, because of the drain on fuel reserves, it was necessary to continue with only two of the Maybach engines running. At 10.20 in the morning the airship landed safely.

[Signed] Scherzer, *Oberleutnant*
and *Kommandant*

Between March and May 1916 only Z XII was serviceable for action. *Sachsen* had been handed over to the Navy as a training ship. LZ 79 was brought to western Germany on 11 September and was finally used over France. During October LZ 85, under the command of *Oberleutnant* Scherzer, destroyed some railway targets by dropping 10,600kg of bombs. The ship was then directed once more against Salonika. During the third raid LZ 85 was damaged in action and stranded in the Wardar Swamps, and the crew were taken prisoner on 5 May 1916. LZ 86 (production number 56) was lost on 5 September 1916 after returning from a raid against Ploesti to its base at Szantandras. Finally there were six very successful missions carried out over Russia.

LZ 81 survived only three sorties before the damaged ship was stranded during its second raid on Tirnova. LZ 101, commanded by *Hauptmann* Gaissert, one of the most

Left: A close-up view of the German Navy's first airship, L 1, which shows three gondolas.

experienced airship leaders, attacked more than seven targets before he moved his ship from Jamboli to Schneidemühl. He needed more than 25hr to cover the distance of 1,800km.

After operations over western Europe had been reduced, the remaining ships were used as reserves. Army airship operations were terminated by the *Oberste Heeresleitung* in June 1917 when it became obvious that the incendiary ammunition being used by the enemy, together with the increased performance of Allied interceptors, was proving too effective, and all the airworthy ships were handed over to the Navy to be used for training. The 'Zeppelin weapon' had nevertheless required the attention of a good many of the enemy's resources, especially fighters for the air defence of major targets in Britain.

Airships of the *Reichskriegsmarine*

After the Zeppelin Z IV made a successful twelve-hour flight on 1 July 1908, the Army became convinced that airships were capable

Below: L 2 (production number LZ 14) was the second Navy airship. It was destroyed after 74 flights.

of flying great distances. The German *Heeresleitung* placed an order for two Army airships and, despite the loss of Z IV a few weeks later on 4 August, the build-up of the Army Zeppelin force continued.

The first Navy ship, L 1, was not completed until 1912, however, because the Admiralty were hitherto undecided whether to enter the Zeppelin era or not. Because the Navy did not own any Zeppelin hangars, L 1 was based at Johannistal near Berlin, where the ship was flight-tested and the first crews were trained by the indefatigable *Dr* Eckener. The ship having satisfactorily completed the initial tests, it was decided to order a larger ship with a 27,000m^3 volume and a payload of about 11,000kg.

During autumn 1913 L 1 took part in the large-scale manoeuvres of the *Hochseeflotte* (High Seas Fleet) in the North Sea. Although its range did not meet the requirements of the German Navy, everybody realized that the new Zeppelin would be a valuable reconnaissance tool for the German fleet. This continued to be the view even when the first Navy airship went down over the North Sea in a violent storm with the loss of all hands.

Peter Strasser, later to become *Führer der Luftschiffe* and whose name was well-known to friend and foe alike, was appointed as the successor to the first commander of the *Marine-Luftschiff-Abteilung, Korvettenkapitän* Metzing. He championed the airship as a new weapon system and stayed in his post until his death in August 1918, by which time he had become the most experienced Zeppelin leader. A second reversal of fortune hit the Navy when the next ship, L 2, blew up only eight days after its first flight, possibly as a result of a gas explosion, on 17 October 1913 at Johannisthal. After this loss of a second crew and many important *Reichsmarineamt* engineers, it seemed that the end of the Zeppelin was near. But the development of new, more up-to-date ships started immediately, Strasser, having no doubts, imposing his

Below: L 3 just after its delivery to the Navy Airship Detachment.
Bottom: LZ 41 was handed over to the Navy and flown as L 11, based at Nordholz and Hage.

Left: L 12 was commanded by *Oberleutnant z.S.* Peterson and was engaged in a raid on London.

will to get this programme under way. Shortly afterwards the third Navy ship, L 3, was ordered to be constructed at Friedrichshafen. The new airship was tested for the first time on 11 May 1914, and following a flight of 36hr it became the first Navy ship to be stationed at Hamburg-Fuhlsbüttel, subsequently becoming operational at Nordholz. Training missions over the North Sea were conducted, but in August 1914 L 3 was still the sole Navy airship.

Long-range reconnaissance was the most important task assigned to the early Zeppelins and during the war, despite the restrictions placed on them by the weather, a total of 70 ships were engaged in about 930 sorties, comprising more than 150 air attacks on enemy vessels over the North Sea and an additional 220 reconnaissance missions, involving about 25 ships, over the Baltic. While mistakes were certainly made regarding the information supplied by airship leaders reporting the disposition of enemy forces, a lot of very useful data was brought back, enabling the Admiralty staff to compile precise situational maps once the improved ships (L 9–24) were in service. The successful raids against London in 1915 notwithstanding, the airship weapon had suffered delays costing one or two years because of the accidents involving L 1 and L 2.

Important missions were nevertheless undertaken during the first phase of the Navy Zeppelin raids. One successful attack took place on 8 September 1915, when L 13, together with L 9, L 14 and another unidenti-

Left: L 12 crashed at Ostend after returning from London on 10 August 1915.

Right: L 15 (production number LZ 48) was based at Nordholz and became stranded at Knock Deep, where the crew were taken prisoner.

fied ship, took part in the fourth *Geschwader-Attack* over England. A total of more than 4,800kg of bombs hit London, Middlesbrough and Norwich, making it the heaviest raid directed against Britain during the whole of the First World War:

Report of the Commander of Airship L13 concerning the attack on the City of London on 8 September 1915

The course to the target was set from the Wash because the wind was blowing from the north-east and only limited counterattacks were anticipated. Navigation from Kings Lynn to London was straightforward because the landscape was completely dark and most of the cities were still lit up. London was still very brightly illuminated and was recognizable from Cambridge. Orientation over the entire capital was very easy because Regent's Park was located precisely and the city centre was lit up as if in peacetime. After passing Regent's Park the crew began dropping bombs near High Holborn at an altitude of about 2,500m.

Immediately twenty searchlights picked out the airship and the English anti-aircraft batteries started to find L 13 with quick-firing rounds. The shell bursts were noticed close to the ship. L 13 climbed to 3,400m and reached a small cloud in order to hide. After all the bombs had been released the airship retired to Cambridge and from there to the coast.

The effect was similar to that of the attack on the night of 7 June 1915. The explosive effect of the 300kg bomb must have been quite extensive, because a large complex of lights went out.

Summary:
Bearing in mind the activities of the air defences around London, the airships could stay only for a short time over the target when the weather was clear. Therefore it was impossible to find single important targets, owing to the lack of time. Because no incendiary shells were used by the enemy, the only danger came from fragmentation shells which punctured the gas cells or damaged the structure of the ship.

[Signed] Mathy

Below: The severely damaged L 20 (LZ 59), ditched off the coast of Norway on 3 May 1916.

The commanding officer, *Kapitänleutnant* Heinrich Mathy, formerly commanded L 9 and took part in more airship raids than any other Navy Zeppelin crewman. After fourteen combat missions and the dropping of about 34,000kg of bombs over Britain, he was shot down in L 31 near London by Lt W. J. Tempest.

From 1916 the German *Oberste Heeresleitung* began to emphasize the importance of Zeppelin missions to the overall war effort and more and more were flown against the

British west coast, but the home defences became ever more effective, the use of aircraft equipped with incendiary bullets especially causing losses to the ships involved (L 31–34). Between January 1915 and the end of the year 30 Navy airship raids were reported; however, after some 37,000kg of bombs in 1915, during the next eighteen raids more than 166,000kg were released by 111 ships over Great Britain. Meanwhile 26 airships had been lost in action or as a result of accident or bad weather.

Before the Navy received its first Zeppelin its airmen were gaining experience in other, smaller dirigibles. The first large airships to be transferred to the German Navy were the non-rigid PL 6, 19 and 25 and the Gross-Basenach M IV (which was modified three times). These ships were employed intensively in anti-submarine warfare and conducted many reconnaissance missions, while a limited raid against the harbour at Libau was also mounted. By October 1916 PL 19 had been lost, but four new ships, the Zeppelin L 5 and the Schütte-Lanz SL 3, 4 and 6, were now based at Seddin. By the end of 1916 L 5 had been scrapped after sustaining damage in its hangar while SL 4 and SL 6 were continuing their duties over the Baltic Sea. This small force was expanded when SL 8, 9, 14 and 20 became operational in September 1917. SL 9 was hit by lightning and exploded, no survivors being found; SL 8 was decommissioned at Seddin since the ship was considered to be

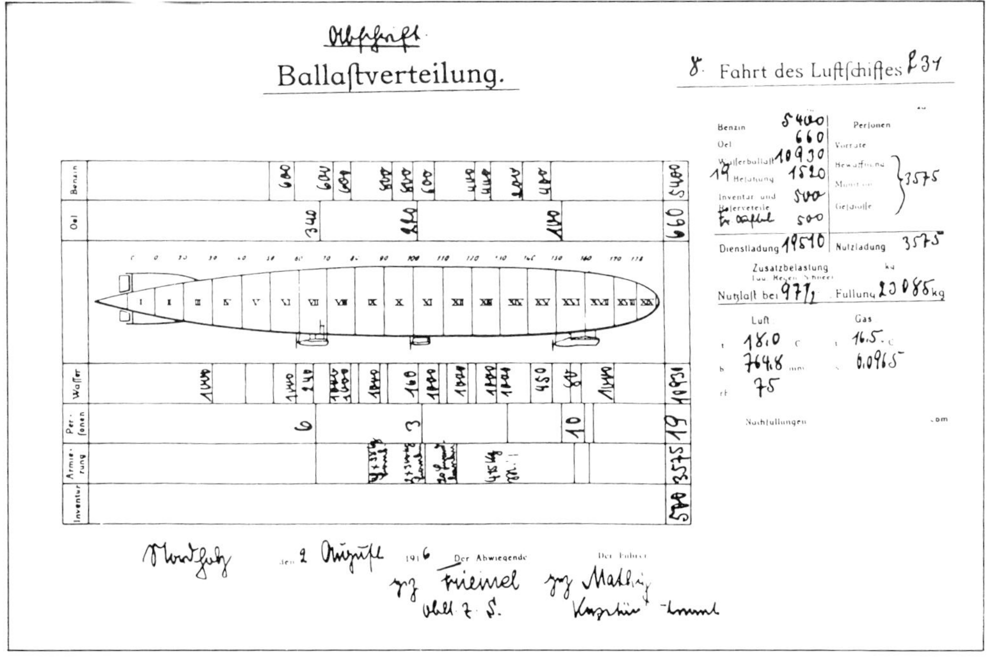

Left: LZ 62 became Navy property in summer 1916 and was engaged in ten offensive and 31 reconnaissance missions. Right: A plan of L 31 as it appeared prior to its eighth mission.

Left: L 31, based at Nordholz, was shot down by Lt Tempest on 2 October 1916 flying a BE 2c.

Left: L 33 was shot down by Lt Brandon of No 39 Home Defence Squadron, which was equipped with BE 2c aircraft.

too old for further useful service; and SL 20, together with four Zeppelins, blew up at Ahlhorn early in 1918.

In an effort to enhance German air power over the Baltic Sea and the Eastern Front, the *Oberste Heeresleitung* assigned further ships – L 30, 37 and 38 and LZ 87, 88, 98, 111 and 113 – to the theatre. The elderly L 30 was commanded by *Oberleutnant zur See* Boedecker and undertook four difficult missions (Sworbe, Wolmar, Salismünde and Pernau) before the ship ceased operations in September 1918. *Kapitänleutnant* Paul Gärtner's L 37 belonged to the 50,000m^3 class of ships and was involved in only three or four offensive sorties, carrying 2,000kg military payloads in combined operations with its sister-ship L30. L 35 and L 36 only had short operational careers in the East – after a few weeks L 35 was brought back to Ahlhorn in order to bolster the attack force there – while L 38 carried out just one mission before being badly damaged on 29 December 1916.

Allenstein and Königsberg were home to the smaller L 87, 88, 98 and 111 but only some of these ships saw combat over the Baltic Sea, damaging an enemy submarine, all four were disarmed by their crews in 1917. Early that year the modern LZ 113 and 120, commanded by *Hauptmann* Falk and *Leutnant zur See* Lehmann respectively, were ready for action, but in September Falk was replaced by *Kapitänleutnant* Zaeschmar and Lehmann by *Kapitänleutnant* von Lossnitzer. Each of these commanders was responsible for six operations against targets in Livonia, on the island of Oesel and around Riga. In November 1918, at the end of the war, LZ 120 was based at Seddin and on 30 November 1920 the ship was handed over to a civilian crew and flown to Italy. On 25 December it arrived in Rome, where it was badly damaged as a result of negligence by Italian personnel. LZ 83 (LZ 113) became a French *prise de guerre* and was transferred to its new owners on 8 October 1920, but after some problematic flights the ship was decommissioned at Maubeuge.

The famous LZ 104, better known as L 59, the *Afrikaschiff*, belonged to the Navy and was one of the busiest airships over the Mediterranean. L 59 was lengthened at Staaken to a reported 226.5m, but when it emerged for service all was not quite what it seemed. The envelope consisted entirely of cotton material, to be used for new uniforms for the Askari soldiers stationed under General Lettow-Vorbeck in East Africa. The material used for the gas cells could be worked into sleeping bags. Sections of the crossbeams and struts were convertible for use as stretchers, and others for constructing a barracks and a large transmission tower for maintaining wireless contact with the *Oberste Heeresleitung* in Germany, the Maybach engines doubling as electricity generators both for wireless communications and other tasks.

Left: The bomb release system aboard L 33, situated at the forward command post.

Left: L 40 (production number LZ 88) was based in northern Germany and was decommissioned after it crashed at Nordholz.

Right: L 48 survived for sixteen flights until it was destroyed by the guns of Lt L. P. Watkins over Suffolk. Below: Only a few German airships made it back to base after being caught by the British air defences.

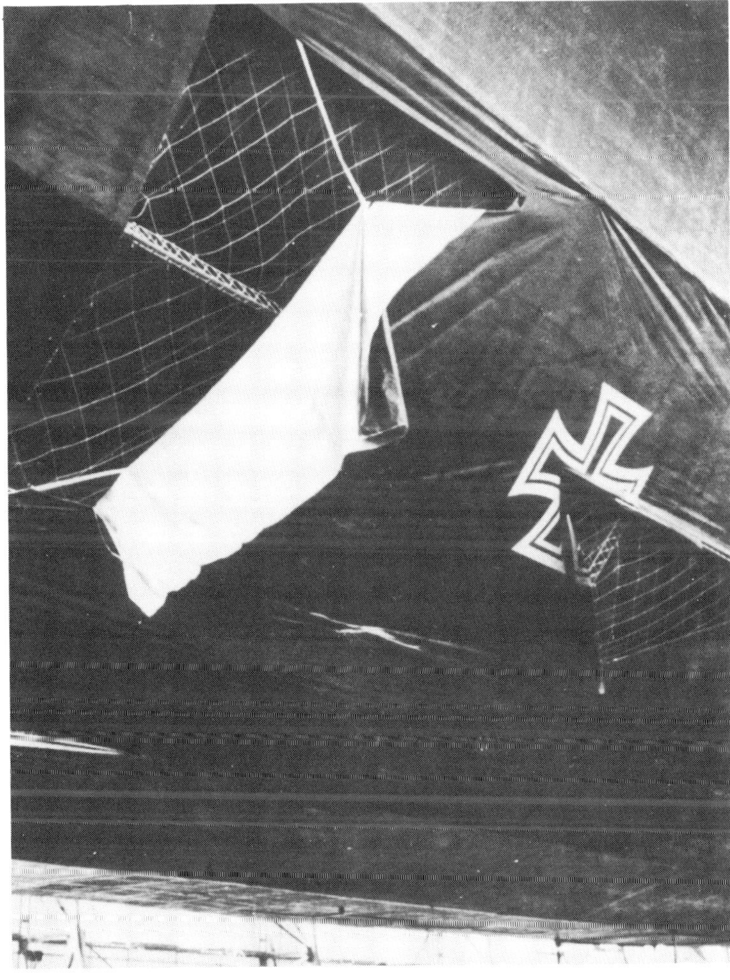

The airship's antenna consisted of three wires, each of them 120m long. The ship's empty weight was 29,594kg, and Ernst Lehmann reported that the payload totalled 49,800kg, comprising 21,790kg of fuel, 1,525kg of oil, 9,160kg of water ballast, 426kg of drinking water, 700kg of food and 16,100kg of military and medical equipment. The last consisted of 311,900 rounds of ammunition in boxes, together with a further 230 boxes of machine-gun ammunition each holding 250 rounds and an additional 54, totalling 13,500 rounds, for automatic weapons. There were 30 machine-guns and nine spare barrels and four new infantry rifles with 5,000 rounds, together with 61 boxes containing first-aid equipment, including surgical instruments and urgently needed medications. Finally, there were some sewing machines, knives and a second wireless set.

The ship was transferred from Berlin-Staaken to Jamboli in Bulgaria on 3 November 1917, landing one day later at 12.55 in the afternoon. In charge was *Kapitanleutnant* Ludwig Bockholt, who in L 23 had succeeded in capturing an English trawler and had earlier commanded L 57. He was assisted by two very experienced chief quartermasters, *Feldwebelleutnant* Grussendorf, from the DELAG, and *Steuermann* Wald, who had served on board the cruiser *Goeben*; the Officer of the Watch was *Leutnant zur See* Walk. *Oberstabsarzt* Zupitza, some government officials and *Dr*

L44

Left: LZ 76 became the Navy ship L 33 and was of the *r* type. It was based at Nordholz and Ahlhorn in 1916
Right: The *t* type LZ 94 became the Navy ship L 46.

Left: L 43's career ended when it crashed into the sea on 14 June 1917 after being shot down by Lt Dickey's H-12.
Right: L 24 was burnt out after a collision with its hangar doors. L 17 and the hangar itself were also destroyed in the conflagration.

Left: L 44, which was lost over Luneville on 20 October 1917 en route to Ahlhorn.
Right: L 48 was shot down over Theberton in Suffolk by Lt Watkins. There were only two survivors.

Eckener joined the airship at Berlin and accompanied Bockholt to Jamboli.

The crew of L 59 were under the impression that the airship was being sent to mount raids over the Eastern Front, but shortly after take-off *Kapitänleutnant* Bockholt informed his men that they were heading for Bulgaria. However, in order to disguise the true reason for transferring the ship, some bombing sorties were planned against lightly defended targets. The war diary records all the important events on board L 59 at that time:

10/10/17	First take-off at Berlin-Staaken.
05/11/17–10/11/17	Overhauling engines and propellers at Jamboli for coming action.
13/11/17	After the loss of water ballast caused by adverse weather the mission was terminated; some Turkish soldiers attacked the ship and were responsible for four hits found during the inspection.
16/11/17–17/11/17	Bombing raid on Panderma prematurely ended after the bombs were jettisoned.
21/11/17	Take-off for long-range mission ordered by the German Admiral Staff at 8.35 in the morning. Going to Adrianople, the Sea of Marmara and the Mediterranean.
22/11/17	Crossing the North African coast near Ras Bulau, then the Farafra Oasis and Dachel, the River Nile near Gubba Selim.
23/11/17	Wireless information about situation in East Africa; returning to Europe.
24/11/17	Passing Golfe of Solum, Cape Caledonia and Constantinople without incident.
25/11/17	Adrianople and back at Jamboli by 07.40.
26/11/17–29/11/17	Overhaul of the airship engines at Jamboli before starting the next raid.
01/12/17	Mine hunting near the coast at Varna.
11/12/17–13/12/17	Transferring to Ahlhorn: 8.43 in the evening, passing Sofia and Vienna.
14/12/17–02/03/18	Various missions over south-east Europe commanded by *Kapitänleutnant* Bockholt.
03/03/18–04/03/18	Bombing raid against Italian targets was stopped by hail and snowy weather.
10/03/18–11/03/18	Attack on harbour at Naples with great success using 6,400kg of bombs from an altitude of 3,650m.
20/03/18–22/03/18	The attack on Port Said was terminated three miles before reaching the town on account of strong winds.

On 7 April 1918 L 59 mysteriously exploded while crossing the Strait of Otranto, the crew having received orders to attack military targets in the main harbour at Malta.

The *Afrika-Flug* was the most important mission carried out by L 59. The distance covered from Jamboli to the turning point over East Africa was reported to be 6,757km, and the flight, lasting over 95hr, was made at an average speed of 71kph (38.3kt). On landing at Jamboli there was enough fuel and oil for a further 64hr or 6,000km, demonstrating that *Dr* Eckener's ideas about long-haul flights between Europe and the United States were entirely practicable. The ship did not land in East Africa because the crew received a wireless message to the effect that the German units were near defeat and that it would be impossible to locate the desperate groups of men in the African bush. Nobody knew that the German forces had in fact just captured the well-defended headquarters of the Portuguese forces, taking 150 white instructors and officers prisoner. Von Lettow-Vorbeck had also succeeded in seizing 30 horses, six machine guns, a large number of rifles and 250,000 rounds of ammunition, together with valuable *matériel* and medical supplies.

Meanwhile in Europe, although the German Army had discontinued raids against England, the Navy had not, bringing into service new ships with a gas volume of more than 60,000m^3 which enabled flights at altitudes of between 6,000 and over 8,000m to be made. The British fighters had no chance of catching these airships, and German losses were reduced, but it was still very difficult successfully to attack predetermined targets, owing to a lack of effective bomb sights; moreover, it seemed impossible to plot positions accurately and to navigate the ship to the correct waypoint or target in the first place. Unfavourable weather, problems with the engines and malfunctioning wireless systems at the increased altitudes all imposed further restraints, while the high ceilings also meant that nausea became a dangerous factor as a reliably effective oxygen system designed to avoid the problems of airsickness had proved impracticable.

After the loss of L 39 and L 48 five other ships were also written off, not as a result of enemy action but because of bad weather and navigational problems. A few months later the Navy lost a further five modern airships during the disaster at Ahlhorn on 5 January 1918. During the next eight months only four big raids over Great Britain were planned and carried out, together with 130 reconnaissance

Right: The huge L 59 was the well-known *'Afrika-Luftschiff'* which was lost in April 1918 over the Mediterranean Sea.

Right: L 63 (production number LZ 110), photographed on 9 March 1918.

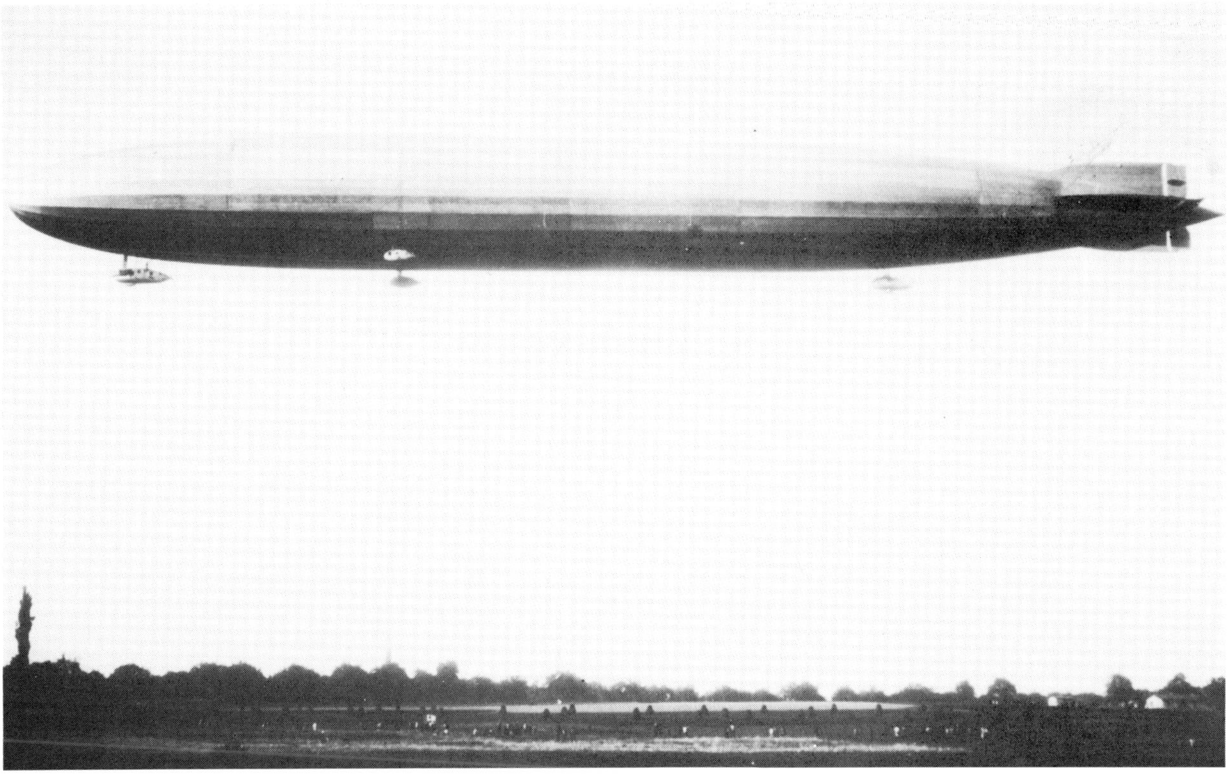

missions over the North Sea, but with no real success. Altogether 40 raids, carrying more than 300,000kg of bombs, were made by the Zeppelin and Schütte-Lanz ships, causing damage amounting to £1,527,000. The thirty-third *Geschwader-Angriff* from 5 to 6 August 1918 marked the end of Navy attacks on England. In it the Navy not only lost a ship, L 70, it also lost its champion, *Fregattenkapitän* Strasser, and with his death the involvement of the *Oberste Heeresleitung* and the *Admiralstab* was brought to an end.

The German Navy lost 74 airship officers, 264 NCOs and 50 men and the Army some 15 officers and 40 men during the First World War. In addition, about 170 airship personnel became prisoners-of-war or were interned in Denmark or the Netherlands.

The Leader and his crews

The first Zeppelin to be handed over to the Army was LZ 3, later designated Z I. It was commanded by officers from one of the five Prussian *Luftschiffer-Bataillone*. The first military commander of Z I was *Major* Sperling, whose Officer of the Watch was *Oberleutnant* Masius who later flew on some raids against Paris. Other experienced commanders were *Hauptmann* George (*Sachsen* and LZ 74), who was responsible for Z II; and *Hauptmann* von Jena, the first commander of the early LZ 9 (Z II *Ersatz*). All the officers and men of the German *Luftschiffer* units were volunteers, and nearly all the Army airship commanders were active officers before the war.

The German Navy only accepted the airship as a reliable reconnaissance vehicle a year before the war. Serious accidents, especially the loss of L 1 (*Kapitänleutnant* Hanne) and L 2 (*Kapitänleutnant* Freyer), caused a further loss of confidence but Peter Strasser's energy, and his ability to assert himself in front of his superiors, led to the building up of a strong Zeppelin fleet within a short period of time. With the assistance of *Dr* Eckener and E. A. Lehmann it proved possible to train many Navy officers before *Kapitän* Strasser was appointed to take over the difficult command of the new force in the autumn of 1913. The *Korvettenkapitän* had served with the Imperial Navy on board SMS *Stein*, *Moltke*, *Mars*, *Blücher*, *Panther*, *Mecklenburg* and *Westfalen*; during these two years he had shown himself to be a first-class gunnery officer, achieving better results than anybody else in the Fleet, and subsequently became the officer responsible for German shipboard and coastal artillery in the *Reichsmarine-Amt*.

Shortly after the loss of the first Navy airship, and with the second one under construction, Peter Strasser assumed command of the *Marine-Luftschiff* detachment. At first Strasser thought that the new command would be, in effect, a demotion, but then he met *Dipl-Ing*. Lehmann who showed him the imposing *Sachsen* being overhauled in a large hangar. Given the loss of L 1 in a thunderstorm and three ships (L 4, L 6 and *Schwaben*) to gas explosions in 1908, 1910 and 1912 respectively, Strasser felt some apprehension about the prospect of having to develop the airship into an effective weapon of war so quickly.

After completing his theoretical training and learning much about the construction and flying characteristics of large airships, the *Korvettenkapitän* got practical experience by assuming command of *Sachsen*. Unfortunately the Navy's second airship, L 2, enjoyed only a brief career before it burst into flames

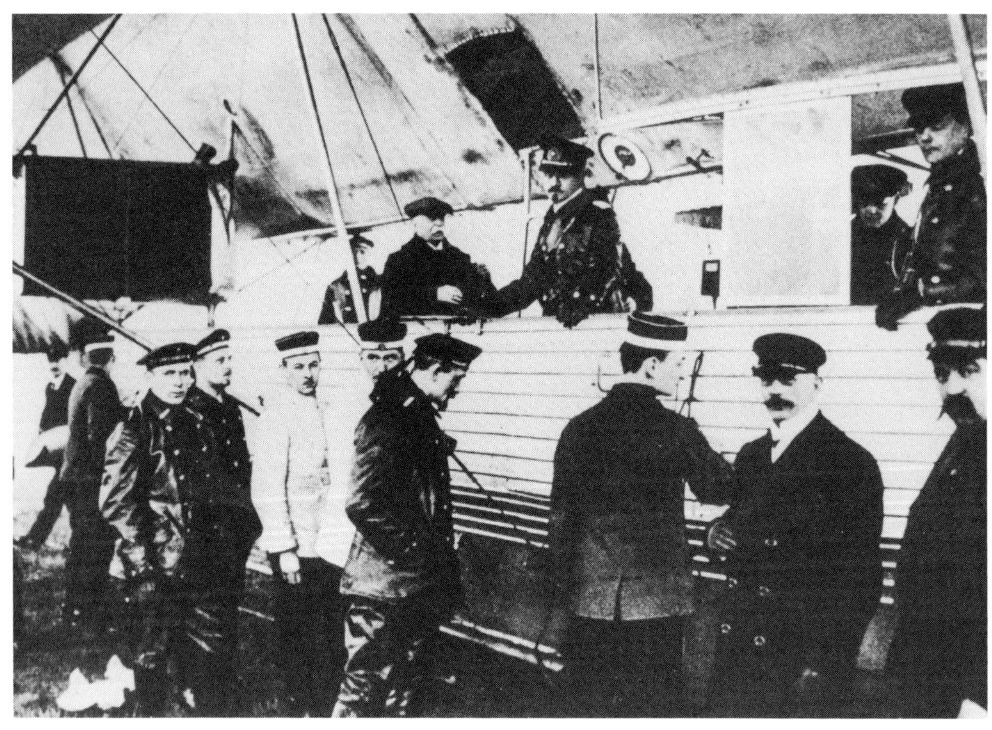

Left: The *Führer der Luftschiffe*, *Korvettenkapitän* Peter Strasser, in the gondola of LZ 27 (the later L 4).

on 17 October 1913. *Luftschiff Zeppelin* 18 (L 2) had been the first experimental ship in a series of ten, and its loss caused further delays to the Navy's programme. Meanwhile Peter Strasser's detachment now had no ships of its own. The Navy's next airship, L 3, was not accepted by the authorities in Berlin because *Reichsmarine* officials were doubtful whether new ships would be of any military value, considering the disasters that had occurred – a matter which was the subject of an argument between the Secretary of State, *Grossadmiral* von Tirpitz, and *Graf* Zeppelin just before the funeral ceremony for the last airship casualties had begun.

Nevertheless, Strasser still believed that such losses were not inevitable. He explained to Lehmann that well-trained crews would soon become available after finishing their course of instruction on board the chartered DELAG airship LZ 13 *Hansa*, and to this end large numbers of Strasser's personnel were immediately transferred to the airship base at Dresden. Meanwhile Berlin gave the go-ahead for the third Navy airship, and this became operational on 11 May 1914. On 28 August L 4 followed, and on 22 September L 5, and a further three ships had been commissioned by the end of the year.

Thus a few weeks before the outbreak of the First World War, the German Navy had just one airship ready for active service with the Fleet. It was transferred to Fuhlsbüttel near Hamburg, where the operational airship base was being constructed, by which time the detachment had been enlarged into a *Luftschiffer-Abteilung*.

Strasser's ship, LZ 24 (L 3), was the only one to participate in the important Imperial Navy manoeuvres just before the war. During August the ship carried out a reconnaissance mission over the North Sea, where it discovered a British submarine 30nm west-north-west of Heligoland. On 28 August, L 3, under the command of *Kapitänleutnant* Fritz, was withdrawn from service because of bad weather and shelling by unknown forces, friend or foe, during the Battle of Heligoland Bight which ended with the loss of the cruisers *Mainz*, *Köln* and *Ariadne*. A few days later, on 31 August, Strasser ordered his men to search for enemy forces during a minelaying operation, and during September further similar missions were flown. By December L 3 had been modernized, prior to setting off on its first offensive raid against British targets in company with *Graf* von Platen's L 4. During the night of 19–20 January 1915 both ships dropped fragmentation bombs over Yarmouth, Sheringham and Kings Lynn with reasonable success, but a few weeks later, on 17 February 1915, L 4 was beached on the

Below: L 71 (production number LZ 113) arrived at Ahlhorn to enter active service on 28 October 1918.

Danish coast during a snowstorm, nearly all the crew members being saved and interned in Danish camps. Because official weather forecasts were very unreliable, Strasser ordered that all his airship commanders and officers of the watch be trained as meteorologists.

Strasser accompanied his men on raids as often as he could, and reports were made by Strasser himself on his return to Germany. The following is typical:

> On 15–16 April 1915 the FdL, *Kapitänleutnant* Hirsch and *Oberleutnant z. S.* von Buttlar-Brandenfels carried out a third raid against British targets. Peter Strasser stood at the bridge of L 7, which was commanded by *Oberleutnant z.S.* Peterson, who noticed that both the other ships were heading to the British Isles too. After extinguishing all lights, L 7 crossed the North Sea and reached the British coast. Strasser and Peterson came across a small town, visible despite the cloud covering. Suddenly huge searchlights tried to pinpoint the German ship and shrapnel exploded nearby. The commanding officer ordered the men to release the bombs and, since some of the Zeppelin's cells had been damaged, Strasser permitted the ship to retreat. He then began working his way through the ship, detailing all the available crewmen as sailmakers, including the commander. Strasser himself took over the controls. Some hours later the crew were convinced that they had reached the island of Borkum but gunfire from coastal batteries indicated that L 7 had in fact approached the coast of the Netherlands. At 23.53 one of the engines failed and Strasser decided to jettison all unnecessary equipment in order to ensure the ship's survival, and the machine guns were taken from their pivots, followed by the empty fuel tanks, surplus clothing and unused food. But the ship was still too heavy and the waves were coming ever closer.
>
> Strasser and his men were very surprised when the engine that had broken down miraculously started up again, and the ship very slowly began to climb. After about 22 hours without sleep the crew finally sighted the German coast. Peterson thought that it would be impossible to land the ship owing to the serious loss of gas, so he ordered all men needed for immediate duties in both gondolas to move into the ship. Peter Strasser took over command and prepared himself for a hard landing. In spite of all his experience the airship was damaged when the gondolas touched the ground and their struts buckled.

The mechanics needed more than a fortnight to repair the damaged ship. Ultimately, after more than 70 reconnaissance missions, L 7 was lost on 4 May 1916.

Meanwhile *Korvettenkapitän* Strasser's *Marine-Luftschiff-Abteilung* had increased its establishment to 7,105 men, twelve bases and nearly twenty ships. Between February and March his men got as far as the city of Liverpool and only two months later his L 20 appeared over Scotland. At the end of March 1916 he boarded L 14, setting off in company with L 9, 11, 13, 14, 15, 16 and 22 which together carried more than 10,000kg of bombs. L9 and L 11 reported engine failure and returned to base, and *Kapitänleutnant* Heinrich Mathy's L 13 was hit by the well-organized British ground defences after he had dropped his bombs in the region of Stowmarket and Lowestoft during his eleventh raid. In a subsequent conversation with Mathy, whose ship had been damaged by two shell hits, on gas cells 10 and 12, Strasser was informed that the British Government had built rows of dummy towns complete with street lights in order to confuse the German airmen.

On 28 November 1916 Peter Strasser received an official cabinet order signed by Emperor Wilhelm II:

> The former commander of the *Marine-Luftschiff-Abteilung* is promoted to *Führer der Luftschiffe* (FdL). He will be responsible for the Navy airships, and the *Marine-Luftschiff-Abteilung* will get a commander of its own. I invest the FdL with the privileges of an Admiral Second Class.
>
> [signed] Wilhelm

Strasser was told on several occasions that it was too dangerous to accompany his men on missions over the British Isles, but he always played down the personal dangers, answering that the soldiers lying in the muddy trenches of the Western Front risked their lives being there. He and his men did not carry parachutes, which were still used on board all *Heeresluftschiffe*, because the Navy believed that it was virtually impossible to escape from a burning ship.

On 23–24 May 1917 L 40, together with L 42, 43, 44 and 45 (with the FdL on the bridge of L 44), headed for England. At 5,000m the British Isles appeared ahead, marked by the white surf along the coastline. Shortly afterwards, over Harwich, the crew noticed a huge fire, and then suddenly two of the engines failed. The ground defences continued to fire at the Zeppelin after one of the searchlights had picked out the ship. Meanwhile L 44 could not be held any longer at 5,000m and began to sink. Shells burst close to the gondolas and Strasser's men began to wonder if they would meet the same fate as Mathy,

Right: An unknown Army crew which was attached to the DELAG before the First World War broke out.

Right: The crew of *Hauptmann* Masius, who was responsible for LZ 72 and 87 during the war.

Peterson, Schramm, Dietrich, Koch and Frankenberg, all of whom had died in action. *Kapitänleutnant* Stabbert ordered the bombs to be released. Because of the altitude, the crew, including Strasser himself, had the appearance of being drunk, and were jolted out of their condition only when L 44 reached the lower layers of the atmosphere again. This airsickness, together with the problems caused by relying on engines which were not intended for use at high altitude, were responsible for L 44's difficulties, forcing Strasser and his staff to look for an improved oxygen system. At the same time it was agreed that all new ships, being built ever larger, required a more effective wireless system.

British countermeasures to the airship threat were developing rapidly by now, with an increasing number of air defence batteries and of fighter units equipped with advanced interceptors. Despite the aggressive defences, however, the FdL and his men took off for six dangerous but well-planned raids during 1917. Only four more followed in 1918, the last, carried out during the night of 6–7 August 1918, being the 33rd in which the Navy's L 53, 56, 63, 65 and 70 took part. Strasser travelled aboard the huge, recently delivered LZ 112, which took the Navy designation L 70. This ship was first flown on 1 July 1918 and was based at Nordholz. On 1 August, commanded by *Kapitänleutnant* von Lossnitzer, it attacked enemy shipping with 100kg bombs and then made off under cover of dense fog.

Early on 6 August 1918 *Fregattenkapitän* Strasser fell victim of the skills of Major Cadbury, who had earlier, on 28 November 1916, shot down L 21. German HQ reported:

> On the night of 6 August *Fregattenkapitän* Strasser, who has often successfully led our airship raids, again hit the east coast of England, making effective attacks on Boston, Norwich and the fortifications in the Humber estuary with one of our units. He probably suffered a heroic death, together with his crew. All the other airships engaged in the attack have returned to their bases, despite the enemy defences. Besides their successful leader and the airship commanders – *Korvettenkapitän* R. Proelss and *Kapitänleutnante* Zaeschmar, Walther, von Freudenreich and Dose – their brave crews were responsible for the achievement.
> Commanding Officer, *Admiralstab* of the Navy

Following these events, the last Navy ship, LZ 113 (L 71), although moved out of its hangar on 29 July 1918, was never flown in combat. It was handed over to the British Government on 30 June 1920.

One of the younger airship commanders to survive the war was *Kapitänleutnant* Horst *Freiherr* Treutsch von Buttlar-Brandenfels:

> Early in September 1913 the first of many Navy airships, L 1, was ready to take part in the autumn exercises conducted by the *Hochseeflotte*. At that time von Buttlar was the wireless officer on board the cruiser *Moltke*. After he had seen L 1 for the first time passing over the cruisers, he wanted to become a member of a Zeppelin crew. Only a few days later the airship was destroyed. Von Buttlar-Brandenfels thought that he would be transferred to submarines, but suddenly, on 1 October, the order came posting him to the *Marineluftschiff* detachment at Johannisthal. Meanwhile L 2 had arrived, ready for its first training mission on 17 October. Von Buttlar was allowed to accompany the crew but was then ordered to leave the ship, giving up his place to *Leutnant* von Bleul, in charge of the ground crew.
>
> A few minutes after lift-off, and only about 1,000m distant, the forward gondola caught fire; within a few minutes the whole ship was burning, oxy-hydrogen gas having built up as result of the hot weather. The airship crashed immediately and the injured survivors died in the hands of the ground crew who had tried to help. A few days later the civil airship *Sachsen*, belonging to the Deutsche Luftschiffahrts AG was chartered.
>
> In mid-October von Buttlar arrived in Dresden, where the DELAG's director, *Dr* Eckener, was training Navy crews. There was such an abundance of new experiences and facts to absorb that nobody had time to be downcast. Later *Sachsen* moved to Hamburg-Fuhlsbüttel, where the Navy rented the huge airship hangar.
>
> *Kapitänleutnant* Fritz was expected to be the leader of the next Navy ship. L 3 was under construction early in April, and on 4 May 1914 the new Zeppelin was ready for take-off. After passing its acceptance trials, it made another flight following the River Rhine from Basel to Mainz and Cologne, then to Hamburg, Heligoland, Stettin, Frankfurt/Oder and back to Johannisthal near Berlin. The long-range mission ended successfully after more than 36 hours. Later the Zeppelin was used mainly for training. Nearly every day the huge ship took off early in the morning with von Buttlar and his men. Because his duties did not occupy all his

Left: The FdL, Peter Strasser, together with *Kapitänleutnant* von Lossnitzer, perished when L 70 (shown) was shot down on 5 August 1918.

time, he would climb up to the platform on the top of the Zeppelin. Machine guns has been proposed for this position but not yet installed, and there was enough space behind the canvas screens for him to sleep . . . L 3 passed over Wismar on the Baltic Sea. Shortly before the airship began its descent he joined the bridge to assist the commander during the last phase of the flight, never knowing whether the officer had noticed his absence.

At the outbreak of war the huge hangars at Nordholz were still under construction. L 3 therefore remained at Fuhlsbüttel, taking part in the first cruiser engagement on 24 August 1914. That same month L 4 joined the *Marine-Luftschiff* detachment. After L 3 was transferred to the makeshift hangars at Nordholz, Buttlar's commander, *Korvettenkapitän* Strasser, made him commanding officer of L 6; by 1918 von Buttlar would have completed several hundred flights, only one crew member, a sailmaker called Heesen losing his life, through gas poisoning while he was repairing a gas cell.

Ten days after the crew arrived at Friedrichshafen the big ship was ready for its first test, the flight to Nordholz marking the first occasion that von Buttlar-Brandenfels had taken over command of an airship. After *Graf* von Zeppelin had wished the crew and the ship all the best, von Buttlar, accompanied by *Dr* Eckener as supervisor, entered the forward gondola. Early in the afternoon L 6 landed at Hamburg-Fuhlsbüttel, from where several reconnaissance missions were carried out, often in appalling weather. On 23 December 1914 the ship was brought to the new station at Nordholz and two days later a new order arrived: while the crew of L 5 had to make a sortie to the west, von Buttlar was ordered to fly north.

That day von Buttlar's crew had their first confrontation with the enemy. Near the island of Amrun they noticed three steamers engaged in minelaying, and about three or four miles away they spotted two small British cruisers in company with eight destroyers. The airship's wireless system failed, but fortunately a German seaplane out from Heligoland appeared and, in poor light, was informed about the presence of the Royal Navy. The aircraft returned to Heligoland and the battlecruiser *Seydlitz* was alerted, sailing to intercept the enemy. Meanwhile von Buttlar's Zeppelin climbed to 1,800m and the commander ordered his Officer of the Watch, *Fähnrich* von Schiller, to drop a 50kg bomb on the last of the minelayers by hand, there being no electrical or mechanical release system. The bomb missed its target by 100m. Immediately all the warships opened fire on L 6, the British crews gathering on deck with rifles and machine guns and loosing off in the direction of the airship. By the time the cruiser got round to firing fragmentation shells von Buttlar's ship had reached 2,500m and disappeared into the clouds. Later, on L 6's return to northern Germany, hundreds of small holes were found all over the Zeppelin's envelope. It took some days to patch them all.

A while later the ship landed in a wood. One of the crew members reported the first few minutes after the accident:

> First the commander thought that he had driven into a gasometer, but then the first boughs and branches became visible. Only one man seemed to be hurt. He had stuck his head out of an opening and his face was smothered with fir needles. The crew noticed a small light below the airship and asked for a position. A man answered: 'In the wood!'. After von Buttlar asked where he came from, he told him: 'Out of the rear gondola, *Herr Oberleutnant!*' It was one of the crew members, who had fallen out when the airship hit the trees.

Von Buttlar subsequently took over the command of the new L 11 at Friedrichshafen and after some training flights the airship landed on the River Elbe. Six raids were carried out in L 11, mainly against targets in southern England, including the British capital. Most of the night raids reached London at about midnight, and from altitudes of about 4,000m more than 14,000kg of bombs were released. After dropping their loads the ships tried to escape into cloud whenever possible, leaving for Germany with engines throttled back. After landing, the necessary reports, some containing seven copies, were written up and sent to the *Führer der Luftschiffe*.

On another occasion on board L 11, von Buttlar was returning from a raid when, on reaching Hull, he met a large, storm-laden weather front. The ship did not have enough fuel for him to go round the front, so he carefully crossed it, taking more than two hours to reach Nordholz. He was given command of the brand new L 30 – the first of the *56,000m³-Luftkreuzer* – on 28 May 1916. *Graf* Zeppelin himself was on board for the delivery flight. Near Heidelberg, on the way, L 30 won a race with a 120kph express train. After a successful landing at Nordholz, the airship was hauled into one of the huge hangars and, after a celebration with his *Luftschiffer*, von Zeppelin left. It was the last time before his death that the *Graf* visited Nordholz.

With the larger airships such as L 30, the service ceiling was raised considerably and now every man was equipped with a personal oxygen set for flights at altitudes over 4,500m. The first missions were armed reconnaissance sorties. One of these required L 30 to reconnoitre the North Sea up to the region of the Firth of Forth. While returning to Germany it was attacked by a British warship disguised as a fishing vessel but despite the low altitude the enemy gunners failed to achieve a hit. After von Buttlar had released most of his ballast, the Zeppelin disappeared in the clouds again; German torpedo-boats later attacked the *U-boot-Falle* (submarine trap).

Von Buttlar carried out eight further raids before the Zeppelins were withdrawn. He took part in the Colchester raid on the night of 1 August 1918, during which he unleashed 25 GP bombs and 20 incendiaries – a total of 1,670kg. On his next mission, on 8–9 August, he succeeded in attacking Hartlepool and also some Royal Navy warships, while during September 1916 he made three further raids over London.

Early in 1917 *Freiherr* von Buttlar-Brandenfels left active service with the *Marine-Luftschiffgeschwader* and was appointed commanding officer of L 35, a post which he was to hold for about eight months. L 35 was undergoing trials with experimental torpedo-gliders, but the results were, in the end, discouraging. He then took over L 54, from 16 September 1917 to 19 August 1918. He was the sole commander to reach Tondern on 19 October 1917, despite the wind causing his ship to drift in the direction of Denmark after he had dropped 2,800kg of bombs. It seems that during this mission some flares caught fire in the forward gondola but were extinguished by quick-thinking crew members.

During the attack on the batteries at Spurn Point, L 54 was hit, Cell IX suffering damage, but the ship reached Germany after nearly all the ballast had been dumped. Later the *Freiherr* was decorated with the Pour le Mérite, having, during the previous month, carried out fourteen reconnaissance missions and two bombing raids. On 19 July 1918 L 54 was destroyed by British bombs, but only two of the seven Sopwith Camels from HMS *Furious* which made the attack, each equipped with two small bombs, returned.

Airships also took part in anti-submarine warfare from 1914, when the young Sergeant Albessard attacked a U-boat in the Channel which was trying to capture an enemy ship. After some small bombs had been dropped on the submarine, the German sailors fired back and the *VA-Ballon* was hit, causing it slowly to descend; as it did so it alerted its own destroyer forces to intercept the submarine.

Throughout the war, German airship commanders reported over 100 sightings of enemy submarines. Five of them were sunk, by L 9, L 10, L 54, L 63 and the Schütte-Lanz SL 3. *Kapitänleutnant* Mathy also made an attack on a group of British submarines, hitting one of them, but his airship was damaged too and he was forced to withdraw.

One of the most famous commanding officers in the *Heeresluftschiff* establishment was Ernst A. Lehmann. He was born at Ludwigshafen-am-Rhein in 1886. After finishing his schooling in 1904 he left his home town and moved to Kiel to become one of the young *Baueleven*, an apprentice shipbuilder. After a year spent working at the Imperial Dockyard, he was transferred to the *Storch*, a cadet training vessel. At the time Lehmann did not know whether to become a Navy officer or a ship constructor, but his experience on board *Storch* – on one occasion, when the ship had lost one of its propellers, Lehmann was ordered to carry out an underwater inspection – decided him in favour of the latter, and he joined the technical university at Berlin-Charlottenburg. A few years later, in 1912, he left Berlin with a degree in marine engineering and was appointed *Marinebauführer* to the Imperial Dockyard at Kiel. Some months earlier he had been promoted to the rank of *Leutnant zur See* in the German Naval Reserve.

But Lehmann was not happy in his profession, and he was therefore delighted when he was approached by *Dr* Eckener, who was looking for somebody qualified to command the airship *Sachsen*, which was still under construction at the time. Lehmann, trained by Eckener himself, was appointed as *Sachsen*'s first commander in the autumn of 1913, and during the winter of that year both men were busy training the young officers and crews of the *Marine-Luftschiff* detachment handling the ship. *Sachsen*'s first six months of service saw Lehmann involved in sightseeing tours from Dresden and Leipzig; from 3 May 1913 to 31 July 1914 the ship made 419 flights,

The crew of *Kapitänleutnant* von Buttlar-Brandenfels, who commanded L 54 (LZ 99).

carrying a total of 9,837 passengers and crewmen.

Soon after this the civil airship was handed over to the German Army following the loss of LZ 21 (Z VI) during *Hauptmann* Kleinschmidt's ill-fated raid on Liége on 6 August 1914. The *Oberste Heeresleitung* had thus lost three ships very early in the war and had appeared to have forgotten its own Zeppelin force at Cologne. As no orders for *Sachsen* had been received, both Gemmingen and Lehmann decided to drive to the German headquarters at Koblenz, where they told the commanding officer that it would be impossible to penetrate enemy air space by day using prewar airships, whose limited performance could guarantee a service ceiling of only about 2,500m. The staff thus allowed the airship commanders themselves to decide which targets to attack on days when the weather conditions were favourable.

Lehmann flew naval reconnaissance missions and made three successful raids on Antwerp, where the Belgians were concentrated in a huge, well-armed base surrounded by the forces of *General* von Beseler. At the end of the war Lehmann wrote about his first military missions over western Europe, including one of these:

> Only a railway line linking the Netherlands and the [Belgian] strongpoint was in the hands of the Western Allies. Therefore I suggested that we load as many bombs as possible aboard *Sachsen* and try to destroy one of the stations along this important lifeline. But the commanding general had no interest in this kind of modern warfare and ordered his cavalry to destroy the railway station, although his ground forces were not strong enough to do the job. Thus it was still possible to evacuate very many Belgian soldiers from Antwerp – men who would subsequently play an important role during the Battle of the Marne. During September the General Staff remembered the airship again and enquired about the possibility of bombing Antwerp.
>
> Further training missions followed, including the first bombing trials, the inert ordnance being released and then gathered up from the fields and used again. A few days later the ordnance officer was ready for the actual combat mission. At first the other airship commanders and I did not have any specially developed military payload: most of the 'bombs' were actually artillery shells with a horse-hide covering over their ends. Hence – by permission of the General Staff – some fragmentation bombs were manufactured and delivered by the ammunition factory at Cologne.
>
> The first of three Antwerp raids was made on the night of 1–2 September 1914. At 11.00 *Sachsen* took off at Cologne and followed the railway line to Aachen, then started climbing, to a service ceiling of only 2,000m. *Sachsen* had been loaded with just 900kg of bombs, but it was nevertheless necessary to land the machine guns in order to take the bombs on board. The crew were armed with automatic pistols and rifles in case of emergency.
>
> Out from Liége the airship passed over the clouds and continued its mission without sighting the ground. Near Antwerp the clouds became thinner and thinner, and in order to avoid the danger of being shot down by enemy ground fire I waited until the moon had disappeared. Only few minutes would remain

from then until dawn. After cruising for more than an hour near the Dutch–Belgian border, the ship became heavier and only with a great effort was it possible to hold *Sachsen* at an altitude of 1,700m. The ship appeared over the fortress with reduced engine power and the air defences started searching for her with big lights but were unable to illuminate her for any length of time. The infantry between both rings of fortifications opened fire using their rifles and machine guns. Without hesitation I ordered the bombing to start, with some of the small 5kg fragmentation bombs thrown by hand on to the lines beyond; *Obersteuermann* Laur dropped one of the 10kg bombs while standing in the forward gondola, and when we were over the fortifications around the town the larger incendiary bombs were used. Finally two of the major inner forts were hit on the way to the main railway station. After spending twenty minutes over the target, *Sachsen* left the town when the crew became aware of the first bright light of dawn breaking on the horizons. After passing the Schelde valley with dense fog covering the landscape, the airship found its way back to Cologne where it landed at 11.00 in the morning, about twelve hours after lifting off.

Together with Z IX, commanded by *Hauptmann* Alfred Horn, we dropped about 5,000kg of bombs over Antwerp during the successful September raids.

Two other missions involving Lehmann's airship would fail. He took over command of LZ 26 (Z XII), in use since 14 December 1914, but moved from Frankfurt to Maubeuge early in March 1915. Lehmann's first raid against British targets ended on 17 March 1915 before he reached his objective, thanks to fog and dense cloud; given the navigational risks, he decided to attack Calais. Because the ceiling of clouds was 1,000m, it was possible to drop 3,000kg of bombs through the cover using the new *Spähkorb* or 'reconnaissance basket'. The ship was damaged while landing and it was not possible to carry out the next attack on Calais until 16 May 1915.

The ship did not have a sufficiently good performance for offensive sorties over western Europe so it was withdrawn to the Eastern Front and based at Allenstein in East Prussia during the summer of 1915. Later, bad weather hindered many operations, but the first raid, against the railway junctions at Bialystock and other vital targets along the Russian lines of communication, took place in August 1915. During one of these attacks Z XII was damaged by ground fire when shrapnel hit some of the gas cells. Lehmann tried to make an emergency landing on a lake in East Prussia, and despite severe damage to the second gondola and the failure of three engines the ship was saved and finally brought back to Allenstein. It was proposed to carry out further missions over Russia, and Ernst August Lehmann was responsible for nine sorties, dropping a total of 17,000kg of bombs.

Above: Two crew members of an unknown Navy airship, photographed in 1917.

Lehmann and his crew were then ordered to take over LZ 60 (military designation LZ 90), which was based at Trier and had entered service on 1 January 1916. After the failure of four raids against French targets near the local front lines, the new ship was reported over Bar-le-Duc on 7 March, over Norwich a couple of weeks later and over the City of London on 2 April 1916. On that last date a second ship, commanded by *Hauptmann* Falk, released its 1,600kg payload over Margate, a seaside town which had been the main target on 25 April 1916 when LZ 88 was found by, but luckily escaped from, British fighters armed with incendiary rounds. (LZ 88 was later lengthened and taken on charge by the *Reichsmarine* under the new designation L 25.)

Before *Hauptmann* Gaissert took command of LZ 90, *Leutnant zur See* Lehmann became the new commander of LZ 98 in April 1916. After just a limited number of flight-tests the ship was ordered to take part in forthcoming attacks on England. Bad weather, however, forced the experienced crew to return from seven missions without reaching British territory, and on one of these the airship was hit by lightning, though suffered only minor damage.

On 2 September 1916, accompanied by *Hauptmann* La Quiante's LZ 90 and *Hauptmann* Schramm's SL XI (which would be shot down), Lehmann's LZ 98 arrived over the City of London to drop 1,500kg of bombs on various targets. On the way back dense fog hampered the airship leader's navigation but with the *Spähkorb* deployed the coast of the Netherlands was discovered. The ship continued on its way, still above the clouds, and landed without any problems. Later the Zeppelin was sent to the Eastern Front and was engaged in some important naval reconnaissance missions over the Baltic.

Ernst Lehmann's last active command began in early 1917. LZ 120's first flight took place on 31 January 1917 and the large 55,200m^3 Army airship was then brought to Seerappen, its new base. From there Lehmann made some seventeen reconnaissance missions. Experimental long-range missions began on 26 July 1917 but once again, because of changeable weather, the first sortie ended earlier than anticipated on 31 July after some 35,600km had been flown, enough fuel remaining for another 33 hours' flying when LZ 120 came down after 101 hours. The reason for such a lengthy mission was the proposed sortie by L 59, which had been selected as a strategic support ship for von Lettow-Vorbeck's *Schutztruppe*. It was probably Lehmann's last wartime mission. *Kapitänleutnant* von Lossnitzer took over the ship and its crew during August 1917 and survived three attacks against targets at Riga and on Oesel, from where many difficult actions would be reported later that year.

In November 1918 LZ 120, now based at Seddin, was taken out of commission. On 30 November 1920 it was flown to Ciampino near Rome by a civilian crew, and it broke in two when the Italians deflated the huge gas cells without taking the necessary precautions. After the war Lehmann remained one of *Dr* Eckener's closest advisers and friends. He was the commander of the famous *Luftschiff Hindenburg* which crashed at Lakehurst.

The end

After severe losses the German Army decided to transfer most of its remaining airships to the Eastern Front and south-east Europe, and after more than 125 missions in the West about 200 followed in the East. The Navy ships were active over Russia on only sixteen occasions, while over the North Sea about 330 sorties were flown, during which enemy forces reacted on 63 occasions. A further 60 missions were flown against British mainland targets, either by single Zeppelin crews or in the so-called *Geschwader-Angriffen* of Peter Strasser's *Marine-Luftschiff-Abteilung*.

General von Hoeppner was told that the *Heeresluftschiffe* had carried more than 160,000kg of ordnance to their designated targets: 44,000kg were released over Belgium and France, 36,000kg over Britain and 80,000kg over Russia and south-east Europe. The Navy meanwhile had carried a total of 360,000kg, the majority on missions over the British Isles. *Dr* Dieckerhoff noted that 307,315kg were directed at enemy vessels in the North Sea and at harbours and towns from Plymouth to Scotland, while only small quantities (58,000kg or so) were dropped over the Baltic, Italy and the Mediterranean.

There is no doubt that the most successful Army ships were Z XII, LZ 38, LZ 39, LZ 77, LZ 79, LZ 81, LZ 85, LZ 86, LZ 90, LZ 97 and LZ 101, together with *Sachsen*. The most active ship was Z XII, led by Lehmann for

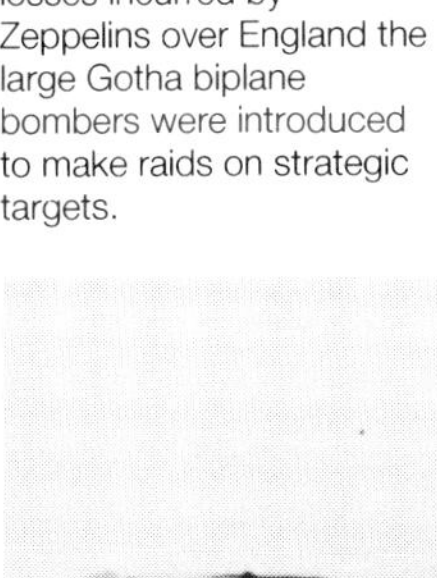

Below: After the severe losses incurred by Zeppelins over England the large Gotha biplane bombers were introduced to make raids on strategic targets.

Above: The giant SSW aircraft L I at Berlin-Staaken in 1918.

nine missions (17,000kg of bombs) and by *Hauptmann* Mirbach who took over the ship in 1916 and carried out two further missions (3,000kg). The comparable Navy airship was L14, flown by *Kapitänleutnant* Böcker on 42 reconnaissance missions, followed by seventeen attacks with a total of 22,000kg of bombs when under the command of the experienced *Hauptmann* Manger and *Kapitänleutnant* Dose. Of the 60 ships from the Navy's 73 which were used in an offensive role, thirteen carried nearly 60 per cent of all the bombs taken aboard L-ships, L 13 having the distinction of causing the most telling damage

Left: The Siemens-Schuckert SSW *Riesenflugzeug* R VIII photographed during its trials.

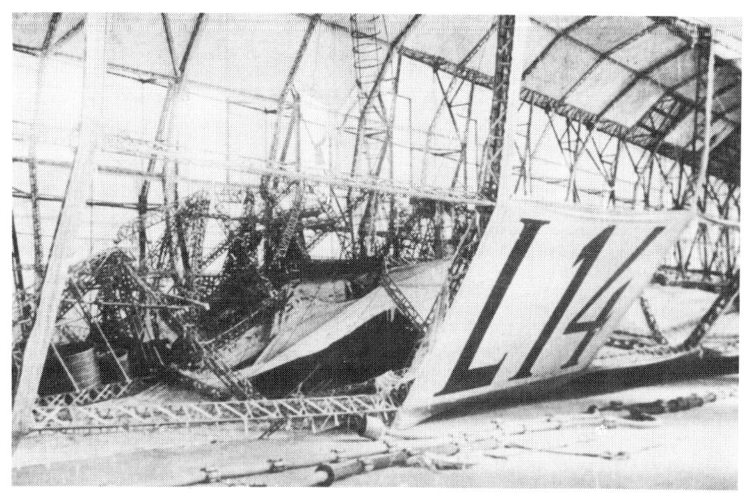

Above: L 14 (production no LZ 46) was destroyed in its hangar on 23 June 1919.

suffered by London during the First World War. *The Times* of 13 January 1919 mentioned the official losses caused by German air raids between 1915 and 1918: besides 498 civilians, 58 soldiers were killed, while 1,913 people were reported as injured.

However, airship losses were extremely high, especially of those belonging to the German Navy – 23 ships as a result of enemy action with another 31 stranded, destroyed in accidents and explosions or hit by lightning. The survivors were either disarmed or handed over to the victorious Allies at the end of the war. Of 37 rigid Zeppelins, ten Schütte-Lanz ships and one Gross-Basenach, plus two non-rigid ships, seventeen were shot down, while nineteen others, too old for further combat, were withdrawn from service.

Of the airships which were written off, nine were destroyed by Allied bombs falling on their bases. The first such loss happened on 8 October 1914, when British aircraft destroyed the Army airship Z IX in its hangar near Düsseldorf. The following year, on 7 June, LZ 37 was bombed by Sub-Lt R. Warneford from a Morane over Gontrode; on the same day LZ 38 was hit whilst in its hangar. After surviving three attacks, L 22 was shot down by a Curtiss H-12 flying boat near Terschelling. During June and August 1917 two more Zeppelins, L 43 and L 23, became victims of, respectively, another H-12 and a Sopwith Pup, which latter had taken off from the gun platform of the cruiser HMS *Yarmouth*. In the hangar at Tondern both L 54 and L 60 were burnt out after two Sopwith Camel pilots succeeded in making direct hits. Lt S. Culley destroyed L 53 near Terschelling on 11 August 1918, having begun his attack from a special lighter towed by a Royal Navy destroyer near the coast.

Only a few ships appeared to be airworthy when the war ended on 11 November 1918 following the events of the November Revolution in Germany, but more than a year was to pass before Germany was forced to hand over some of her huge Zeppelins to the Allies. Many had in the meantime been destroyed by their crews after *Konteradmiral* von Reuter had permitted his men to scuttle their ships at Scapa Flow on 21 June 1919. However, some remained.

LZ 75, operated by the Navy as L 37, was first flown on 9 November 1916 but its construction did not meet the demands of the *Reichsmarine* and it played only a minor role in four attacks on Livonia and Lithuania during 1917. In August 1920 the ship was disarmed and dismantled at Seddin and the parts were shipped to Japan as war booty. The last Navy airship, L 71, arrived at Ahlhorn on 28 October 1918, only a few days before the war ended, the ship having been taken over by the Imperial Navy on 29 July that year. It was enlarged to a volume of 68,500m^3 and the number of engines was reduced from seven to six, though it could now carry a larger payload than hitherto. The ship remained at Ahlhorn until being brought to Pulham, England, for trials.

LZ 90 (alias LZ 120), which was based at Seerappen in East Prussia, made seventeen reconnaissance sorties covering an aggregate distance of 35,600km. The ship held an unofficial world record for a long-distance flight of about 6,100km, made between 26 and 31 July 1917; there was enough fuel for more than one further day's flying, but the weather did not permit the mission to continue. The airship was subsequently flown by von Lossnitzer during the bloody struggles on Oesel and at Riga. Moved to Seddin, on 30 November 1918 LZ 90 was decommissioned by the German Navy and mothballed to await the future. On 27 November 1920 it was brought to Staaken near Berlin and from there taken to Italy, where it arrived on 24 December 1920. A few days later the ship, now called *Ausonia*, took off for some long-distance flights under the command of Major Valle. In June 1921 the ship was severely damaged in its hangar, and shortly afterwards the Italians decommissioned it.

LZ 106, the second airship handed over to Italy after the war, had been flown under the tactical designation L 61 by *Kapitänleutnant* Ehrlich. He took part in nine reconnaissance missions and two bombing raids over England. The ship bombed a steel plant at Sheffield on 13 April 1918 and escaped an attacking fighter by climbing to an altitude of some 7,000m. On 21 May 1920 the ship was flown to Italy, where it received the name *Italia* and was placed under the authority of Commandant Brivonesi. On its first flight, carried out from Rome-Ciampino on 27 August 1921, it crashed in front of the Italian king as a result of aircrew error. The structure of the *Italia* was totally wrecked and it was decided to scrap the ship because the damage seemed irreparable.

The third airship to be handed over to Italy was LZ 120, named *Bodensee*. The first of two small civil ships which had been constructed for the DELAG in 1919, it was lengthened in 1921 from 121m to 132m to cover an additional gas cell to accommodate an exclusive compartment for first-class passengers. After its first trials on 20 August 1919, the ship made 100 flights between Friedrichshafen and Berlin and one from Berlin to Stockholm. During a total of 103 flights, *Bodensee* transported 4,050 people. After its modification, the ship left Germany on 3 July 1921 by order of the Allies. Under the command of *Dr* Eckener, it crossed Zürich, then Lausanne, followed the Rhône and reached the Mediterranean coast, where it passed San Remo, flew from Corsica to Elba and from there landed at Ciampino, where it was taken over by the Italian Army. LZ 120 received the name *Esperia* some days after its 12.5hr, 1,329km journey. During the second half of 1921 the ship was again flown on a number of occasions, but in 1922 the gas cells began to leak and it was necessary to deflate them. It took until 20 August 1923 to effect repairs. *Esperia* flew again that month, but after some further flights, one carried out by General Nobile, the ship was scrapped in 1925.

The next ship to be handed over to the Allies was LZ 121 *Nordstern*. This was another small ship, with a length of 132m, thirteen gas cells and three piston engines. This airship, which was completed on 8 June 1921, was proposed for airline duty between Berlin and Stockholm, but after only one test-flight it left Germany on 13 June 1921 for St Cyr in France. The ship had been allocated to the French Army, but it was damaged when towed out of its new hangar just before its first flight under French management. It was repaired by German personnel and given the name *Mediterrannée*; now handed over to the French Navy, it was stationed at Cuers near Toulon, from where many test-flights were conducted until the ship was dismantled during 1927.

In addition to *Mediterranée*, LZ 114 (L 72) was assigned to the French armed forces. This huge ship had not joined the German Navy until the end of the First World War, and on 9 July 1920 it was tested by Eckener himself, being flown to Mauberge the next day. In August 1923 the Zeppelin lifted off for the first time in France, the delay caused by the material used for the gas cells, produced during the last days of the war, being of insufficient quality and French technicians needing a considerable period of time to make corrections. The first journey, under *Commandant* Jean du Plessis, was made from the Navy's airship dock in Toulon on 2 August, and, the ship following the southern coast of France, lasted some 18hr; for the next flight, on 9 August, the island of Corsica was circumnavigated. The third sortie lasted 60hr and took the ship from Toulon to Algiers, Tunis, Sardinia and Corsica. On the fourth trip (29–30 September 1923) the Mediterranean Sea was crossed for a second time and interesting parts of the Sahara Desert were surveyed from aloft. One month later the ship took part in Navy exercises and on 24 November was caught in a dangerous thunderstorm near Cap Ferrat.

On 18 December 1923 LZ 114, named *Dixmude* by the French, set off on an important long-distance flight. Leaving Toulon, the crew followed the coast of northern Tunisia and flew across the Sahara to the oasis of In Salah. A storm ahead was noted, and the airship moved to near Bou Saâda in the north and then tried to fly to the east of the Atlas Mountains. *Dixmude* was seen for the last time over the Gulf of Gabès. Some days later, near the southern coast of Sicily, parts of the ship were found together with the body of the commander. There was no sign of the crew, which comprised more than 50 men: the ship had disintegrated in a gigantic explosion. With the disappearance of *Dixmude*, interest in airship aviation in France ended. The accident led many to believe that airship flight was still a dangerous undertaking when using inflammable gas, but only in the USA was there an alternative on offer.

Above: LZ 62 (tactical code L 30), decommissioned in 1917 and handed over to Belgium in 1920.

Right: LZ 120 *Bodensee* was constructed at Friedrichshafen, indicated by the legend 'D I' on the fin.

GERMAN CIVIL AIRSHIPS

From DELAG to DZR

On 23 June 1919 the remaining German airship force of seven craft was destroyed by the crews in their hangars in order to prevent them from falling into Allied hands; on 18 August the DELAG officially started up operations again. During these days *Dr* Eckener, the organization's experienced director, noted that

> The Deutsche Luftschiffahrts Aktien Gesellschaft (DELAG), a well-known airship transport company with its ships *Viktoria Luise, Hansa* and *Schwaben*, making flights all over Germany and carrying more than 14,000 passengers without accident, will continue operations by establishing a regular service between Berlin and Friedrichshafen from 18 August this year. The Swiss ferries will meet the Zeppelin ships at Friedrichshafen and connect them to the railway network. The airship *Bodensee* is a new, improved type of Zeppelin, built with the benefit of experience gained during the Great War, and has been designed purely for passenger service. Unfortunately not a single ship could be commissioned until today because of the strikes.

The published timetable was as follows:

> (a) Berlin to Friedrichshafen (on dates with odd-numbers) at 09.00 at Staaken near Berlin, arriving at Friedrichshafen at about 16.00.
> (b) Friedrichshafen to Berlin (every other day) at 17.00 at the local airship hangar, arriving at Berlin-Staaken at 10.00.

The prices were as follows:

(a) Berlin–Munich–Friedrichshafen	450 marks
(b) Berlin–Friedrichshafen	400 marks
(c) Berlin–Munich	350 marks
(d) Munich–Friedrichshafen	150 marks
(e) Munich–Friedrichshafen–Munich	250 marks

> No return tickets will be available for the routes between Berlin and Munich and between Berlin and Friedrichshafen. Each passenger can take along, free of charge, luggage weighing 15kg. The prices do not include transport to and from the airship hangars.

On 20 August 1919 LZ 120 *Bodensee* took off for the first time at Friedrichshafen. From the beginning the new scheduled services connecting the three towns were very reliable, and *Dr* Eckener tried to stimulate interest in his idea of a European airline system using more Zeppelins – the first route could be that to Stockholm, which he had visited on 8 October 1919 – but all thoughts of expansion using LZ 121 *Nordstern* had to be abandoned almost immediately when, after one test flight on 13 June 1921, this ship was transferred to France by order of the Allies.

Only 103 commercial flights, covering an aggregate distance of 51,258km and carrying a total of 2,380 passengers, were made by *Bodensee*, between August and December 1919. LZ 120 had a gas capacity of only 20,000m^3, though this was enlarged to match the size of *Nordstern* (22,500m^3). The ship was also seized by the Western Allies, and

Below: The command cabin of *Bodensee*.

Right: LZ 120 being lengthened in 1921. The ship was transferred to Italy on 3 July the same year.

then handed over to Italy. Work on LZ 115 to LZ 119 ceased, as did the construction of LZ 122 to LZ 125, for which only a few components had been produced by the end of the war.

ZR III

The best-known 'reparations airship', ZR III (Zeppelin Rigid No III, manufacturer's designation LZ 126), was produced after hostilities had ceased. This Zeppelin was allocated to the United States, and was later handed over to the US Navy who christened it *Los Angeles*. Prior to the airship's completion, test runs of the Maybach engines produced good results, and on 27 August 1924 ZR III was moved out of its hangar at Friedrichshafen. It had a length of 200m, a maximum diameter of 27.64m and a gas volume of 70,000m^3. It was propelled by five Maybachs, each developing 400hp, to give the ship a maximum speed of about 125kph (67.5kt) and a range of 8,500km with a hydrogen-filled envelope (less with helium). A. Wittemann, the navigation officer of LZ 126, reported on the new ship's first test-flights:

> With the advent of LZ 126, a German airship was seen over Friedrichshafen again after an interruption of a few years. The ship rose and was steered to Lindau. It was a day with dark

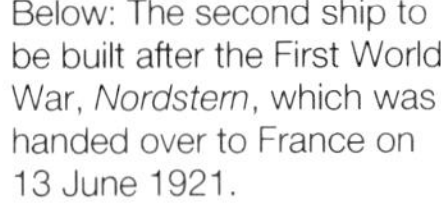

Below: The second ship to be built after the First World War, *Nordstern*, which was handed over to France on 13 June 1921.

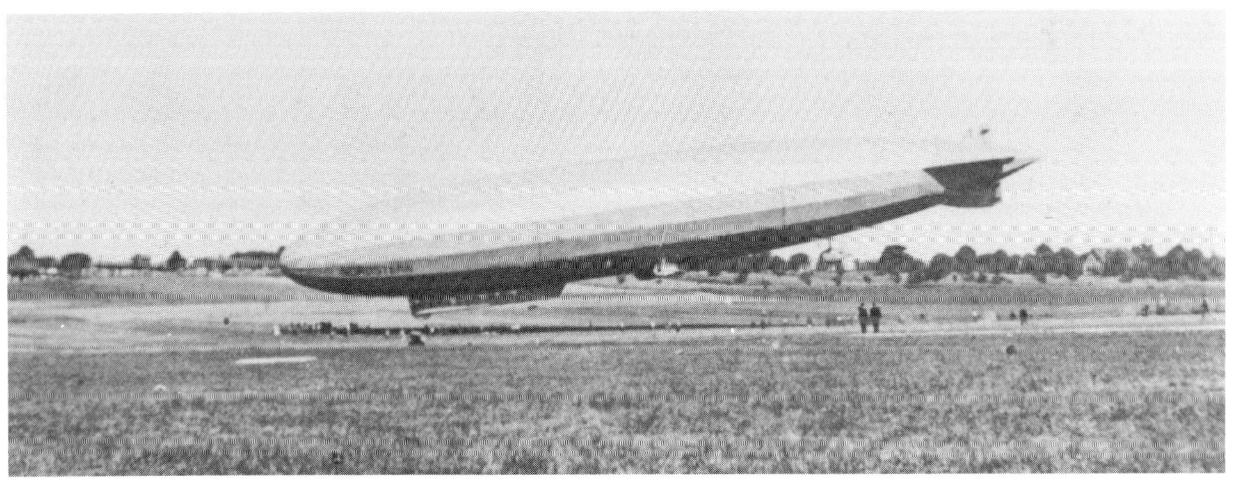

Left: LZ 126 under construction at Friedrichshafen, 20 October 1923.

clouds, the air waiting for the rain. After a short time it started raining and a strong wind pushed the water through the front window seals of the command post. Steadfastly, *Dr* Eckener navigated the ship along the Swiss side of Lake Constance.

Meanwhile the sun was coming through and near Reichenau the weather cleared up. Despite the stormy weather, and despite one of the Maybach engines having failed because of poor maintenance, LZ 126 was returned to Friedrichshafen by a crew brimming with self-confidence.

The second test-flight was carried out early in September 1924. Lifting off at Friedrichshafen to the sounds of a *Reichswehr* band, having been towed out with the help of German soldiers, the ship passed a railway train near Ravensburg at 09.45, crossed Kempten at 10.20 and only 40 minutes later passed the Ammersee, and then the Starnberger See, followed by the eyes of thousands and thousands of people on the ground below. To the 'hurrahs' of the inhabitants of the Bavarian metropolis, the ship turned over Munich at about 11.30 and disappeared in the direction of Landshut. At 12.40 Kehlheim was sighted by the 86 men on board, and then LZ 126 went on to Nuremberg, Stuttgart, Esslingen and Urach. It returned over the Jura and landed again at Friedrichshafen.

The next test-flight took place on 11 September. Despite the strong wind blowing from the north-east, the ship was brought out of its hangar by the ground crew, and at 10.00 eighty people rose into the sky. The Rheinfall at Schaffhausen was photographed by most of the passengers, and some 30 minutes later Basel was reached; the last Zeppelin to visit the old town was the Navy's L 3 on 21 May 1914, more than ten years ago. At 15.30 the people on board had a good view of Zürich, the crew receiving a welcome from the local broadcasting station. Passing the village of Winterthur and the monastery of St Gallen, the Zeppelin crossed Lake Constance and landed again at home base.

Rolf Brandt, the special correspondent for the *Berliner Lokal-Anzeiger*, reported on LZ 126's last flight over Germany on 25 September 1924:

In the afternoon the ship was ready for further action, but the start of the long-distance flight was postponed until the next day because of the strong winds. The ground crew pulled the ship, with 73 people on board, out of its hangar and then LZ 126 started its ascent. After an hour, all five engines were still running and the ship moved forward to Sigmaringen and attempted to cross the Jura Mountains to reach Tübingen. Far away the Black Forest, with dark clouds covering the mountains, could only be imagined as LZ 126 continued on its way. Then the ship appeared over Heidelberg and its world-famous castle at noon. At Darmstadt the passengers had a view of the large market below. At 12.30 the Zeppelin crossed Frankfurt, and near Cassel two aircraft approached, made some circuits around the large ship and then flew away again.

Peacefully, and with a kind of majesty, LZ 126 made its way to Hanover, the sleepy passengers sitting in the roomy compartment. At three o'clock in the afternoon the ship flew over the airport at Hanover and made its way along the Weser to Bremen harbour. Everywhere people were waiting for the *Amerikaschiff* on its way to Hamburg. From there it turned in a northerly direction over Schleswig to Flensburg; at the controls, *Dr* Eckener was assisted by E. A. Lehmann. At 7 o'clock in the evening the old battleship *Hannover*, was seen making her way across the Baltic Sea. As LZ 126 passed over Warnemünde, tea and hot dogs were served by the crew at an altitude of about 1,600m. After sighting a sloop, the ship appeared over the River Oder near Stettin and set course for a real sea of buildings, the German capital Berlin. At a constant altitude of only 300m the shouts of many thousands of people were audible, the crowd standing everywhere to greet LZ 126 and its passengers. Unfortunately the ship could not go to Königsberg, where its arrival was awaited by more crowds, because of bad weather.

Some time later LZ 126 returned to Friedrichshafen to be prepared for its handing over to the Western Allies.

On 12 October 1924 the ship was ready to fly across the North Atlantic. The previous day 30,000kg of fuel, 2,000kg of oil and a generous supply of food and groceries had been stowed aboard the ship, which was inflated to such a pressure that a good deal of gas escaped from the relief valves again. At 06.00 there was a test-run with all engines, and at 06.35 the ship lifted off and climbed through a fogbank. At an altitude of about 350m it left the fog behind and emerged into blazing sunshine. A. Wittemann revealed much fascinating detail about the days that followed:

> It was very difficult to bring ZR III [i.e. LZ 126] over the hills and mountains because there was nothing on board the ship that could be jettisoned: the higher peaks of the Côte d'Or were circumvented, because the ship's weight was still too great to cope. Later the Zeppelin moved over St Armand and crossed Cognac with its famous vineyards. At 3 o'clock in the afternoon the mouth of the Gironde was spotted at a great distance. The weather was still excellent, and 29 minutes later the shores of the Atlantic Ocean were passed. The crew were divided into two watches, similar to the practice on a real ocean liner.
>
> The wireless operator also had to act as cook. The first dinner consisted of turtle soup, Hungarian goulash with different vegetables, coffee and pudding. Because no regular passengers were being carried, there was plenty of room for an excellent meal.

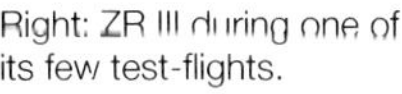
Right: ZR III during one of its few test-flights.

Right: LZ 126 about to depart for Munich, 6 September 1924.

Finally Cape Ortegal was reached and the night closed in; all the navigation lights were switched on. Suddenly the wind arose, shaking the crew for the next few hours. Near the Azores two freighters were sighted and an exact fix on their position was relayed by one of the officers on board the ships.

Thanks to the wind, ZR III moved along at a spanking pace. Over São Miguel, one of the Azores, two postal bags were thrown off at Angra, the main settlement. At 6 o'clock in the evening the crew passed the mid-point of the journey (38°50′N, 32°10′W). The next morning a wind speed of Force 8 to 9 was measured by the crew, and during the next few hours it started raining. The weather situation, relayed by an unknown steamer west of Newfoundland, enabled *Dr* Eckener set a new course in a northerly direction at last.

Near the Grand Banks, off Newfoundland, ZR III entered a region of dense fog. All five Maybach engines were running smoothly, and no faults were reported by the personnel in the gondolas.

At 22.18 the American coast, indicated by a lighthouse, was reached at 43° 42′ N and 59° 48′ W. Early in the morning the Zeppelin appeared over the skyline of New York and at 07.45 the ship passed over the Statue of Liberty; ten minutes later the Hudson River was reached. At 09.15 the flight ended at Lakehurst. The ship was taken over by the American Government immediately after the customs officers had left.

The Zeppelin abroad

In addition to Germany and Great Britain, the United States was interested in developing intercontinental airship operations, while the Netherlands perceived an opportunity to create a fast service between Europe and Dutch colonies in the Far East. As Germany's airships were beginning their scheduled service between Friedrichshafen and Recife de

Left: A close-up photograph of a Maybach VL I engine being installed in one of LZ 126's gondolas.
Centre left: The roomy command post aboard LZ 126, in a photograph taken just before the ship's flight to the United States in October 1924.
Below left: LZ 126 arriving at Lakehurst.
Below: The huge rings of LZ 127's framework, seen during the early stages of the ship's construction.

Pernambuco, French craft were operating a postal service from Paris to Dakar in Africa while at Natal in northern Brazil letters and parcels were being put aboard aircraft bound for Rio de Janeiro and other destinations in South America. However, following the loss of the R 101 and the scrapping of the R 100, it began to look as though all the ambitious schemes for creating a world-wide airship service would need much more time before they could be fulfilled.

Meanwhile, various proposals had been made to build a fleet of sixteen Zeppelins and to organize an ambitious multi-national service, but these came to nothing because clearance for the sale of its (non-flammable) helium was not granted by the US Government. Germany therefore continued its own attempts to set up the promised air-link between the Old World and both parts of the American continent.

LZ 127 *Graf Zeppelin*

Dr Eckener's huge civil airship LZ 127, constructed at Friedrichshafen and based on the standard Zeppelin, was proposed for use in developing a world-wide commercial air service. The design, by *Dr* Dürr, was limited in size only by the dimensions of the ship's assembly hall. Taking his cue from *Graf* Zeppelin himself, Dürr succeeded in raising finance and within a short period of time had amassed 2.5 million Reichsmarks; the German Government added a further 1 million. Ferdinand von Zeppelin's only child, his daughter Hella, christened LZ 127 on 8 July 1928, her father's birthday. She named it *Graf Zeppelin*.

The first flight did not occur until 18 September that year. For its fifth test-flight the ship remained aloft for 34hr and covered a distance of about 3,150km, overflying Nuremberg, Würzburg, Cologne, Hamburg, Amsterdam, the English Channel, Harwich, Bremerhaven and Berlin. Then it moved on to Leipzig and Dresden before returning to Nuremberg again. LZ 127 was prepared for its first Atlantic crossing early in October 1928. On board were a few reporters and official guests, plus some officers who would receive instruction on the way to America, but only two fare-paying passengers. On 13 October, after LZ 127 had passed the Azores, bad weather blew up and the stabilizer fabric was ripped off in a number of places. There was a danger that canvas from the hull could jam the rudder system, and by mid-Atlantic some of the crew had to climb up and effect repairs, even though, because the storm was still blowing, it was impossible to reduce speed. However, in spite of all difficulties, *Graf Zeppelin* reached New York and landed at Lakehurst. The airship had covered a distance of 9,926km and stayed aloft for nearly 112hr. *Dr* Eckener and his men received a warm welcome on the streets of New York. After repairs, the ship travelled back to Germany at the end of the month, taking only 71hr, and following a promotional tour over the German capital and a further test-flight, LZ 127 was taken out of service until the next year.

Between 25 and 28 March 1929 the airship made a non-stop return flight from Germany via Lyons, Marseilles, Corsica, Rome,

Naples, Cyprus, Jerusalem, the Dead Sea, the Levantine coast, Crete, Athens, Corfu, the Dalmatian Coast, the Austrian Alps and Vienna. It returned to its base after some 81hr. More journeys over Austria, Germany, the Netherlands and Switzerland quickly followed. During April 1929 the ship went round Spain, although the mechanics had to fight against engine failure and repair one of the Maybachs during flight after its propeller had come off. None of the passengers noticed the problems.

On 16 May 1929 the second *Amerika-Fahrt* began. Following the River Rhône, LZ 127 reached the western part of the Mediterranean but near Alicante the second engine suddenly failed when the main shaft snapped. Eckener was forced to abandon the trip and went back to the Rhône valley, where a strong *mistral* was blowing. Near Valence a third engine failed, and soon afterwards the fourth gave out, leaving the huge airship reliant on a single Maybach for propulsion. There was now no real chance of reaching Geneva: the last remaining engine was able to hold LZ 127's position but not move the ship onward. The French Government allowed the Zeppelin to enter the naval airship base at Cuers near Toulon, where new engines, all of them brought from Friedrichshafen, were immediately installed. In the light of these events Eckener suggested that the drive shafts of his ship be improved – a time-consuming task. On 1 August 1929 a 95-hour transatlantic flight was under way.

From Lakehurst in the USA, *Graf Zeppelin* began its voyage around the world on 7 August. Friedrichshafen was reached after a record-breaking flight of only 55hr, the ship averaging 127.5kph over the 7,068km journey. A few passengers, each of them paying $9,900, had joined the press entourage, occupying rooms equipped with modern conveniences. After all the systems had been tested, the ship rose again on the morning of 15 August. Nuremberg, Leipzig and Berlin were passed, then Danzig and Königsberg. After crossing East Prussia, it flew steadily on over Lithuania and Latvia, Russia and then the Urals, the natural boundary between Europe and Asia. The flight continued along the River Ob, where gigantic forest fires were noticed, passing the Rivers Yenisey and Yakutsk and the easternmost part of the Soviet Union. The ship finally crossed the Sea of Japan, and on the afternoon of 19 August the people of Tokyo welcomed the German airship. Compared with a four-week sea voyage or a two-week journey in an old railway carriage across Asia, LZ 127 had covered the distance, 11,250km, in 102hr.

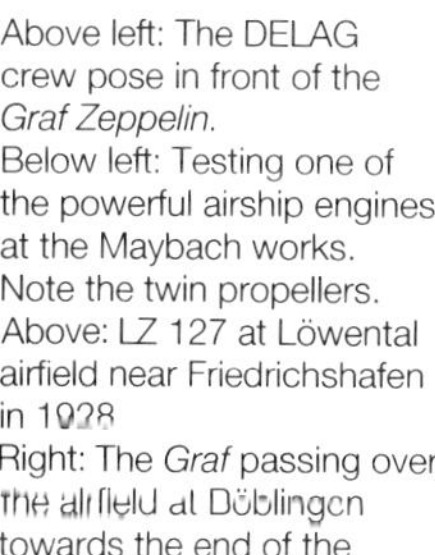

Above left: The DELAG crew pose in front of the *Graf Zeppelin*.
Below left: Testing one of the powerful airship engines at the Maybach works. Note the twin propellers.
Above: LZ 127 at Löwental airfield near Friedrichshafen in 1928
Right: The *Graf* passing over the airfield at Döblingen towards the end of the 1920s.

After some minor problems with the weather while leaving the naval hangar at Kasumigaura, the Zeppelin appeared off the American West Coast near San Francisco, and after giving its personnel a view of the Golden Gate Bridge the ship was moored at the US Navy's airship base at Los Angeles. The third segment of the journey had ended after a further 9,635km. The Zeppelin then flew east, crossing Arizona, New Mexico, Texas, Oklahoma, Missouri, Illinois, Michigan, Ohio and Pennsylvania, finally descending at Lakehurst early in the morning of 29 August. The circumnavigation ended after a total of 32,790km. Early in September E. A. Lehmann brought his ship back to Friedrichshafen, where it arrived 20 days after it first took off, having spent rather more than twelve of them in the air. The *Graf Zeppelin* undertook only minor promotional work for the rest of the year, one tour being made over the Netherlands and another over countries of southern Europe. The crew were met with great acclaim wherever the ship was seen. A year later LZ 127 became the first airship to reach South America, arriving at Recife de Pernambuco after a flight lasting 62hr. It then moved south and made some circuits over Rio de Janeiro before setting course back to Recife.

After LZ 127's so-called *Nordlandfahrt* in July 1930, for which General Nobile was one of the passengers, and a long-range sortie over the Baltic, about 90 short flights were made over Germany and Western Europe. In July

Left: A close up photograph of LZ 127's gondola, showing the command position and the passenger compartment. Right: The huge airship hangars at Frankfurt-Main airport.

SÜDAMERIKA-FAHRPLAN DER DEUTSCHEN ZEPPELIN-REEDEREI 1936

Fahrt Nr.	Angabe der Postbeförderung (LC Briefpost, Drucksachen u. Pakete; AOP nur Drucksach. u. Paketpost)	EUROPA—SUDAMERIKA: Dienst der Deutschen Zeppelin-Reederei			Flugzeug-Anschluß der Syndicato Condor Ltda. (3 motorige Junkers Ju 52) Jederzeitige Aenderungen vorbehalten.				SUDAMERIKA—EUROPA: Flugzeug-Anschluß der Syndicato Condor Ltda. Jederzeitige Aenderungen vorbehalten.				Dienst der Deutschen Zeppelin-Reederei		
		Frankfurt a. M.	Recife (Pernambuco)	Rio de Janeiro	Rio de Janeiro	Porto Alegre	Porto Alegre	Montevideo Buenos Aires	Buenos Aires Montevideo	Porto Alegre	Porto Alegre	Rio de Janeiro	Rio de Janeiro	Recife (Pernambuco)	Frankfurt a. M.
		Mittw. Donnerstg. ab	Samstag an ab	Sonntag an	Montag ab	Montag an	Dienstag ab	Dienstag an	Dienstag ab	Dienstag an	Mittwoch ab	Mittwoch an	Mittwoch bzw. Donnerstag ab	Donnerstag Freitag an ab	Montag/Dienstag an
7	LC	24./25. Juni	27. Juni	28. Juni	29. Juni	29. Juni	30. Juni	30. Juni	30. Juni	30. Juni	1. Juli	1. Juli	1. Juli	2./3. Juli	6./7. Juli
8	LC	8./9. Juli	11. Juli	12. Juli	13. Juli	13. Juli	14. Juli	14. Juli	14. Juli	14. Juli	15. Juli	15. Juli	15. Juli	16./17. Juli	20./21. Juli
9	AOP (Olympiafahrt)	20./21. Juli (ausnahmsw. Mont./Dienst.)	—	24. Juli (ausnahmsweise Freitag)	26. Juli (ausnahmsweise Sonntag)	26. Juli	26. Juli	26. Juli	23. Juli (ausnahmsweise Donnerstag)	23. Juli	23. Juli	23. Juli	25. Juli (ausnahmsw. Samstag)		30. Juli (ausnahmsw. Donnerstag)
10	LC	29./30. Juli	1. August	2. August	3. Aug.	3. Aug.	4. Aug.	4. Aug.	4. Aug.	4. Aug.	5. Aug.	5. Aug.	5. August	6./7. August	10./11. August (ausnahmsweise an Friedrichshafen)
11	LC	12./13. August (ausnahmsweise ab Friedrichshafen)	15. August	16. August	17. Aug.	17. Aug.	18. Aug.	18. Aug.	18. Aug.	18. Aug.	19. Aug.	19. Aug.	19. August	20./21. Aug.	24./25. Aug.
12	LC	26./27. August	—	30. August	31. Aug.	31. Aug.	1. Sept.	1. Sept.	1. Sept.	1. Sept.	2. Sept.	2. Sept.	3. Sept.		7./8. Sept.
13	LC	9./10. Sept.	12. Sept.	13. September	14. Sept.	14. Sept.	15. Sept.	15. Sept.	15. Sept.	15. Sept.	16. Sept.	16. Sept.	16. Sept.	17./18. Sept.	21./22. Sept.
14	LC	23./24. Sept.	26. Sept.	27. September	28. Sept.	28. Sept.	29. Sept.	29. Sept.	29. Sept.	29. Sept.	30. Sept.	30. Sept.	30. Sept.	1./2. Okt.	5./6. Okt.
15	LC	7./8. Okt.	10. Okt.	11. Oktober	12. Okt.	12. Okt.	13. Okt.	13. Okt.	13. Okt.	13. Okt.	14. Okt.	14. Okt.	14. Okt.	15./16. Okt.	19./20. Okt.
16	LC	21./22. Okt.	—	25. Oktober	26. Okt.	26. Okt.	27. Okt.	27. Okt.	27. Okt.	27. Okt.	28. Okt.	28. Okt.	29. Okt.	—	2./3. Nov.
17	LC	28./29. Okt.	31. Okt.	1. November	2. Nov.	2. Nov.	3. Nov.	3. Nov.	3. Nov.	3. Nov.	4. Nov.	4. Nov.	4. Nov.	5./6. Nov.	9./10. Nov.
18	LC	4./5. Nov.	—	8. November	9. Nov.	9. Nov.	10. Nov.	10. Nov.	10. Nov.	10. Nov.	11. Nov.	11. Nov.	12. Nov.	—	16./17. Nov.
19	LC	11./12. Nov.	14. Nov.	15. November	16. Nov.	16. Nov.	17. Nov.	17. Nov.	17. Nov.	17. Nov.	18. Nov.	18. Nov.	18. Nov.	19./20. Nov.	23./24. Nov.
20	LC	18./19. Nov.	—	22. November	23. Nov.	23. Nov.	24. Nov.	24. Nov.	24. Nov.	24. Nov.	25. Nov.	25. Nov.	26. Nov.	—	30. Nov./1. Dez.
21	LC	25./26. Nov.	28. Nov.	29. November	30. Nov.	30. Nov.	1. Dez.	1. Dez.	1. Dez.	1. Dez.	2. Dez.	2. Dez.	2. Dez.	3./4. Dez.	7./8. Dez.
22	LC	2./3. Dez.	—	6. Dezember	7. Dez.	7. Dez.	8. Dez.	8. Dez.	8. Dez.	8. Dez.	9. Dez.	9. Dez.	10. Dez.	—	14./15. Dez.

Jederzeitige Aenderungen vorbehalten.

Luftschiff-Einsatz: Im Südamerika-Dienst hauptsächlich LZ 127 „Graf Zeppelin" und bei den Fahrten Nr. 9, 17, 16, 18, 20, 22 voraussichtlich LZ 129 „Hindenburg". Nähere Auskunft bei den Dienststellen der Deutschen Zeppelin-Reederei und in den Reisebüros.

Die **Abfahrt des Zeppelin-Luftschiffes** erfolgt bei der Reise **Nr. 9** von dem Flug- und Luftschiffhafen Rhein-Main bei Frankfurt am M. in ausnahmsweise **in der Nacht von Montag auf Dienstag**, bei den Reisen **Nr. 7 und 8 sowie Nr. 10—22 in der Nacht von Mittwoch auf Donnerstag.** Am Tage der Einschiffung versammeln sich die Fahrgäste ab 17 Uhr im Hotel Frankfurter Hof in Frankfurt a. M., für die Fahrt Nr. 11 im Kurgarten-Hotel in Friedrichshafen a. B.

Landung in Sevilla erfolgt nur bei Bedarf; es müssen mindestens 4 Fahrgäste für Sevilla gebucht sein.

Fahrpreise
für den Zeppelin-Dienst (einschließlich Verpflegung und Trinkgelder):
Frankfurt – Recife (Pernambuco) RM 1400.—, Frankfurt – Rio de Janeiro RM 1500.—

Flugzeug-Anschluß der Syndicato Condor Ltda.
Rio de Janeiro – Montevideo RM 330.—
Rio de Janeiro – Buenos Aires RM 360.—
Bei diesen Anschluß-Flügen findet eine Uebernachtung der Fluggäste in Porto Alegre statt. Die Kosten für alle Auto-Zubringerfahrten vom Flugplatz zum Hotel und umgekehrt sowie die Uebernachtungskosten und Verpflegung sind in dem Flugpreis mit einbegriffen.

Flugzeug-Anschluß nach der Westküste
Rio de Janeiro – Santiago RM 375.— + $ 100.— (zum Tageskurs) einschließlich Verpflegung und Uebernachtung in Porto Alegre und Buenos Aires. Der Anschluß von Buenos Aires nach Santiago wird durch den bestehenden Dienst ausgeführt. Start von Buenos Aires nach Santiago Mittwochs, von Santiago nach Buenos Aires Sonntags.

Jederzeitige Aenderungen vorbehalten.

Fluganschlüsse in Europa: Von und nach Frankfurt a. M. (Flug- und Luftschiffhafen Rhein-Main) Friedrichshafen an das Streckennetz der Deutschen Lufthansa.

Fahrpreisermäßigungen: Bei gleichzeitiger Buchung von Hin- und Rückreise wird eine Ermäßigung von 20% auf die Rückfahrkarte gewährt, deren Gültigkeit 12 Monate beträgt; dies gilt auch für den Flugzeug-Anschluß.

Kinder zahlen, sofern nicht Unterbringung in einem normalen Bett verlangt wird, bis zum Alter von 6 Jahren ein Viertel des Fahrpreises, bis zum 12. Lebensjahr die Hälfte des Fahrpreises.

Reisegepäck: Die Beförderung von Reisegepäck bis zum Gewicht von 120 kg ist im Fahrpreis eingeschlossen. Davon können 20 kg kostenlos im Luftschiff mitgenommen werden, die restlichen 100 kg werden kostenlos mit einem deutschen Seeschiff befördert.

Post- und Frachtbeförderung: Der Zeppelin-Dienst bietet einen sicheren und schnellen Weg zur Beförderung Ihrer eiligen **Briefe, Drucksachen** und **Pakete** nach Uebersee.

Auskunft über Postanschlüsse und Tarife ist bei den Postanstalten erhältlich.

Für die **Beförderung von Frachtgütern** steht ein besonderer Prospekt der Deutschen Zeppelin-Reederei auf Anforderung zur Verfügung.

Zeppelin-Sonder-Fahrten nach Nordamerika siehe letzte Seite.

1931 a planned visit to Iceland, continuing the journey to try to reach Greenland shortly afterwards, had to be abandoned on account of bad weather. On 24 July 1931 the ship set off on its now-famous Arctic flight of exploration, which ended seven days later. On board were *Professor* Samoilowitch and fifteen well-known scientists with 15 tons of instruments and equipment. The ship left Leningrad in the morning of 26 July, travelling over the Barents Sea to Franz Josef Land and then Severnaya Zemlya. *Graf Zeppelin* managed to find the most northerly point of Siberia in spite of the dense fog, and on the way back hitherto unexplored parts of Novaya Zemlya were mapped and photographed.

Between 29 August and 10 December 1931 the ship was in permanent service across the

Left: LZ 127 at Frankfurt-Rebstock, summer 1934. Above: The timetable for LZ 127, connecting Frankfurt and Rio de Janeiro by both airship and aircraft. Right: After the LZ 129 disaster, LZ 127 was consigned to an airship museum at Frankfurt-Main.

South Atlantic, linking Friedrichshafen and Rio de Janeiro, and some forty flights over Germany were made that year as well. During 1932 LZ 127 completed nine successful flights over the South Atlantic, one sortie over England and twenty other short commercial flights covering a total of 180,000km.

On 1 May 1932 – dubbed *Tag der Arbeit* – LZ 127 was again involved in trips across the South Atlantic, and between 27 April and 2 November 1933 the ship made 123 flights, and during 1934 twelve more, to South America. The year 1934 also saw a further eleven sorties around Europe, while in 1935 the ship travelled some 350,000km in total, which included sixteen flights to South America and the one-hundredth transatlantic crossing. In 1937 a record 60 Atlantic crossings were made, fifteen by LZ 127. The grand total was 590 flights, covering more than 1,695,000km and transporting 13,100 fare-paying passengers.

On 18 June 1937, following the *Hindenburg* disaster, the *Graf Zeppelin* was transferred to Frankfurt, where it went on display as a huge museum-piece in honour of *Graf* von Zeppelin and his work. On 29 February 1940 *Fliegerstabsingenieur* Lucht, under orders from *Reichsmarschall* Hermann Göring, informed the *Deutsche Zeppelin Reederei* (DZR) that the ship had to be scrapped immediately.

LZ 129 *Hindenburg*

On 4 March 1936 LZ 129 *Hindenburg* (there have been rumours of a suggestion that it be named *Adolf Hitler*) rose for the first time at Friedrichshafen. On board were 56 crew members and 31 passengers, and after about three hours' flying the ship returned, having covered a distance of 180km. Five experimental flights followed up to 23 March, and three days later *Hindenburg* made a promotional flight carrying 59 passengers.

Plans were laid for the airship's first flight to South America, and, with 37 passengers, 61kg of postage and 1,269kg of freight, it departed on 4 April 1936; one month later it flew from Friedrichshafen to Lakehurst to complete its first North American trip, a second starting from Frankfurt on 17 May. This was followed by a journey to Rio and some flights over Germany. At the end of June and during July 1936 the *Hindenburg* made four more long-distance flights.

On 27 April 1936 LZ 129 participated in an experiment undertaken by Ernst Udet to test

Left: LZ 129 *Hindenburg* under assembly at Friedrichshafen.

Right: LZ 129 leaves the large construction hall at Friedrichshafen for the first time, 4 March 1936.

an idea for speeding up airmail services. Udet had taken off at Darmstadt-Friesheim in a small Fw 44 Stieglitz (D-EUTE), a large hook fitted to the centre of the biplane's upper wing. The *Hindenburg*, commanded by the experienced Max Pruss, approached the aircraft from its Frankfurt base at an altitude of 700m. The first attempt at a connection failed, but the second approach was more successful, Udet's *Stieglitz* hooking itself under the vast hull of the airship. After about five minutes the aircraft was released again and returned to Darmstadt.

Immediately after the *Olympiafahrt*, which started and ended at Rhein-Main and transported 65 passengers and 778kg of mail, three journeys to the Americas were made. On 14 September 1936 the ship flew from Friedrichshafen to Nuremberg, returning the same day, and two days later it moved to Frankfurt in preparation for the eighth *Nordamerikafahrt*. After its arrival again at Lakehurst, LZ 129 made a sortie with more than 100 passengers over the American East Coast. Three more flights ending at Rio and Recife de Pernambuco were made up to December 1936. The ship was engaged in a total of ten commercial flights to Lakehurst, from where a 9hr flight over the western United States was begun in August 1936.

Regular passengers had to pay between 1,600 and 1,800 Reichsmarks to travel to New York; the maximum fare for the return journey from Germany to Lakehurst was 3,200 marks, the fare to Recife de Pernambuco was 1,400 marks; and from there to Germany cost 2,650 marks. By late 1936 *Hindenburg* had carried more than 1,000 passengers, nearly all the flights being fully booked. The actual cost of flying the ship from Germany to the United States was reported to be about $28,000; this was enough to cover fuel, taxes, insurance, landing fees and other fixed charges. When 50 passengers flew in the Zeppelin they paid a total of $20,000; the remaining $8,000 was met by transporting mail or other freight.

During the winter of 1936–37 the *Hindenburg*'s passenger compartments and lounges were rebuilt to enable 72 passengers to be accommodated instead of only 50. Between 16 and 27 March 1937, the airship, fully booked, was flown under the command of Eckener, Pruss, von Schiller and *Kapitän* Albert Sammt, the First Officer, on the South Atlantic route to Brazil. Some days later *Hindenburg* appeared over the Rhineland and western Germany, on a promotional tour. The ship was now based at Frankfurt and Friedrichshafen-Löwental, from where both LZ 127 and LZ 129 crossed the South Atlantic on 46 occasions.

Left. Another view of LZ 129 under construction. An engine gondola is prominent.

On 6 May 1937 LZ 129 approached Boston after passing over Nova Scotia, then overflew Long Island and crossed New York after making a circuit of the city. In command was the experienced *Kapitän* Max Pruss, assisted by both Ernst A. Lehmann and Anton Wittemann; Albert Sammt was once again the First Officer. At about 22.30, as the huge airship approached Lakehurst, the manager of the local station, Charles Rosendahl, sent a message to the airship commander that the weather would allow landing to begin. During the airship's descent phase the wind changed direction and Pruss was forced to approach again from the opposite direction. The airship was at first too heavy, but after some ballast and more gas had been released it was finally balanced. The hand-ropes fell and were connected up with the larger ropes leading to the mooring post. The ship shook a little for a few seconds.

On the upper part of the covering, near the fin, a small flame suddenly appeared. It became larger and larger and then yellow flames began to engulf the rear part of the ship. Albert Sammt did not allow the release of any more ballast in order to bring the ship into balance once again: he ordered the ship brought down as fast as possible. Many of the passengers and crew members jumped out of the inferno, to be saved by courageous helping hands, but within 32 seconds 170,000m^3 of hydrogen had completely burnt up.

At midnight United Press reported: '*Hindenburg* crashed burning at Lakehurst'. At

02.40 the naval wireless station at Chatham broadcast, verbatim:

CQ de WCC: Special Bulletin CQ
An explosion destroyed the German dirigible Hindenburg and it went crashing in flames Thursday night a loss of nearly one hundred lives – period – There were approximately one hundred passengers and crew members aboard – period – Navy communication at Washington announced there were some survivors but their number could not be determined immediately – period – The disaster occurred just as the huge airship had dropped ground lines in preparation for landing its passengers upon arrival from Frankfurt comma Germany which it left last Monday night – period – The blast shook the surrounding area and the flames engulfed the ship – period – Medical assistance and police reinforcements were rushed from all nearby cities – period – Radiomarine Corporation of America.

Left: *Hindenburg* over Lake Constance in the summer at 1936.
Below far left: The sailplane *Präsident*, being hung under LZ 129.
Below left: The Fw 44 at Frankfurt Airport, showing the large hook fitted on its upper wing.

Right: Two views of the burning *Hindenburg* at Lakehurst on 6 May 1937 show the last moments of the ship.

At 02.55, after a period of silence, the *Deutsche Zeppelin Reederei* received a new message:

> Told you she arrived at 22.30. At about that time she was approaching downward towards the mooring at Lakehurst; within about 100 feet she exploded and burst into flames. The latest report says fifteen passengers, 35 crew, including three commanding officers, saved. – USF

An hour later Chatham reported to the *Fahrtenbüro* at Frankfurt-Main airship base:

> 50 men saved, 50 men lost – period – Commander Pruss saved. – USF

The disaster in fact killed 34 passengers and crew members together with one man from the ground handling crew, but 62 others survived the formidable explosion. Ernst A. Lehmann died of his injuries the following morning, as did *Oberfunkinspektor* Speck, who had been a crew member aboard LZ 126; *Kapitän* Pruss survived, but he suffered serious burns. The dead were the first victims of German civil airship aviation. *Kapitän* Hans von Schiller had just set course from Recife de Pernambuca when the wireless station received the message about the disaster. He gave the news to his men but kept it from the passengers, who were informed after LZ 127 had landed at Friedrichshafen.

The *Deutsche Zeppelin Reederei* decided to cancel all scheduled flights to the United States of America and to Brazil until the cause of the loss of LZ 129 was discovered. The ship destroyed at Lakehurst had made a total of 63 flights, covering 337,129km.

Right: LZ 130 *Graf Zeppelin* (II) under final assembly at Friedrichshafen.
Far right: The powerful Daimler-Benz DB 602 (LOF 2) airship engine, which produced 1,200hp.

LZ 130 *Graf Zeppelin* (II)

LZ 130 was ready for take-off on 14 September 1938 and, following *Dr* Eckener's recommendation, was, like LZ 127, named *Graf Zeppelin*. The United States was at the time the only country producing helium, and it gave special permission for LZ 130 to be inflated using this gas – thus requiring the ship to be modified. However, before the gas was sent to Germany, the US Government found itself under domestic pressure to reverse the decision as a protest against Germany's National Socialist regime, and the agreement was duly terminated. LZ 130 had to be converted once again, therefore, so as to accommodate the more dangerous hydrogen.

Right: The command gondola of LZ 130 during the first part of the ship's evaluation.
Far right: The wireless operators of LZ 130, about their daily work.

After the Lakehurst disaster the German Government forbade the carrying of passengers aboard airships; permission was given only for transporting mail and attending air shows over Germany – and no flights over foreign territory were allowed by the *Reichsregierung*. LZ 130 was based first at Friedrichshafen-Löwental, then, from 1 November 1938, at Frankfurt-Main under the authority of *Kapitän* Sammt and *Dr* Eckener.

Left: The forward hull of LZ 130 *Graf Zeppelin* (II).

Right: A photograph of the ship taken on 14 September 1938 over Frankfurt-Main.

Left: A photograph of LZ 130 taken at Löwental.

Left: LZ 130 approaching its mooring mast, 1939.

In 1937 secret wireless experiments involving centimetre-band amplitude-modulated (AM) radio waves were conducted, involving *Dr* Ernst Breuning, who was responsible for the military interception service belonging to *General* Udet's office. A contract was made between the *Reichsluftfahrtministerium* (RLM) and the *Deutsche Zeppelin Reederei* under which LZ 130 was equipped with 24 work stations for experienced radio specialists, and on 22 September 1938, just before Austria had become absorbed into the *Grossdeutsches Reich*, the ship began a series of radio reconnaissance sorties, protected by four 'Police Green'-painted 'civilian' Bf 109 fighters. Those top-secret missions continued into 1939, and after some successful trials intercepting foreign radio stations, a new series of experiments was started. Because LZ 130's metal construction prevented the location by radio of foreign civil and military broadcasting stations, the specialists looked for a different approach and then remembered the *Spähkorb* used during the First World War. A wooden so-called *Messkorb* was developed, equipped with a special radio system. One of the earliest trials took place on 13 April 1939, another between 12 and 14 July which lasted about 45hr, and a third in early August. A few weeks before the outbreak of the Second World War, the silver Zeppelin flew along the east coast of Britain exploring the well-camouflaged air defence radar sites. However, the German radio operators were often disturbed by their own radar frequencies – the *Oberkommando* of the *Luftwaffe* had not allowed defensive radar sites on the North Sea to be switched off during the reconnaissance flight – and few positive results were achieved.

LZ 130 was also engaged in German Government propaganda work. When Adolf Hitler arrived at Reichenberg for the result of the Sudetenland referendum, for example, LZ 130 stood-to over the town dropping small swastika flags. During the last few weeks of peace the ship undertook public relations tours all over Germany. The last of these, to Königsberg in East Prussia on 26 July 1939, was cancelled and the ship was transferred to Frankfurt. It had flown on only 30 occasions, covering an aggregate distance of 36,550km and spending more than 400hr in the air.

The ship was placed in storage at its huge hangar in Frankfurt for a while but was scrapped on the personal orders of Hermann Göring in the spring of 1940 together with the museum-ship LZ 127. The large airship hangars at Frankfurt were destroyed on 6 May that year.

LZ 131

LZ 131 was never completed, only some structural components being manufactured at the Friedrichshafen works: the RLM did not permit the completion of a fourth mighty Zeppelin, and the finished sections were taken over by the *Reich* and paid for immediately.

Right: Only a few components for LZ 131 were produced at Friedrichshafen and all were later scrapped.

Left: The damaged *Graf Zeppelin* (II) in its hangar at Frankfurt during the Second World War.

The airship would have had a gas volume of 223,000m^3, 23,000m^3 more than that of LZ 129 and 118,000m^3 more than that of the first *Graf Zeppelin.*

The transworld airship projects

A lesser-known constructor of airships was Otto Brinkmann, who endeavoured to raise money in order to fulfil his ambition of building a large commercial ship and a huge hangar near Speyer. In June 1937 the hangar structure was erected and the first components of the ship assembled. The first of three proposed designs showed a maximum length of 97m, had accommodation for 60 passengers, all of whom were kitted out with parachutes, and was expected to achieve a range of about 3,200km with three Jumo 5 engines. However, on 3 January 1939 the *Landgericht* (district court) at Frankenthal found Brinkmann guilty of contravening a number of German laws in the methods he used to obtain money from abroad.

Meanwhile both Schütte-Lanz and Zeppelin produced many designs for civil airships after the First World War, the former concern proposing their 'Transatlantic', 'Panamerica', 'Pacific' and 'Kentucky' and the latter their 'Hensly'. From November 1920 the engineers at Schütte-Lanz had been studying the possibility of building an airship with a capacity of more than 100,000m^3. Their most recent ships had been SL 23 (64,000m^3) and SL 24 (78,000m^3); neither had been completed by the end of the war, and many of their design features were adopted for the larger craft. *Professor* Johann Schütte also decided to utilize a tubular framework: this would be stronger, and thus more reliable, than the girder-type framework favoured by Zeppelin.

After the war the big Schütte-Lanz factory was dismantled and sold, the owner claiming 936 million Reichsmarks for the expense involved in constructing the works and the twenty completed airships. Only a small sum, however, was paid to him by the Weimar Republic, successor to the former Imperial *Deutsches Reich*.

Taking the shape of the 62,200m^3 Zeppelin airship as a starting point – and this was subsequently enlarged to 92,000m^3 – the Schütte-Lanz team had by February 1921

Below: The remains of LZ 130 at Frankfurt Airport. The large hangars were destroyed early in 1940 on orders of Göring.

designed a 101,700m^3 ship. The length of the proposed new ship, SL 101, was 228.5m and its diameter 28.78m – much larger dimensions than those of any previous airship – and an average speed of about 130kph (70kts) was envisaged. It was suggested that, using this ship, a regular service from Western Europe to the USA and South America could be established. Schütte-Lanz had also proposed the SL 102 'Panamerica' (a project which dated from 21 January 1921), with a gas capacity of 220,000m^3, a length of 298m and a maximum diameter of 38.54m. This ship would have been so big that the rudder controls would have required the strength of two crew members to operate them. The SL 103 design, or 'Pacific', was also proposed in early 1921. It was smaller than the 'Panamerica', with a gas capacity of 150,000m^3, a reported diameter of 34.77m and a length of 274.5m.

There was no chance of these projects being realized because the Allies did not permit airships of that size to be built. *Professor* Johann Schütte's company built only twenty airships, but his research proved very important in the development of more advanced rigid vehicles.

The Zeppelin works proposed their LZ 124 design in 1921–22. This huge 235m-long ship would have had a gas volume of 100,000m^3, divided among sixteen cells installed in the 29.1m-diameter envelope. The ship was proposed for a fast transatlantic service, capable of covering distances of about 10,000km at an average speed of 150kph (81kt). Power for Project 'Hensley' would have been provided by twelve Maybach piston engines each rated at 240hp; only LZ 129 had greater total power, at 4,200hp. The design featured eleven ventral gondolas, one for the command station and ten for the motors. The Allies, with bitter memories of the part Zeppelins played during the war, withheld permission for the project to proceed.

German airships after 1945

Eleven years after the end of the Second World War an 'L' Class Goodyear Blimp was modified for civilian use and engaged in promotional tours over West Germany; subsequently registered D-LAVO, it was operated by the Underberg Corporation and three years later it was enlarged and flew for the *'Güldenring'*. In September 1960 the ship, now D-LISA, was chartered by the Schwab

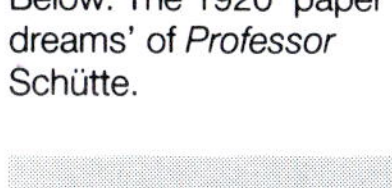

Below: The 1920 'paper dreams' of *Professor* Schütte.

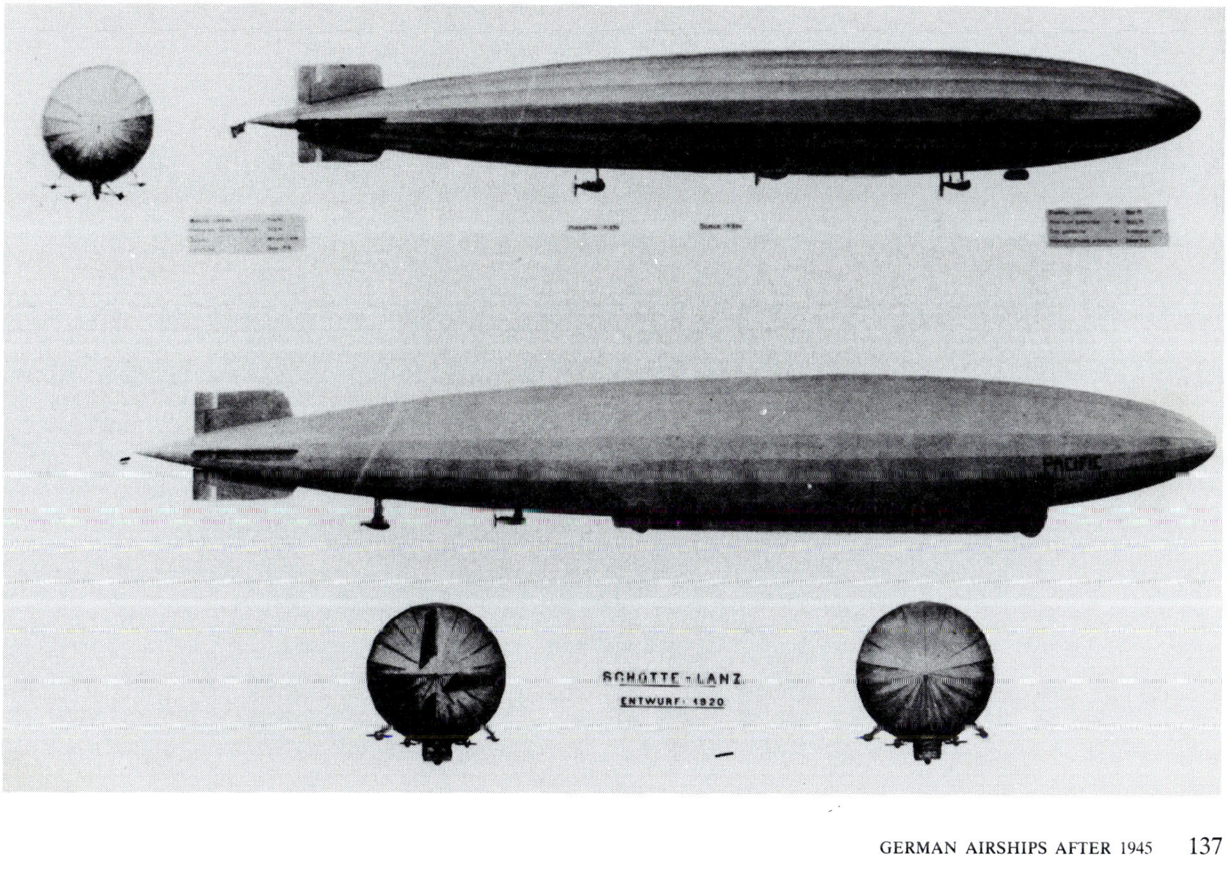

company until it was damaged on 26 July 1960 and put out of action. It was eventually sold to Japan, where it was destroyed on 9 April 1969.

The first German airship to be constructed after the Second World War was assembled at the Schempp-Hirth Sportflugzeugbau works at Kirchheim-Teck. The hull was manufactured by Augsburger Ballonfabrik, the former Riedinger works well known all over Germany to this day. D-LEDA took off for the first time on 1 December 1956, propelled by one 215hp Franklin engine. The ship survived for only about six months, managing a total of 43hr in the air: after 26 flights it was completely destroyed at Stuttgart on 21 June 1957

The Monheim Corporation therefore decided to finance a new airship, to be built by Zeppelin-Metallwerke; the hull, again was ordered from Augsburger Ballonfabrik. Powered by two 180hp Warner-Scarab engines, it was flown for the first time on 17 August 1958 sporting the name 'Trumpf', a well-known German confectionery. After more than 3,400hr in the air, it was decommissioned in 1963, but during the winter of 1968–69 it was prepared for a fresh tour of duty and was flown until 1972 by Theo Wüllenkemper.

Wüllenkemper, Chairman of the Westdeutsche Luftwerburg, considered the possibility of constructing his own non-rigid airships, reflecting that these ships could be used for more than mere promotional tours over Western Europe. Accordingly, a modern production plant was built near Essen-Mühlheim Airport, and between January 1970 and April 1971 the first ship, WDL 1 (named *Der Fliegende Musketier*), was developed and assembled. WDL 1 (D-LDFM) took off at Mühlheim for the first time, with Konrad Hess at the controls, on 12 August 1972, and by the time it had flown for about 650hr – with great success – a second airship, WDL 2 (D-LDFN, *Der Fliegende Nippon*), started its career on 17 August 1972. Both ships were inflated with non-flammable helium. The two craft completed nearly 3,000hr of trouble-free flying during a year's steady use.

A thunderstorm on 13 November 1972 caused damage to both ships, severe in the case of WDL 1 though only minor to WDL 2. The airship hangar, however, was destroyed, and Theo Wüllenkemper was obliged to build

Above: D-LEDA (right) together with an L class blimp, photographed in southern Germany.

Left: D-LEDA 'Trumpf', the first airship built after the Second World War.

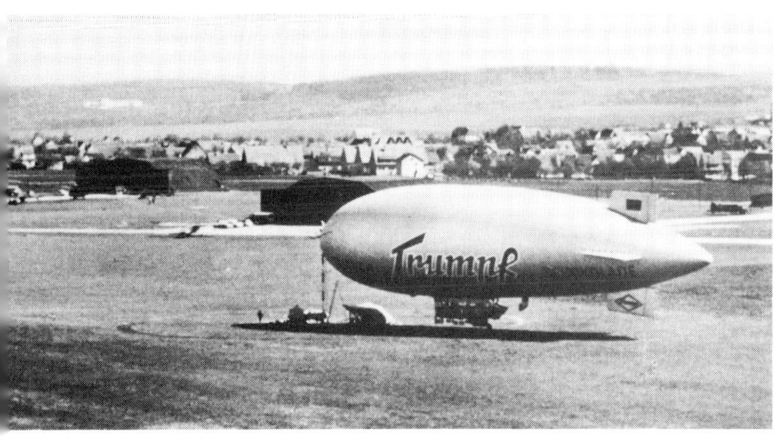

a new one. On 2 April 1973, however, the hangar was again destroyed in a storm, although many of WDL 1's component parts, for example the gondola and both 180hp Continental engines, fortunately had been stored in another hall and only very minor damage to the hull resulted, easily repaired within a few days. On 28 April 1973 the repaired D-LDFM was ready for flight again, now bearing the name 'Wicküler', a well-known German beer. The 56m-long ship had a diameter of 14.25m and a helium capacity of 6,000m^3. It could lift a payload of about 1,500kg. Meanwhile *Der Fliegende Nippon* was dismantled and taken to Japan for further publicity work under the management of the Orient Lease Corporation and carrying the code JA 1002. It was damaged during a thunderstorm on 26 August 1974 and never took off again. All the usable parts were sent back to Germany and incorporated into WDL 1a (D-LDFO), which was flying again by 1981.

In 1976, WDL 1 took part in development projects in Ghana and Upper Volta. Three years later it was moved back to Mühlheim for an overhaul and then transferred to Japan, where it spent some time in traffic control work. From 1985 it was used in Germany again for more advertising, this time promoting Stuttgarter Hofbräu beer; by 1 June 1985 D-LDFM had spent 10,000hr in the air.

Larger ships have been projected in recent years and one with a length of 59m, a diameter of 15.2m and a gas volume of 6,904m^3 went to final assembly in the summer of 1989. Currently, WDL are proposing much larger non-rigid ships with accommodation for 14–16 passengers, to be built over the next few years.

Right: The non-rigid airship 'Fuji Film' during maintenance work in WDL Luftschiffgesellschaft's hangar at Mühlheim.

CONCLUSION

Military airships

Before the First World War broke out, 25 Zeppelin, four Gross-Basenach and a small number of Parseval and Schütte-Lanz airships had been built; during the war no fewer than 88 further military Zeppelins left the manufacturers. Altogether some 61 Zeppelins were built at Friedrichshafen, 23 at Löwental, one at Frankfurt, sixteen at Potsdam and twelve at Staaken near Berlin, and compared with this output all the other constructors made but a minor contribution to the war effort. The unpopular non-rigid Parseval ships did see very limited service with the German armed forces because the rigid, wooden Schütte-Lanz types could not fulfil their operational duties successfully owing to the effects of maritime weather conditions.

Following the first raids against Continental European targets, British towns and military targets were attacked in 1914–15. During the difficult Antwerp attacks the former DELAG ship *Sachsen* used newly developed incendiary and fragmentation bombs after experimenting with modified artillery shells. There was close co-operation with the Imperial German Navy on long-range reconnnaissance missions, especially during sorties behind the lines of the Eastern Front, which were bombed to some effect. *Korvettenkapitän* Strasser's Naval Airship Division and the Army ships, both types operating from large bases in northern Germany, carried out several difficult missions all over Europe. At first the British air defences appeared to be very poorly organized but within a short period of time incendiary shells for ground-based anti-aircraft weapons had been issued and were proving their worth against all kinds of balloons filled with inflammable hydrogen, aided by the widespread deployment of powerful searchlights. Later the British authorities established squadrons of interceptor aircraft armed with incendiary ammunition and endeavoured to destroy the huge Zeppelins from the air. Significant results were achieved by the British defences in the second half of the war, several German airships being forced down because of damage they had suffered. Moreover, despite the introduction to service of larger and larger combat airships and the improvements made to the Maybach piston engines and the ships' own defensive capabilities, it still proved impossible to raise service ceilings sufficiently to escape the tenacious British airmen. Furthermore, the giant 'Super Zeppelin' was unable to climb to more than about 7,000m. Neither the increased speeds nor the improved oxygen systems for the crews made very much difference, while engine failures caused by the low pressures at high altitudes, navigational problems and poor bomb-aiming accuracy combined to make missions even more difficult for all involved.

On 5 August 1918 the dream of a strategic Zeppelin force ended in an instant with the death aboard L 70 of Peter Strasser during

Below: *Graf Zeppelin* over Friedrichshafen, 1935.

Right: The WDL 1B ship, which is propelled by two Continental IO-360CB piston engines and has enough room for eight people, including a crew of one.

a raid against British targets. His ship caught fire at about 6,000m after being intercepted by RAF aircraft from Great Yarmouth. Four days later another German ship was destroyed by enemy fighters. The British Official History, recorded after the First World War, made the following comment concerning the German airships:

> The threat of their raiding potentialities compelled us to set up at home a formidable organization which diverted men, guns and aeroplanes from more important theatres of war. By the end of 1916 there were, specially retained in Great Britain for home anti-aircraft defence, 17,341 officers and men. There were twelve RFC squadrons comprising approximately 200 officers, 2,000 men and 110 aeroplanes. The anti-aircraft guns and searchlights were served by 12,000 officers and men who would have found a ready place with continuous work in France or in other war theatres.

The officers at German HQ knew that their own offensive raids would involve heavy losses, but it seemed to them to be very important to avoid releasing further well-trained British forces for service on the continent.

Civil airships

First formed in 1910, the Deutsche Luftschiffahrts AG operated 34 flights with the rebuilt LZ 6, carrying 726 passengers, before the ship was burnt out in its hangar at Baden-Oos. The DELAG and the Deutsche Zeppelin Reederei flew a total of eleven civilian ships of different sizes and configurations until the disaster at Lakehurst. Before the First World War *Schwaben*, *Sachsen* and *Hansa* became very familiar sights over Germany, demonstrating the enormous potential of the airship by transporting thousands of passengers in accident-free tours over the homeland and neighbouring countries. After the war the DELAG tried to set up a regular airship service between Germany and Sweden, and with the advent of the famous LZ 127 interest in passenger-carrying flights spread across the world. The crossing of the North and South Atlantic were crucial events in the history of civil aviation, these long-range flights paving the way for the world-wide air service we know today.

Apart from Germany, responsible for the famous *Graf Zeppelin*, *Hindenburg* and *Graf Zeppelin* (II), Great Britain produced a number of rigid ships, but none of the other industrial nations engaged in airship construction on a noteworthy scale. With the scrapping of LZ 127 and LZ 130 a fascinating era was brought to an end. On his eightieth birthday on 10 August 1948, Hugo Eckener told former employees of the Zeppelin-Luftschiffbau:

> You must consider the age of airships definitely over. If you wish to cling to the idea of airships, that means abolishing modern traffic systems on the streets and returning to the age of horse-drawn transport.

In September 1986 a conference took place in Vancouver in which the rebirth of the airship was discussed. Although several interesting ideas were put forward, none of the airships proposed at the conference has yet been realized. Small, non-rigid ships have been built in England and Germany, but nothing more has been done.

Has the age of dirigibles ended?

APPENDICES

APPENDIX I: CAREER DETAILS OF ZEPPELIN AIRSHIPS

Production no.	Military/civil designation	Type	First flight	Where built	Decommissioned/ lost	Commander(s)
LZ 1	–	*a*	02/07/00	Manzell	Autumn 1901	*Graf* von Zeppelin
LZ 2	–	*b*	17/01/06	Manzell	17/01/06	*Graf* von Zeppelin
LZ 3	Z I	*b*	09/01/06	Manzell	March 1913	*Graf* von Zeppelin, *Hptm.* Sperling, *Hptm.* George, *Hptm.* Lohmüller
LZ 4	–	*c*	20/06/08	Manzell	05/08/08	*Graf* von Zeppelin
LZ 5	Z II	*c*	26/05/09	Manzell	25/04/10	*Graf* von Zeppelin, *Major* Sperling, *Hptm.* von Jena
LZ 6	None (DELAG)	*d*	25/08/09	Friedrichshafen	14/09/10	*Dr* Dürr, *Kapt.* Hacker
LZ 7	*Deutschland*	*e*	19/06/10	Friedrichshafen	28/06/10	*Dr* Dürr, *Dr* Eckener *et al*
LZ 8	*Deutschland*	*e*	30/03/11	Friedrichshafen	16/05/11	*Dr* Eckener, *Dr* Dürr *et al*
LZ 9	Z II (*Ersatz*)	*f*	02/10/11	Friedrichshafen	01/08/14	*Dr* Dürr, *Hptm.* Horn, *OLt* v.d.Leyen, *Lt* v.d.Haegen
LZ 10	*Schwaben*	*f*	26/06/11	Friedrichshafen	28/06/12	*Dr* Eckener, *Dipl-Ing.* Dörr *et al*
LZ 11	*Viktoria Luise*	*g*	14/02/12	Friedrichshafen	08/10/15	*Dr* Lempertz *et al*
LZ 12	Z III	*f*	25/04/12	Friedrichshafen	01/08/14	*Hptm.* Lohmüller
LZ 13	*Hansa*	*g*	30/07/12	Friedrichshafen	01/08/14	*Dipl-Ing.* Dörr, *Ing.* Reinen
LZ 14	L 1	*h*	07/10/12	Friedrichshafen	09/09/13	*Dr* Eckener, *Kplt* Hanne
LZ 15	Z I (*Ersatz*)	*h*	16/01/13	Friedrichshafen	19/03/13	*Hptm.* Horn
LZ 16	Z IV	*h*	14/03/13	Friedrichshafen	Autumn 1916	*Hptm.* F. Jacobi, *Lt* Grussendorf, *Hptm.* von Quast
LZ 17	*Sachsen*	*h*	03/05/13	Friedrichshafen	Autumn 1916	*Ing.* E.A. Lehmann, *Kapt.* Hacker
LZ 18	L 2	*i*	09/09/13	Friedrichshafen	17/10/13	*Ing.* E.A. Lehmann, *Kplt* Gluud
LZ 19	Z I	*h*	06/06/13	Friedrichshafen	13/06/14	*Ing.* E.A. Lehmann, *Hptm.* Horn, *Hptm.* Kleinschmitt
LZ 20	Z V	*h*	08/07/13	Friedrichshafen	28/08/14	*Hptm.* Lange, *Hptm.* Grüner

Theatre(s) of operations	Base(s)	Remarks
S. Germany	–	Decommissioned after only three flights owing to lack of funds.
S. Germany	–	One flight only: damaged 30/11/05 at Manzell; destroyed at Kisslegg by storm.
Germany	Metz	Third experimental ship; 45 flights before taken over by Army. First night flight 1–2/04/09. Rebuilt at Metz, used as training ship. Scrapped (obsolete).
Germany	–	Proposed for German Army. Burnt after being stranded by weather at Echterdingen.
Germany	Cologne	Second Zeppelin Army airship; 16 flights with Army crew. Took part in Frankfurt ILA. Stranded at Weiburg by weather; decommissioned immediately.
Germany	Baden-Oos	Flown to Berlin on 29/08/09; at ILA 11/09/09. Lengthened to 144m, handed over to DELAG. Total 73 flights (34 with DELAG). Burnt at Oos.
Germany	Düsseldorf	7 passenger flights with DELAG (total 1,035km, 212 pasengers). Stranded in Teutoburger Forest by bad weather.
Germany	Baden-Oos, Cologne	Named *Deutschland* (Ersatz) by DELAG after loss of LZ 7. Only 24 flights. Collided with hangar at Düsseldorf; decommissioned.
Germany	Baden-Oos, Cologne, Metz, Gotha	Rebuilt 21/10/11–23/11/11 (lengthened); used as training ship by Army. Scrapped (obsolete).
Germany	Frankfurt/Main, Gotha, Berlin, Düsseldorf	224 flights (479hr). Damaged while entering hangar at Düsseldorf, burst into flames; scrapped.
Germany	Baden/Oos, Gotha, Hamburg, Leipzig, Dresden, Potsdam, Liegnitz	Total 64,125km, 22,039 passengers. Training ship 01/08/14; used by Army and Navy. 1,000th flight 15/06/15. Destroyed while entering hangar at Liegnitz.
Germany	Rebstock, Baden-Oos, Metz, Gotha, Hamburg	Army ship. 10.5hr flight Friedrichshafen–Hamburg 31/12/12. Disarmed August 1914 at Metz (obsolete).
Germany	Gotha, Leipzig, Dresden, Berlin, Jüterbog, Fuhlsbüttel	DELAG until 31/07/14 (399 flights, 44,437km), 8,321 passengers). To Army for training in Central Germany; decommissioned (obsolete).
Germany	Berlin-Johanisthal, Hamburg-Fuhlsbüttel	First Navy Zeppelin; 74 flights, 13,409km. Trials with 210hp engines. Brought down by thunderstorm (14 dead, 6 survivors).
S. Germany	Baden-Oos	33 flights from Baden-Oos. Stranded near Karlsruhe by strong headwind. Decommissioned.
Central Germany; East Prussia; Lorraine	Königsberg, Gotha, Jüterbog	Fourth Army ship. Emergency landing at Lunéville (France) 03/04/13, reconnaissance during Battle of Tannenberg (10/08–23/09/14). Trials with bombing gear. Training airship 24/02/15. Disarmed at Jüterbog (obsolete).
Germany	Leipzig, Potsdam, Baden-Oos, Königsberg, Hamburg, Dresden	DELAG ship until 31/07/14 (419 flights, 9,837 passengers). Enlarged to 148m. First parachute drop from an airship. Army training ship Sept. 1915. Decommissioned at Düren.
Germany	Friedrichshafen, Berlin-Johannisthal	Second Navy ship with bombing system; 10 flights (1,727km). Destroyed during take-off near Johannisthal after engine fire.
Germany	Frankfurt, Rebstock, Königsberg, Posen, Leipzig	Replacement for Z I. Stranded during thunderstorm at Diedenhofen; immediately decommissioned by Army.
Germany	Posen, Rebstock, Berlin, Potsdam	In action over Eastern Front (reconnaissance and offensive missions). Shot down by AA, emergency landing near Mlawa; crew taken POW by Eastern Allies.

Production no.	Military/civil designation	Type	First flight	Where built	Decommissioned/ lost	Commander(s)
LZ 21	Z VI	*k*	10/11/13	Friedrichshafen	06/08/14	*Hptm.* Masius, *Hptm.* Gaissert, *Hptm.* Kleinschmitt
LZ 22	Z VII	*l*	08/01/14	Friedrichshafen	21/08/14	*Hptm.* Gaissert
LZ 23	Z VIII	*l*	21/02/14	Friedrichshafen	21/08/14	*Hptm.* Andree
LZ 24	L 3	*m*	11/05/14	Friedrichshafen	17/02/15	*Kplt* Fritz
LZ 25	Z IX	*m*	29/07/14	Friedrichshafen	08/10/14	*Hptm.* Horn
LZ 26	Z XII	*n*	14/12/14	Frankfurt	08/08/17	*Ing.* E.A. Lehmann, *Hptm.* von Mirbach, *Hptm.* Heerlein, *Hptm.* Bruns, *Hptm.* Sommerfeldt, *Hptm.* Dassel
LZ 27	L 4	*m*	28/08/14	Friedrichshafen	17/02/15	*Kplt* von Platen
LZ 28	L 5	*m*	22/09/14	Friedrichshafen	06/08/15	*Kplt* Hirsch, *Kplt d.R.* Boecker, *Kplt* Ehrlich
LZ 29	Z X	*m*	13/10/14	Friedrichshafen	21/03/15	*Hptm.* Gaissert, *Hptm.* Horn
LZ 30	Z XI	*m*	11/11/14	Potsdam	20/05/15	*Hptm.* Gaissert
LZ 31	L 6	*m*	03/11/14	Friedrichshafen	16/09/16	*OLt* von Buttlar-Brandenfels, *Kplt* Breithaupt
LZ 32	L 7	*m*	20/11/14	Friedrichshafen	04/05/16	*OLt* Petersen, *Kplt* Dietrich, *Kplt* Stabbert, *Kplt* Sommerfeldt, *Kplt* Hempel
LZ 33	L 8	*m*	17/12/14	Friedrichshafen	05/03/15	*Kplt* Meyer, *Kplt* Beelitz
LZ 34	LZ 34	*m*	06/01/15	Potsdam	21/05/15	*Hptm.* Jacobi
LZ 35	LZ 35	*m*	11/01/15	Friedrichshafen	14/04/15	*Hptm.* Masius
LZ 36	L 9	*o*	09/03/15	Friedrichshafen	16/09/16	*Kplt* Mathy, *Kplt* Loewke, *Kplt* Proelss, *Hptm.* Stelling, *Kplt* Kraushaar, *Kplt* Ganzel, *Kplt* Hollender, *Kplt* Gayer
LZ 37	LZ 37	*m*	28/02/15	Potsdam	07/06/15	*OLt* von de Haegen
LZ 38	LZ 38	*p*	03/04/15	Friedrichshafen	07/06/15	*Hptm.* Linnarz
LZ 39	LZ 39	*o*	25/04/15	Friedrichshafen	18/12/15	*Hptm.* Horn, *Hptm.* Falck *Hptm.* Schramm, *Hptm.* Wilhelm
LZ 40	L 10	*p*	13/05/15	Friedrichshafen	03/09/15	*Hptm.* Hirsch
LZ 41	L 11	*p*	07/06/15	Löwental	25/04/17	*OLt* von Buttlar-Brandenfels, *Korvkpt.* Schütze, *Kplt* Hollender
LZ 42	LZ 72	*p*	15/06/15	Potsdam	16/02/17	*Hptm.* Masius, *Hptm.* Jacobi, *Hptm.* Bode

Theatre(s) of operations	Base(s)	Remarks
Central Germany, W. Germany	Cologne	Decommissioned near Bonn after rough landing caused by shrapnel damage during raid on Liège.
S. Germany, France	Baden-Oos, Rebstock, Dresden	Reconnaissance missions over France. Shot down by French AA, stranded at St Quirin; scrapped.
W. Germany	Baden-Oos, Trier	Operated from Trier. Shot down near Bavonville emergency landing; scrapped by Army.
Germany, W. Europe	Fuhlsbüttel, Nordholz	Sole Navy airship at outbreak of war. First German Zeppelin over England (18–19/01/15). 78 flights (31,559km). Stranded near Fanö (Denmark) by bad weather following reconnaissance sortie.
Central Germany	Dresden	Proposed for active service over the Western Front.
W. Germany	Düsseldorf	Destroyed by Allied bombs in hangar at Düsseldorf 08/10/14.
Germany, W. Front E. Front	Frankfurt, Mauberge Gotha, Allenstein, Warsaw, Königsberg	First Dural ship; closed command gondola; equipped with *Spähkorb*. Eleven raids, last in Autumn 1916; 20,000kg of bombs dropped. Decommissioned August 1917 when Army airship activities terminated by German High Command.
N. Germany	Fuhlsbüttel	Emergency landing on Danish coast when fuel ran out after first attack on East Coast of England.
N. Germany E. Prussia	Nordholz, Fuhlsbüttel Seddin	47 reconnaissance missions; mine-hunting over Baltic. Damaged by the Russian defence forces and forced into emergency landing at Plungjany near Mitau.
W. Europe	Düsseldorf, Bruxelles-Evère	Attack on Calais 21/02/15, Paris 21/03/15. Stranded following enemy action near St Quirin.
E. Europe	Posen	Raids against Warsaw, Grodoni, Kowno etc. Severely damaged at Posen while leaving hangar; burnt and scrapped May 1915.
N. Europe	Fuhlsbüttel, Nordholz, Dresden	91 flights (73,921km) up to 03/08/15; 36 reconnaissance missions, one raid. Training ship 04/08/15. Caught fire while being inflated at Hamburg
NW Europe, Brit. Isles, N. Sea	Leipzig, Nordholz, Tondern	Survived Friedrichshafen raid 21/11/15; 166 flights (48,531km). Damaged by British cruisers *Galatea* and *Phaeton* near Horns Reef; 11 dead, 7 POW.
Germany, W. Front	Düsseldorf, Gontrode	22 flights (1,423km). Only reconnaissance missions over W. Europe. Damaged by enemy action, stranded at Tirlemont; scrapped.
Central Germany E. Prussia	Potsdam Königsberg	Some combat missions over the E. Front (raids on Kowno and Grodno). Gas leaks caused by enemy action; burnt during emergency landing.
W. Germany	Cologne, Gontrode	Attacks on Paris 20/03/15 and Poperinghe 13/04/15. Raid on Brit. Isles (failed): emergency landing at Ypern; destroyed by storm near Aeltre.
N. Germany	Hage, Tondern, Fuhlsbüttel	First Navy ship with closed command cabin and revised engine gondola. 74 reconnaissance and four attack missions. Raid on Hull 06/06/15 (British submarine bombed). Destroyed while being inflated at Fuhlsbüttel.
W. Germany Belgium	Cologne Brussels	Damaged during training mission April 1915. Used against Western targets. Shot down by Sub-Lt R. A. J. Warneford near Ghent (1 survivor).
E. Prussia W. Germany	Königsberg Düsseldorf, Bruxelles-Evère	Used over Western Front (first airship over City of London (31/05/15). New motor gondola with 3 engines. Destroyed in British air raid in hangar at Bruxelles-Evère
W. Europe E. Front	Düsseldorf, Bruxelles-Agathe, Namur Posen, Allenstein, Warsaw	Missions against Calais, Harwich. Later used in East; attacks on Nowo, Minks, Kowno (too heavy to carry increased payloads). Stranded following enemy action at Luck, decommissioned
Northern Germany	Nordholz	Used over North Sea and Brit. Isles (29 flights, 53,639km). First Navy ship over British capital. Hit by lightning and ignited (no survivors).
N. Germany	Nordholz, Hage	Used in West, over N. Sea and Brit. Isles: 394 flights, inc. twelve attacks on English targets (15,543kg of bombs), 31 reconnaissance missions and 276 training missions. Decommissioned at Hage 1917 (obsolete).
Germany	Düsseldorf, Spich, Jüterbog, Dresden	Training ship only, owing to structural defects. Decommissioned at Jüterbog Feb. 1917.

Production no.	Military/civil designation	Type	First flight	Where built	Decommissioned/ lost	Commander(s)
LZ 43	L 12	*p*	21/06/15	Friedrichshafen	10/08/15	*OLt z. S.* Peterson
LZ 44	LZ 74	*p*	08/07/15	Löwental	08/10/15	*Hptm.* George
LZ 45	L 13	*p*	23/07/15	Friedrichshafen	25/04/17	*Kplt* Mathy, *Kplt* Eichler, *Kplt* Schwonder, *OLt z. S.* Fleming
LZ 46	L 14	*p*	08/09/15	Löwental	23/06/19	*Kplt* Boecker, *Hptm.* Manger, *Kplt* Dose
LZ 47	LZ 77	*p*	24/08/15	Friedrichshafen	22/02/16	*Hptm.* Horn
LZ 48	L 15	*p*	09/09/15	Löwental	01/04/16	*Kplt* Breithaupt
LZ 49	LZ 79	*p*	02/08/15	Potsdam	30/01/16	*Hptm.* Gaissert
LZ 50	L 16	*p*	23/05/15	Friedrichshafen	19/10/17	*OLt z. S.* Peterson, *Kplt* Sommerfeldt, *Kplt* Gayer
LZ 51	LZ 81	*p*	07/10/15	Löwental	27/09/16	*Hptm.* Jacobi, *Hptm.* Barth
LZ 52	L 18	*p*	03/11/15	Löwental	17/11/15	*Kplt* M. Dietrich
LZ 53	L 17	*p*	20/10/15	Friedrichshafen	28/12/16	*Kplt* Ehrlich, *Kplt* Kraushaar
LZ 54	L 19	*p*	27/11/15	Friedrichshafen	02/02/16	*Kplt* Loewe
LZ 55	LZ 85	*p*	12/09/15	Potsdam	05/05/16	*Hptm.* Scherzer
LZ 56	LZ 86	*p*	10/10/15	Löwental	04/09/16	*Hptm.* Linnarz, *Hptm.* W. Wolff
LZ 57	LZ 87	*p*	06/12/15	Löwental	28/07/17	*Hptm.* Steegmann, *OLt* Gerstenberg, *OIng.* Langrehr
LZ 58	LZ 88/L 25	*p*	14/11/15	Potsdam	15/09/17	*Hptm.* Falck, *OLt* Gerstenberg, *Kplt* von Buttlar-Brandenfels, *Kplt* Flemming
LZ 59	L 20	*p*	21/12/15	Friedrichshafen	03/05/16	*Kplt* Stabbert
LZ 60	LZ 90	*p*	01/01/16	Potsdam	07/11/16	*Hptm.* Gaissert, *Hptm.* La Quiante, *OIng.* Langrehr
LZ 61	L 21	*q*	10/01/16	Löwental	28/11/16	*Kplt* M. Dietrich, *Hptm.* Stelling, *OLt z. S.* Frankenberg
LZ 62	L 30	*r*	28/05/16	Friedrichshafen	17/11/17	*Kplt* von Buttlar-Brandenfels, *Olt z. S.* Friemel, *Kplt* Boedecker

Theatre(s) of operations	Base(s)	Remarks
N. Germany	Nordholz, Hage	Used over W. Front and Brit. Isles: 12 flights (4,112km). Damaged during *Geschwaderangriff* on London, stranded in sea near Ostend; scrapped.
Germany	Darmstadt, Mauberge, Namur, Hage	Used over W. Europe and Brit. Isles (2 raids). Stranded after colliding with mountain near Orthe (most crew members injured). Decommissioned Oct. 1915.
N. Germany	Wittmundhaven, Hage	Most successful Navy airship used over W. Europe and Brit. Isles: 159 flights (69,100km). Attack on London caused £530,000 damage. Decommissioned 1917 at Hage after 15 sorties.
N. Germany	Nordholz	Operated over the N. Sea and Brit. Isles: 42 reconnaissance missions, 17 raids. Total 127 operational flights plus 399 training flights after 05/04/17 (63,742km). Decommissioned 08/09/18; destroyed June 1919.
Germany, France	Spich, Namur, Hage, Düsseldorf	*Spähkorb* experiments autumn 1915. 6 raids over France (12,610kg). Shot down by AA fire near Brabant-le-Roi, crashed at Révigny (no survivors).
N. Germany	Nordholz, Hage	Three successful attacks (5,780kg), two on London; 8 reconnaissance missions. Stranded near Knock Deep (N. Sea); one crew member killed, remainder POW.
Germany, France	Düren, Posen, Maubeuge, Namur	Used over W. and E. Fronts 10 and 25/08/15 (Brest), 30/01/16 (Paris). Stranded at Ath after direct hit by Allied AA fire.
N. Germany	Nordholz, Hage	132 operational flights, 103 training flights (total 49,146km). Twelve raids and 44 reconnaissance missions. Damaged while landing at Nordholz; decommissioned.
Germany, France, SE Front	Szentandras, Düsseldorf, Namur	Operational in SE theatre early 1916; rebuilt at Dresden (240hp engines); operations W. Europe. Stranded at Tirnowa while attacking Bucharest.
N. Germany	Tondern	Four flights only (1,060km). Burnt out while taking on extra gas at Tondern.
N. Germany	Nordholz, Tondern	Used over N. Sea and Brit. Isles: 80 flights, inc. 9 raids (10,724kg) and 27 reconnaissance missions. Burnt out at Tondern after collision with hangar door.
Germany	Dresden, Tondern	14 missions, inc. one 02/02/16 against targets in English Midlands (1,600kg of bombs). Damaged by AA fire, stranded in the N. Sea near Ameland. Trawler *King Stephen* failed to rescue crew, all of whom perished.
Germany, E. Front	Liegnitz, Allenstein, Szentandras	Raids on Minsk, Riga and Dünaburg, three on Salonika. Stranded as result of enemy action in Vadar Swamps; all crew POW.
Germany, E. Front	Schneidemühl, Allenstein, Szentandras	Successful raids on Dünaburg, Minsk, Ploseti. Enlarged May 1916 at Dresden. At Szentandras August 1916. Crashed owing to pilot error; few survivors.
Germany	Darmstadt, Namur, Königsberg, Jüterbog	Used in W. and E. theatres. Lengthened at Dresden, then training ship. Handed over to Navy; 12 missions over Baltic (6,200km). Decommissioned summer 1917 (obsolete).
Germany, France	Hanover, Jüterbog, Maubeuge, Cologne, Seddin, Königsberg, Wainoden, Dresden, Potsdam	47 missions as Army airship (Verdun, Harwich, Margate, Arensburg). Lengthened summer 1916 at Dresden; 14 reconnaissance missions over Baltic, then experimental ship (L 25) for testing remote-controlled weapons and new torpedo-gliders. Decommissioned Sept. 1917 at Jüterbog.
Germany	Tondern, Seddin	Operated over Brit. Isles, N. Sea and Baltic (19 flights, 7,211km); only 2 successful raids on England plus 2 reconnaissance missions. Stranded near Stavanger (out of fuel); personnel interned in Norway.
Germany, France	Hanover, Spich, Trier, Namur, Mannheim, Dresden, Wittmundhaven	Four raids only (8,860kg). Lengthened summer 1916 at Dresden. Broke away from mooring at Wittmundhaven and disappeared over N. Sea (no crew on board).
N. Germany, E. Prussia	Nordhoz, Seddin, Tondern	Used over the N. Sea, Baltic and Brit. Isles (10 raids, 14,442kg), total 74 flights (35,751km). Shot down by British aircraft (1 Lt Cadbury) over N. Sea off Norfolk.
N. Germany, E. Prussia	Ahlhorn, Nordholz, Tondern, Seerappen	First ship of *r*-type (56,000m³); ten guns, bomb capacity 5,000kg. Total 123 flights (55,226km); 10 raids, 31 reconnaissance missions. Withdrawn from active service 17/11/17; dismantled 1920, handed over to Belgium.

Production no.	Military/civil designation	Type	First flight	Where built	Decommissioned/ lost	Commander(s)
LZ 63	LZ 93	*q*	23/02/16	Potsdam	Summer 1917	*Hptm.* Bode, *Hptm.* Schramm, *Hptm.* Wilhelm
LZ 64	L 22	*q*	03/03/16	Löwental	14/05/17	*Kplt* M. Dietrich, *Kplt* Hollender, *Kplt* Hankow, *Kplt* U. Lehmann
LZ 65	LZ 95	*q*	01/02/16	Potsdam	21/02/16	*Hptm.* George
LZ 66	L 23	*q*	08/04/16	Potsdam	21/08/17	*Kplt* Schubert, *Kplt* Ganzel, *Kplt* Stabbert, *Kplt* Bockholt, *OLt z. S.* Dinter
LZ 67	LZ 97	*q*	04/04/16	Löwental	05/07/17	*Hptm.* Linnarz, *OLt* Weidling, *Hptm.* Bruns
LZ 68	LZ 98	*q*	28/04/16	Löwental	August 1917	*OLt z.S.d.R.* Lehmann, *OLt Frhr.v.* Gemmingen
LZ 69	L 24	*q*	20/05/16	Potsdam	28/12/16	*Kplt* Koch, *OLt z. S.* Friemel
LZ 70	–	*q*	–	Löwental	–	–
LZ 71	LZ 101	*q*	29/06/16	Potsdam	August 1917	*Hptm.* Gaissert, *OLt* Koreuber
LZ 72	L 31	*r*	12/07/16	Löwental	02/10/16	*Kplt* Mathy
LZ 73	LZ 103	*q*	08/08/16	Potsdam	August 1917	*Hptm.* Falck
LZ 74	L 32	*r*	04/08/16	Friedrichshafen	24/09/16	*Kplt* Peterson
LZ 75	LZ 37	*r*	09/11/16	Staaken	24/12/17	*Kplt* Proelss, *Kplt* Gärtner
LZ 76	L 33	*r*	30/08/16	Friedrichshafen	24/09/16	*Kplt* Boecker
LZ 77	LZ 107	*q*	16/10/16	Potsdam	07/07/17	*Hptm.* Sommderfeldt, *OLt* Reinstrom
LZ 78	L 34	*r*	22/09/16	Löwental	28/11/16	*Hptm.* M. Dietrich
LZ 79	L 41	*r*	15/01/17	Staaken	23/09/19	*Hptm.* Mawger
LZ 80	L 35	*r*	20/10/16	Friedrichshafen	Sept. 1918	*Kplt* Ehrlich, *Kplt* Sommerfeldt
LZ 81	LZ 111	*q*	02/12/16	Potsdam	10/08/17	*Hptm.* Barth
LZ 82	L 36	*r*	01/11/16	Friedrichshafen	07/02/17	*Korvkpt.* Schütze, *Kplt* Eichler
LZ 83	LZ 113	*r*	22/02/17	Staaken	08/10/20	*OLt* Weidling, *Hptm.* Falck, *Kplt* Zaeschmar, *Kapt.* von Schiller, *Kapt.* Heinen
LZ 84	L 38	*r*	22/11/16	Löwental	29/12/16	*Kplt* M. Dietrich

Theatre(s) of operations	Base(s)	Remarks
Germany, France	Hanover, Düsseldorf, Namur, Spich, Cologne, Dresden	Operational over W. Europe (3 raids). Lengthened summer 1916 at Dresden, again based at Düsseldorf. Scrapped at Trier.
N. Germany	Tondern, Nordholz, Hage, Wittmundhaven	Used mainly in W. theatre and over Brit. Isles; 8 raids (9,215kg), 30 reconnaissance missions; total 81 flights (38,200km). Shot down near Terschelling by 1 Lt Galpin.
Germany, France	Düsseldorf, Namur	Severely damaged en route to first target, emergency landing south of home base Namur.
N. Germany		Mostly used over the N. Sea and Brit. Isles; 101 flights (48,700km), inc. three raids and 51 reconnaissance missions. One sailing ship captured north of Horns Reef. Shot down by Lt B. A. Smart near Jutland.
Germany, France	Mannheim, Namur, Wittmundhaven, Darmstadt, Szentrandras	Missions over France, Brit. Isles, N. Sea, Romania, Italy. Raids on London (25/04/16, 23/08/16), Boulogne (22/09/16), Bucharest (23/10/16, 1,500kg). Decommissioned Aug. 1917 at Jüterbog.
Germany, France	Hanover, Namur, Ahlhorn, Wildeshausen, Wainoden, Allenstein	15 reconnaissance missions, some aborted raids on Brit. Isles. Used by Navy from May 1917. Decommissioned summer 1917 at Schneidenmühl.
N. Germany	Tondern	45 flights (26,373km) up to end 1916. Four successful raids on Brit. Isles (8,510kg); 19 reconnaissance missions. Burnt at Tondern.
–	–	Not completed owing to advent of Type *r* ship.
Germany, E. Front	Hanover, Spich, Szentrandras, Jamboli, Schneidemühl, Jüterbog	Used over Romania and Aegean Sea; 3 attacks on Bucharest summer 1916. Total 7 offensive raids (11,934kg). Decommissioned 1917 at Schneidemühl.
N. Germany	Nordholz, Ahlhorn	Used over W. Europe and Brit. Isles (6 raids, 19,411kg). Reconnaissance over Sunderland 19/08/16; shot down by Lt W. J. Tempest (BE 2c); no survivors.
Germany	Hanover, Spich, Wittmundhaven, Königsberg	Raid on Calais 01/10/16; other proposed attacks against targets in N. France failed. Decommissioned 1917 at Königsberg.
N. Germany	Nordholz, Ahlhorn	Took part in *Geschwaderangriff* against London with 15 other airships 03/09/16. Shot down by Lt F. Sowrey 24/09/16 over London.
N. Germany, E. Prussia	Ahlhorn, Tondern, Nordholz, Seddin, Seerappen, Wainoden	First ship at Staaken (near Berlin). 4 attacks on Livonia and Riga, 13 reconnaissance missions; total 70 flights (29,090km). Withdrawn from service Dec. 1917; parts handed over to Japan, 1920.
N. Germany	Nordholz, Ahlhorn	Used over NW Europe (8 flights, 1,688km). Stranded at Mersea (Essex) following enemy action. Crew POW.
W. Germany	Jüterbog, Düren, Hanover	Took part in Boulogne raid 16/02/17 (*Spähkorb*). Decomissioned July 1917 at Darmstadt.
N. Germany	Nordholz	Total of 8 missions (6,007km), inc. 3 reconnaissance sorties over W. Europe and N. Sea. Shot down near Hartlepool by Lt I. Pyott.
N. Germany	Nordholz	36 raids; total 54 flights. Training ship from 11/12/17; 15 reconnaissance missions. Withdrawn from service 29/05/18; destroyed 1919.
N. Germany, E. Prussia	Ahlhorn, Seerappen, Jüterbog	88 flights (35,393km), inc. 13 reconnaissance and some raids. Trials ship from 26/09/17. Declared obsolete Sept. 1918 at Jüterbog.
E. Prussia	Schneidemühl, Königsberg, Seddin	Proposed for Army service but transferred to Navy 29/04/17: 7 reconnaissance missions over Baltic. Handed over to Army 07/08/17; decommissioned.
N. Germany	Nordholz	1 aborted raid, 4 reconnaissance missions. Crashed on iced-up River Aller near Rethem, damaged; later scrapped.
Germany, E. Prussia	Jüterbog, Seddin	Proposed for action in E. theatre but handed over to Navy: 15 reconnaissance sorties from Seddin, three raids on Oesel (6,000kg). Withdrawn from active service 08/10/18 and stored at Seddin. Delivered to France 08/10/20.
N. Germany, E. Prussia	Ahlhorn, Wainoden, Seerappen	Total 10 flights (4,460km) over N. Sea and Baltic. Raids on Reval and St Petersburg. Stranded at Seerappen (Kurland); decommissioned.

Production no.	Military/civil designation	Type	First flight	Where built	Decommissioned/ lost	Commander(s)
LZ 85	L 45	*r*	12/04/17	Senaken	20/10/17	*Kplt* Koelle
LZ 86	L 39	*r*	11/12/16	Friedrichshafen	07/03/17	*Kplt* Koch
LZ 87	LZ 47	*r*	01/05/17	Staaken	05/01/18	*Kplt d. R.* Wolff, *Kplt* Freudenreich
LZ 88	L 40	*r*	03/01/17	Friedrichshafen	16/06/17	*Kplt* Sommerfeldt
LZ 89	L 50	*r*	09/06/17	Staaken	20/10/17	*Kplt* Schwonder
LZ 90	LZ 120	*r*	31/01/17	Löwental	24/12/20	*Olt z. S. d. R.* Lehmann, *Kplt* Lossnitzer
LZ 91	L 42	*s*	21/02/17	Friedrichshafen	23/06/19	*Kplt* M. Dietrich
LZ 92	L 43	*s*	06/03/17	Friedrichshafen	14/06/17	*Kplt* Kraushaar
LZ 93	L 44	*t*	01/04/17	Löwental	20/10/17	*Kplt* Stabbert
LZ 94	L 46	*t*	24/04/17	Friedrichshafen	05/01/18	*Kplt* Hollender
LZ 95	L 48	*u*	22/05/17	Friedrichshafen	17/06/17	*Kplt* Eichler
LZ 96	LZ 49	*u*	13/06/17	Löwental	20/10/17	*Kplt* Gayer
LZ 97	L 51	*u*	06/07/17	Friedrichshafen	05/01/18	*Kplt* Dose
LZ 98	L 52	*u*	14/07/17	Staaken	23/06/19	*Olt z. S.* Friemel
LZ 99	L 54	*u*	13/08/17	Staaken	19/07/18	*Kplt* Bockholt, *Kplt* von Buttlar-Brandenfels
LZ 100	L 53	*v*	08/08/17	Friedrichshafen	11/08/18	*Kplt* Proelss
LZ 101	L 55	*v*	01/09/17	Löwental	20/17/17	*Kplt* Flemming
LZ 102	L 57	*w*	26/09/17	Friedrichshafen	08/10/17	*Kplt* Bockholt
LZ 103	L 56	*v*	24/09/17	Staaken	23/06/19	*Hptm.* Stelling, *Kplt* Zaeschmar
LZ 104	L 59	*w*	10/10/17	Staaken	07/04/18	*Kplt* Bockholt

Theatre(s) of operations	Base(s)	Remarks
N. Germany	Tondern	Damaged while searching for mines over N. Sea, total 27 flights (20,776km). Stranded by lack of fuel near Sisteron (France); ship destroyed, crew POW.
N. Germany,	Ahlhorn	Total 24 flights (5,057km), inc. 2 reconnaissance sorties and 1 raid on Compiègne (17/03/17). Shot down by AA fire at 3,500m; no survivors.
N. Germany	Ahlhorn	Total 44 flights, inc. 12 reconnaissance missions and 3 raids; 'Silent Raid' on Nottingham 19/10/17. Exploded and burnt out at Ahlhorn.
N. Germany	Ahlhorn, Wittmundhaven	Total 30 flights (8,093km). Attacked by British flying boats (H-12) without success. Decommissioned following bad landing at Nordholz.
N. Germany	Ahlhorn, Wittmundhaven	After 'Silent Raid', drifted at more than 5,000m and later collided with mountain near Dammartin (France), losing two gondolas with 16 crew; 4 crew in hull disappeared with ship over Mediterranean.
Germany, E. Front	Jüterbog, Kowno, Seerappen, Seddin	Failed raid on St Petersburg (bad weather). 101hr flight to prepare for Africa mission (26–31/07/17, 6,105km). 17 reconnaissance sorties (35,391km). Stored at Seerappen 08/10/17. Handed over to Italy; destroyed 1921.
N. Germany	Ahlhorn, Nordholz	First high-altitude ship with a designed structure and modified engines. Total 65 flights, 53 on active service (inc. 20 reconnaissance, 5 bombing, 12 training). Declared obsolete 09/11/18; destroyed 23/06/19 at Nordholz.
N. Germany	Nordholz, Ahlhorn	Hull of new design. Total 14 flights (10,614km) over N. Sea and Brit. Isles. Shot down by Lt. Hobbs and Lt. Dickey (H-12) over N. Sea; no survivors.
N. Germany	Nordholz, Ahlhorn	Operational over France and Brit. Isles (5 raids; further 8 reconnaissance missions). Shot down over Luneville/St Clément while returning to Ahlhorn; no survivors.
N. Germany	Ahlhorn	Action over N. Sea and Brit. Isles: 36 flights (25,887km). Problems with oxygen supply. Burnt out at Ahlhorn following gas explosion.
N. Germany	Nordholz	Modified gondolas. Total 16 flights (6,099km). Shot down by Lt. L. P. Watkins over Theberton (Suffolk); 3 survivors (POW).
N. Germany	Ahlhorn, Nordholz	Total 15 flights (1,330km). After 2 reconnaissance missions, ship captured by French at Bourbonne-les-Bains with only minor damage on return from London after fuel ran out.
N. Germany	Nordholz, Ahlhorn	Total 21 flights over W. Europe (9,324km). Damaged during test-flights at 6,800m. Destroyed at Ahlhorn following explosion.
N. Germany	Wittmundhaven, Nordholz	Used over N. Sea and Brit. Isles (over 40 flights, 30,000km, inc. 20 reconnaissance missions and one bombing raid over English Midlands). Withdrawn from service Nov. 1918; destroyed 23/06/19.
N. Germany	Tondern, Wittmundhaven	Total 52 flights with no test-flights (20,271km). Only ship to return to home base from 'Silent Raid'. Hit by bombs at Tondern from Camel aircraft from HMS *Furious*.
N. Germany	Nordholz	Total 51 recorded flights (30,928km), inc. 19 reconnaissance sorties and 4 raids (11,930kg). Shot down by Lt S. Culley near Terschelling; no survivors.
N. Germany	Nordholz, Ahlhorn	Used over N. Sea and Brit. Isles (4,800km); Skinningrove raid. Forced up to 7,600m by enemy action; stranded at Tiefenort near River Werra; decommissioned.
N. Germany	Jüterbog	Proposed for long-distance flight to Africa but only four test-flights after lengthening (by 15m). Damaged when being moved into hangar at Jüterbog and burnt out.
N. Germany	Wittmundhaven, Nordholz	Operated over Brit. Isles and N. Sea: 17 reconnaissance missions, 1 raid (2,600kg; shook off flying boat by climbing to 6,600m). Destroyed June 1919 by own personnel at Wittmundhaven.
Germany Bulgaria	Jüterbog Jamboli	Moved to Jamboli after 4 test flights; mission to Africa (21–25/11/17); 23 raids against Italian targets (24,000km). Crashed in flames into sea near Otranto (Corsica), possibly after being struck by lightning (noticed by crew of *U53*).

Production no.	Military/civil designation	Type	First flight	Where built	Decommissioned/ lost	Commander(s)
LZ 105	L 58	*v*	29/10/17	Friedrichshafen	05/01/18	*Korvkpt.* Schütze
LZ 106	L 61	*v*	12/12/17	Friedrichshafen	Dec. 1920	*Kplt* Ehrlich, *Kplt* Bodecker, *OLt d. R.* von Schiller
LZ 107	L 62	*v*	19/01/18	Löwental	10/05/18	*Hptm.* Manger
LZ 108	L 60	*v*	18/12/17	Staaken	19/07/18	*Kplt* Flemming
LZ 109	L 64	*v*	11/03/18	Staaken	21/07/20	*Korvkpt.* Schütze, *OLt z. S.* Frey
LZ 110	L 63	*v*	04/03/18	Friedrichshafen	23/06/19	*Kplt* von Freudenreich
LZ 111	L 65	*v*	17/04/18	Löwental	23/06/19	*Kplt* Dose, *OLt z. S.* Vermehren
LZ 112	L 70	*x*	01/07/18	Friedrichshafen	05/08/18	*Kplt* Lossnitzer
LZ 113	L 71	*x*	29/07/18	Friedrichshafen	01/07/20	*Kplt* M. Dietrich
LZ 114	(L 72)	*x*	09/07/20	Löwental	22/12/23	*Dr* Eckener, *Kapt.* Heinen, *Lt* de Grénédan
LZ 115–LZ 119 Not built (by order of Allies)						
LZ 120	*Bodensee*	*y* (D I)	20/08/19	Friedrichshafen	1928	*Dr* Eckener, *Kapt.* E. A. Lehmann, *Kapt.* Flemming, *Kapt.* Heinen, *Gen* Nobile
LZ 121	*Nordstern*	*y* (D II)	08/06/21	Friedrichshafen	1927	*Dr* Eckener, *Kapt.* E. A. Lehmann, *Kapt.* Ingwardsen
LZ 122–LZ 125 Not built (by order of Allies)						
LZ 126	ZR III	*z*	27/08/24	Friedrichshafen	Aug. 1940	*Dr* Eckener
LZ 127	*Graf Zeppelin*	–	18/09/28	Friedrichshafen	Apr. 1940	*Dr* Eckener, *Kapt.* E. A. Lehmann, *Kapt.* Flemming, *Kapt.* von Schiller, *Kapt.* Wittemann, *Kapt.* Pruss
LZ 128 Not built						
LZ 129	*Hindenburg*	–	04/03/36	Friedrichshafen	06/05/37	*Dr* Eckener, *Kapt.* E. A. Lehmann, *Kapt.* Pruss
LZ 130	*Graf Zeppelin* (II)	–	14/09/38	Friedrichshafen	Apr. 1940	*Dr* Eckener, *Kapt.* von Schiller, *Kapt.* Oammt
LZ 131	–	–	–	Friedrichshafen	–	–

Theatre(s) of operations	Base(s)	Remarks
N. Germany	Ahlhorn	First ship with new high-altitude engines (MB IVa). 2 reconnaissance missions only. Destroyed in explosion at Ahlhorn 05/01/18.
N. Germany	Wittmundhaven, Nordholz	Total 32 recorded flights, inc. 9 reconnaissance missions and 2 raids (4,500kg bombs). Escaped from British fighter aircraft 13/04/18 by climbing to 7,100m. Handed over to Italy Aug. 1920.
N. Germany	Nordholz	Total 19 flights (6,463km) inc. 2 reconnaissance missions and 2 raids. Destroyed by fire over Heligoland (lightning or enemy action); no survivors.
N. Germany	Tondern	Over 23 flights (about 16,000km). Took part in *Geschwaderangriff England Mitte* 13/04/18 (Hull Grimsby); further 11 reconnaissance missions over N. Sea. Destroyed in air raid.
N. Germany	Ahlhorn, Nordholz	Operated over Brit. Isles and N. Sea; total 26 flights plus some test-flights (about 18,000km), inc. 13 reconnaissance missions and 1 raid (2,800kg); air battle with 6 enemy fighters. Handed over to Britain; destroyed in storms at Fulham.
N. Germany	Ahlhorn, Nordholz	Total 39 flights: 13 test-flights, 26 missions (25,294km). 16 reconnaissance missions plus 3 raids over Brit. Isles, inc. Humber 05/08/18. Destroyed at Nordholz June 1919 to prevent being taken by Allies.
N. Germany	Nordholz	Actions over Brit. Isles, N. Sea; total 28 flights (25,158km), inc. 10 reconnaissance missions and only 1 raid (Kings Lynn 05–06/08/18). Decommissioned 15/08/18; destroyed at Nordholz 23/06/19.
N. Germany	Nordholz	Total 27 flights (27,806km) over Brit. Isles, N. Sea reported. Shot down by Maj. Cadbury and Capt. Leckie using incendiary ammunition: FdL Peter Strasser and crew killed in action.
N. Germany	Ahlhorn	Rebuilt Oct. 1918, transferred to Ahlhorn 28/10/18. Total 8 flights only. Flown to Fulham 01/07/20; decommissioned.
Germany France	Lowental Toulon	Completed after WWI; proposed for German Navy but handed over to French 10/07/20. Destroyed by fire.
Germany Italy	Friedrichshafen, Staaken Ciampino/Roma	First DELAG ship built after WWI; lengthened 10m early 1921. Total 103 commercial flights Friedrichshafen–Berlin and back (51,258km). Handed over to Italian Government 09/07/21.
Germany, France	Friedrichshafen *et al*	Proposed for commercial service Berlin–Stockholm but seized by Allies and handed over to France 13/06/21. Some flight trials. Scrapped 1927.
Germany, USA	Friedrichshafen, Staaken *et al*	Built as reparation for US; taken over by US Navy after flights over Germany and Sweden Sept. 1924. Arrived Lakehurst Oct. 1924. Total 331 flights (4,398hr). Withdrawn from service 1932, trials only thereafter.
Worldwide service		Total 590 flights (over 1,690,000km, about 34,000 passengers); 136 crossings of S. Atlantic, 7 of N. Atlantic, 1 of Pacific. Destroyed on orders of *Reichsmarshall* Göring.
Germany, USA	Frankfurt, Lakehurst *et al*	Total 63 flights Europe–S/N America (about 340,000km, 30,000 passengers, 1 car, 1 aircraft), 1 promotional tour over Germany. Caught fire during final approach at Lakehurst 06/05/37; 35 dead, 62 survivors.
Germany	Friedrichshafen, Frankfurt	Total 30 flights reported (36,550km, 409hr), mostly wireless and other trials. Rebuilt for helium autumn 1937 but no gas provided by US. Scrapped on orders of Göring Apr. 1940. Last flight 20/08/39 at Essen.
–	–	Some structural parts manufactured; work abandoned by order of German Government.

APPENDIX II: CAREER DETAILS OF SCHÜTTE-LANZ AIRSHIPS

Designation	Type	Begun	First flight	Service entry	Decommissioned/ lost	Commander(s)
SL 1	*A1*	Nov. 1909	01/10/11	17/12/12	17/01/13	*Hptm.* von Jena
SL 2	*B1*	June 1913	28/02/14	27/05/14	12/01/16	*Hptm.* von Wobeser
SL 3	*C1*	Sept. 1914	04/02/15	05/02/15	01/05/16	*Kplt* Boemarck, *Kplt* G. Wolff, *Kplt* Koch, *Kplt* von Wachter
SL 4	*C2*	30/11/14	02/05/15	11/05/15	14/12/15	*Kplt* R. Wolff
SL 5	*C3*	08/12/14	21/05/15	–	05/07/15	*Hptm.* Pochhammer
SL 6	*D1*	16/03/15	09/10/15	23/10/15	10/11/15	*Kplt* Boemarck
SL 7	*D2*	05/04/15	03/09/15	28/09/15	06/03/17	*Hptm.* Pochhammer
SL 8	*E1*	03/10/15	30/03/16	13/04/16	20/11/17	*Kplt* G. Wolff, *Kplt* von Kachter
SL 9	*E2*	Nov. 1915	09/06/16	09/06/16	30/03/17	*Kplt* R. Wolff, *Kplt* Kölle, *Kplt* Jülmke
SL 10	*E3*	15/10/15	17/05/16	16/06/16	28/07/16	*Hptm.* von Wobeser
SL 11	*E4*	10/04/16	01/08/16	12/08/16	03/09/16	*Hptm.* Schramm
SL 12	*E5*	July 1916	09/11/16	14/11/16	28/12/16	*Kplt* Kölle
SL 13	*E6*	01/06/16	29/10/16	–	08/02/17	*Hptm.* Pochhammer*
SL 14	*E7*	16/05/16	23/08/16	23/08/16	18/05/17	*Kplt* von Wachter
SL 15	*E8*	20/08/16	04/11/16	29/11/16	Aug. 1917	*Hptm.* Laquiante
SL 16	*E9*	04/09/16	18/01/17	09/02/17	Aug. 1917	*Hptm.* Härtlein
SL 17	*E10*	Nov. 1916	23/03/17	19/04/17	Aug. 1917	*OLt* Gerstenberg
SL 18	*E11*	09/12/16	–	–	–	–
SL 19	*E12*	–	–	–	–	–
SL 20	*F1*	05/11/16	10/09/17	20/10/17	05/01/18	*Kplt* G. Wolff
SL 21	*F2*	Mar. 1917	26/11/17	–	Feb. 1918	–
SL 22	*F3*	?	05/06/18	–	June 1920	–
SL 23	*G1*	?	–	–	–	–
SL 24	–	?	–	–	–	–

*Proposed.

Theatre(s) of operations	Base(s)	Remarks
Germany	Mannheim	Trials ship. Destroyed after being stranded following thunderstorm and insecure mooring by ground crew.
Germany	Liegnitz, Trier, Brussels	Higher performance than Zeppelins. Lengthened May–June 1915 at Mannheim. Stranded at Luckenwalde owing to lack of fuel.
Germany, N. Sea, Baltic	Seddin	First unofficial take-off 02/02/15. Total 30 reconnaissance missions, 1 raid. Structurally degraded by sea air, stranded near Riga.
Germany, Baltic	Seddin	Total 21 reconnaissance missions, 2 raids against enemy harbours in the East. Destroyed in hangar at Seddin when roof collapsed under weight of snow.
Germany	Darmstadt	Structure damaged during first trial; second flight 21/05/15. Stranded at Giessen by bad weather. No missions flown.
Germany, E. Front	Seddin	Total 6 reconnaissance missions. Exploded over Seddin, cause unknown; no survivors.
Germany, W. Front, E. Front, Baltic	Königsberg	3 reconnaissance missions, 3 raids. Structural defects, ship possibly lengthened. Decommissioned at Jüterbog 1917 when Army terminated airship operations.
Germany, Brit. Isles, W. Front, E. Front, Baltic	Seddin	First 38,000m^3 ship, 4 motor gondolas. 34 reconnaissance missions, 3 raids (4,000kg). Decommissioned at Seddin.
Germany, Brit. Isles, N. Sea, Baltic	Seddin	13 reconnaissance missions, 4 raids (4,230kg). Crashed into Baltic Sea (possibly set on fire by lightning).
Germany	Jamboli (from June 1916)	Unofficial first take-off 15/05/16. 16hr reconnaissance missions to Zongguldag; went missing during attack at Sevastopol (due to weather ?).
Germany, Brit. Isles	Spich	Shot down over Hertfordshire by Lt W. L. Robinson in BE 2c armed with incendiary ammunition.
Germany, Brit. Isles, N. Sea	Ahlhorn	Obsolete before completion: flew only on reconnaissance missions. Badly damaged after hitting gasometer near own hangar.
Germany	Leipzig	Used in trials only (unfit for active duty). Badly damaged by hangar collapsing under weight of snow.
Germany/E. Front	Seerappen, Wainoden	2 reconnaissance missions, 2 raids; attack on Riga terminated after engine failure. Rebuilt Feb. 1917; damaged 09/05/17 at Wainoden; scrapped 18/05/17 at Seerappen.
Germany	Mannheim	No active service. Decommissioned summer 1917 at Sandhofen (Mannheim).
Germany	Spich	No missions; not used by Army. Laid up at Spich; scrapped Aug. 1917 near Cologne.
Germany	Allenstein	No missions; not used by Army. Laid up at Allenstein; scrapped summer 1917.
Germany	Leipzig	Construction completed but ship destroyed when roof of hangar collapsed 08/02/17.
Germany	Leipzig	Not built (no hangar space available following collapse of hangar at Leipzig).
Germany/Baltic	Alhorn	2 reconnaissance missions. Burnt in hangar at Ahlhorn 05/01/18.
Germany	Zeesen	Used as a static ship after some brief flights. Decomissioned 1918 at Zeesen.
Germany	Gegen	Not accepted by Navy (poor payload). Decommissioned 1920.
Germany	–	First SL ship with tubular aluminium structure. Assembly complete at end of WWI.
Germany	–	Tubular aluminium structure. Completed after WWI.

APPENDIX III: SPECIFICATIONS OF ZEPPELIN AIRSHIPS

Production no.	Military/civil designation	Operator	Length (m)	Diameter (m)	Gas capacity (m^3)	Performance (m/sec)	Service (m)	Range (km)	Payload (tonnes)	No/type of engines (hp)
LZ 1	–	LZ	128.0	11.7	11,300	9.0	950	–	–	2 Daimler (12)
LZ 2	–	LZ	128.0	11.7	11,300	11.0	–	–	2.80	2 Daimler (85)
LZ 3	–	LZ	128.0	11.65	12,200	11.0	–	–	2.90	2 Daimler (85)
	Z I (rebuilt)	Army	136.0	11.65	–	–	–	–	–	2 Daimler (100)
LZ 4	–	LZ	136.0	13.0	15,000	13.5	–	–	4.6	2 Daimler (105)
LZ 5	Z II	Army	136.0	13.0	15,000	12.5	–	200	4.65	2 Daimler (105)
LZ 6	–	LZ	136.0	13.0	15,000	13.5	–	200	4.5	2 Daimler (125)
	– (rebuilt)	DELAG	144.0	13.0	16,000	–	–	200	4.37	2 Daimler (115) 1 Maybach (140)
LZ 7	*Deutschland*	DELAG	148.0	14.0	19,300	16.7	–	1,600	6.8	3 Daimler (120)
LZ 8	*Deutschland (Ersatz)*	DELAG	148.0	14.0	19,300	16.7	–			
LZ 9	–	DELAG	132.0	14.0	16,550	21.7	–	1,600	4.6	3 Maybach (125)
	ZII (*Ersatz*)	Army	140.0	14.0	17,800	21.0	–	1,600	6.0	3 Maybach (125)
LZ 10	*Schwaben*	DELAG	140.0	14.0	17,800	21.0	–	1,600	6.20	3 Maybach (145)
LZ 11	*Viktoria Luise*	DELAG	148.0	14.0	18,700	22.2	–	1,100	6.5	3 Maybach (170)
LZ 12	Z III	Army	140.0	14.0	17,800	21.2	–	1,600	6.2	3 Maybach (170)
LZ 13	*Hansa*	DELAG	148.0	14.0	18,700	22.2	–	1,100	6.5	3 Maybach (170)
LZ 14	L 1	Navy	158.0	14.9	22,470	21.2	–	2,800	9.5	3 Maybach (165)
LZ 15	Z I (*Ersatz*)	Army	142.0	14.9	19,500	21.8	–	2,700	7.2	3 Maybach (170)
LZ 16	Z IV	Army	142.0	14.9	19,500	21.8	–	2,700	7.2	3 Maybach (170)
LZ 17	*Sachsen*	DELAG	140.0	14.9	19,500	21.8	–	2,700	7.0	3 Maybach (170)
	Sachsen (rebuilt)	Army/ Navy	148.0	14.9	20,900	21.0	–	2,800	7.4	3 Maybach (180)
LZ 18	L 2	Navy	158.0	16.6	27,000	21.0	–	2,100	11.1	4 Maybach (180)
LZ 19	Z I (*Ersatz*)	Army	140.0	14.9	19,500	20.5	–	2,700	7.0	3 Maybach (165)
LZ 20	Z V	Army	140.0	14.9	19,500	20.5	–	2,700	7.0	3 Maybach (170)
	Z V (rebuilt)	Army	148.0	14.9	20,870	20.0	–	–	7.5	3 Maybach (180)
LZ 21	Z VI	Army	148.0	14.9	20,900	21.0	–	1,900	7.8	3 Maybach (170)
LZ 22	Z VII	Army	156.0	14.9	22,100	20.0	–	2,000	8.8	3 Maybach (180)
LZ 23	Z VIII	Army	156.0	14.9	22,100	20.0	–	2,000	8.8	3 Maybach (180)
LZ 24	L 3	Navy	158.0	14.9	22,500	22.4	2,500	2,200	9.2	3 Maybach (220)
LZ 25	Z IX	Army	158.0	14.9	22,500	22.4	2,500	2,200	9.2	3 Maybach (220)
LZ 26	Z XII	Army	161.2	16.0	25,000	22.5	–	3,300	11.2	3 Maybach (210)
LZ 27	L 4	Navy	158.0	14.9	22,500	22.5	2,500	2,200	9.0	3 Maybach (210)
LZ 28	L 5	Navy	158.0	14.9	22,500	22.5	2,500	2,500	9.5	3 Maybach (210)
LZ 29	Z X	Army	158.0	14.9	22,500	22.5	2,500	2,200	9.0	3 Maybach (210)
LZ 30	Z XI	Army	158.0	14.9	22,470	22.5	2,500	2,200	9.0	3 Maybach (210)
LZ 31	L 6	Navy	158.0	14.9	22,500	22.4	2,500	2,200	9.2	3 Maybach (210)
LZ 32	L 7	Navy	158.0	14.9	22,500	22.4	2,500	2,200	9.2	3 Maybach (210)
LZ 33	L 8	Navy	158.0	14.9	22,500	22.4	2,500	2,200	9.2	3 Maybach (210)
LZ 34	LZ 34	Army	158.0	14.9	22,470	22.4	2,500	2,200	9.2	3 Maybach (210)
LZ 35	LZ 35	Army	158.0	14.9	25,000	22.4	2,500	2,200	9.2	3 Maybach (210)
LZ 36	L 9	Navy	161.4	16.0	24,900	23.6	3,000	2,800	11.1	3 Maybach (210)
LZ 37	LZ 37	Army	158.0	14.9	22,500	22.6	2,500	2,200	9.0	3 Maybach (210)
LZ 38	LZ 38	Army	163.5	18.7	31,900	25.0	3,200	4,300	15.0	3 Maybach (210)
LZ 39	LZ 39	Army	161.4	16.0	25,000	22.0	3,200	2,800	10.0	3 Maybach (210)
LZ 40	L 10	Navy	163.5	18.7	31,900	26.7	3,200	4.300	16.2	4 Maybach (210)
LZ 41	L 11	Navy	163.5	18.7	31,900	26.7	3,200	4,300	16.2	4 Maybach (210)
LZ 42	LZ 72	Army	163.5	18.7	31,900	26.7	3,200	4,300	16.2	4 Maybach (210)
LZ 43	L 12	Navy	163.5	18.7	31,900	26.7	3,200	4,300	16.2	4 Maybach (210)
LZ 44	LZ 74	Army	163.5	18.7	31,900	26.7	3,200	4,300	16.2	4 Maybach (210)
LZ 45	L 13	Navy	163.5	18.7	31,900	26.7	3,200	4,300	16.2	4 Maybach (210)
LZ 46	L 14	Navy	163.5	18.7	31,900	26.7	3,200	4,300	16.2	4 Maybach (210)
LZ 47	LZ 77	Army	163.0	18.7	31,900	26.7	3,200	4,300	16.2	4 Maybach (215)
LZ 48	L 15	Navy	163.5	18.7	31,900	27.7	3,200	4.300	16.2	4 Maybach (240)
LZ 49	LZ 79	Army	163.0	18.7	31,900	27.0	3,200	4,300	16.2	4 Maybach (240)
LZ 50	LZ 81	Army	163.0	18.7	31,900	27.0	3,200	4,300	16.2	4 Maybach (240)
LZ 51	LZ 81	Army	163.0	18.7	31,900	27.0	3,200	4,300	16.2	4 Maybach (240)
	LZ 81 (rebuilt)	Army	178.5	18.7	35,800	26.5	–	4,900	17.9	4 Maybach (240)
LZ 52	L 18	Navy	163.5	18.7	31,900	27.0	3,200	4,300	16.2	4 Maybach (240)
LZ 53	L 17	Navy	163.5	18.7	31,900	27.0	3,200	4,300	16.2	4 Maybach (240)
LZ 54	L 19	Navy	163.5	18.7	31,900	27.0	3,200	4,300	16.2	4 Maybach (240)
LZ 55	LZ 85	Army	163.5	18.7	31,900	27.0	3,200	4,300	16.2	4 Maybach (240)

Production no.	Military/civil designation	Operator	Length (m)	Diameter (m)	Gas capacity (m^3)	Performance (m/sec)	Service (m)	Range (km)	Payload (tonnes)	No/type of engines (hp)
LZ 56	LZ 86	Army	163.5	18.7	31,900	27.0	3,200	4,300	16.2	4 Maybach (240)
	LZ 86 (rebuilt)	Army	178.5	18.7	35,800	26.5	–	4,900	17.5	4 Maybach (240)
LZ 57	LZ 87	Army	163.5	18.7	31,900	27.0	3,200	4,300	16.2	4 Maybach (240)
	LZ 87 (rebuilt)	Army	178.5	18.7	35,800	27.0	–	4,900	17.5	4 Maybach (240)
LZ 58	LZ 88	Army	163.5	18.7	31,900	27.0	3,200	4,300	16.2	4 Maybach (240)
	L 25 (rebuilt)	Navy	178.5	18.7	35,800	26.2	–	4,900	17.5	4 Maybach (240)
LZ 59	L 20	Navy	178.8	18.7	35,800	26.5	3,500	4,900	17.9	4 Maybach (240)
LZ 60	LZ 90	Army	163.5	18.7	31,900	26.5	3,200	4,300	16.2	4 Maybach (240)
	LZ 90 (rebuilt)	Army	178.8	18.7	35,800	26.5	3,500	4,900	17.5	4 Maybach (240)
LZ 61	L 21	Navy	163.5	18.7	31,900	26.5	3,200	4,300	16.2	4 Maybach (240)
	L 21 (rebuilt)	Navy	178.5	18.7	35,800	26.5	3,500	4,900	17.5	4 Maybach (240)
LZ 62	L 30	Navy	198.0	23.9	55,200	28.7	4,000	7,400	32.5	6 Maybach (240)
LZ 63	LZ 93	Army	163.5	18.7	31,900	26.5	3,200	4,300	16.0	4 Maybach (240)
	LZ 93 (rebuilt)	Army	178.8	18.7	35,800	26.5	3,500	4,300	17.5	4 Maybach (240)
LZ 64	L 22	Navy	163.5	18.7	31,900	26.5	3,200	4,300	16.2	4 Maybach (240)
	L 22 (rebuilt)	Navy	178.8	18.7	35,800	26.5	3,500	4,900	17.5	4 Maybach (240)
LZ 65	LZ 95	Army	178.5	18.7	35,800	26.5	3,500	4,900	17.9	4 Maybach (240)
LZ 66	L 23	Navy	178.5	18.7	35,800	26.5	3,500	4,900	17.9	4 Maybach (240)
LZ 67	LZ 97	Army	178.5	18.7	35,800	26.5	3,500	4,900	17.9	4 Maybach (240)
LZ 68	LZ 98	Army	178.5	18.7	35,800	26.5	3,500	4,900	18.2	4 Maybach (240)
LZ 69	L 24	Navy	178.5	18.7	35,800	26.5	3,500	4,900	17.9	4 Maybach (240)
LZ 70	L 26	Navy								
LZ 71	LZ 101	Army	178.5	18.7	35,800	26.5	3,500	4,900	18.4	4 Maybach (240)
LZ 72	L 31	Navy	198.0	23.9	55,200	27.5	4,000	7,400	30.0	6 Maybach (240)
LZ 73	LZ 103	Army	178.5	18.7	35,800	26.5	3,500	4,900	18.4	4 Maybach (240)
LZ 74	L 32	Navy	198.0	23.9	55,200	27.5	4,000	7,400	32.5	6 Maybach (240)
LZ 75	L 37	Navy	198.0	23.9	55,200	27.5	4,000	7,400	32.5	6 Maybach (240)
LZ 76	L 33	Navy	198.0	23.9	55,200	27.5	4,000	7,400	32.5	6 Maybach (240)
LZ 77	LZ 107	Army	178.5	18.7	35,800	26.5	3,500	4,900	18.4	4 Maybach (240)
LZ 78	L 34	Navy	198.0	23.9	55,200	27.5	4,000	7,400	32.5	6 Maybach (240)
LZ 79	L 41	Navy	198.0	23.9	55,200	27.5	4,000	7,400	32.5	6 Maybach (240)
LZ 80	L 35	Navy	198.0	23.5	55,200	27.5	4,000	7,400	32.5	6 Maybach (240)
LZ 81	LZ 111	Army	178.5	18.7	35,800	27.5	3,500	4,900	18.4	4 Maybach (240)
LZ 82	L 36	Navy	198.0	23.9	55,200	27.5	4,000	7,400	32.0	6 Maybach (240)
LZ 83	LZ 113	Army	198.0	23.9	55,200	28.5	4,000	7,400	32.5	6 Maybach (240)
LZ 84	L 38	Navy	198.0	23.9	55,200	28.5	4,000	7,400	32.5	6 Maybach (240)
LZ 85	L 45	Navy	198.0	23.9	55,200	28.5	4,000	7,400	32.5	6 Maybach (240)
LZ 86	L 39	Navy	198.0	23.9	55,200	28.5	4,000	7,400	32.5	6 Maybach (240)
LZ 87	L 47	Navy	198.0	23.9	55,200	28.5	4,000	7,400	32.5	6 Maybach (240)
LZ 88	L 40	Navy	198.0	23.9	55,200	28.5	4,000	7,400	32.5	6 Maybach (240)
LZ 89	L 50	Navy	198.0	23.9	55,200	28.5	4,000	7,400	32.5	6 Maybach (240)
LZ 90	LZ 120	Army/ Navy	198.0	23.9	55,200	28.5	4,000	7,400	32.5	6 Maybach (240)
LZ 91	L 42	Navy	196.5	23.9	55,500	28.7	5,500	10,400	36.4	5 Maybach (240)
LZ 92	L 43	Navy	196.5	23.9	55,500	28.7	5,500	10,400	36.4	5 Maybach (240)
LZ 93	L 44	Navy	196.5	23.9	55,800	28.9	5,500	11,500	37.8	5 Maybach (240)
LZ 94	LZ 46	Navy	196.5	23.9	55,800	28.9	5,500	11,500	37.8	5 Maybach (240)
LZ 95	L 48	Navy	196.5	23.9	56,000	29.5	5,500	12,200	39.0	5 Maybach (240)
LZ 96	L 49	Navy	196.5	23.9	56,000	29.5	5,500	12,200	39.0	5 Maybach (240)
LZ 97	L 51	Navy	196.5	23.9	56,000	28.7	6,800	12,200	39.0	5 Maybach (240)
LZ 98	L 52	Navy	196.5	23.9	56,000	28.7	5,500	12,200	39.0	5 Maybach (240)
LZ 99	L 54	Navy	196.5	23.9	56,000	28.7	5,500	12,200	39.0	5 Maybach (240)
LZ 100	L 53	Navy	196.5	23.9	56,000	31.8	6,500	13,500	40.0	5 Maybach (260)
LZ 101	L 55	Navy	196.5	23.9	56,000	31.8	6,500	13,500	40.0	5 Maybach (260)
LZ 102	L 57	Navy	211.5	23.9	62,200	36.5	7,000	12,000	43.5	5 Maybach (240)
	L 57 (rebuilt)	Navy	226.5	23.9	68,500	28.6	6,850	16,000	52.1	5 HSLu (240)
LZ 103	L 56	Navy	196.5	23.9	56,000	30.0	6,500	13,500	40.0	5 Maybach (260)
LZ 104	L 59	Navy	211.5	23.9	62,200	36.5	7,000	12,000	43.5	5 Maybach (240)
	L 59 (rebuilt)	Navy	226.5	23.9	68,500	28.6	6,850	16.000	52.1	5 Maybach (240)
LZ 105	L 58	Navy	196.5	23.9	56,000	32.0	6,500	13,500	40.0	5 MB IVa (240)
LZ 106	L 61	Navy	196.5	23.9	56,000	32.0	6,500	13,500	40.0	5 MB IVa (240)
LZ 107	L 62	Navy	196.5	23.9	56,000	32.0	6,500	13,500	40.0	5 MB IVa (240)
LZ 108	L 60	Navy	196.5	23.9	56,000	32.0	6,500	13,500	40.0	5 MB IVa (240)
LZ 109	L 64	Navy	196.5	23.9	56,000	32.0	6,500	13,500	40.0	5 MB IVa (240)

Production no.	Military/civil designation	Operator	Length (m)	Diameter (m)	Gas capacity (m^3)	Performance (m/sec)	Service (m)	Range (km)	Payload (tonnes)	No/type of engines (hp)
LZ 110	L 63	Navy	196.5	23.9	56,000	32.0	6,500	13,500	40.0	5 MB IVa (240)
LZ 111	L 65	Navy	196.5	23.9	56,000	32.0	6,500	13,500	40.0	5 MB IVa (240)
LZ 112	L 70	Navy	211.5	23.9	62,200	36.5	7,000	12,000	43.5	7 MB IVa (240)
LZ 113	L 71	Navy	211.5	23.9	62,200	36.5	7,000	12,000	43.5	7 MB IVa (260)
	L 71 (rebuilt)	Navy	226.5	23.9	68,500	–	–	–	51.0	6 Maybach (240)
LZ 114	L 72	LZ	211.5	23.9	62,200	36.5	7,000	12,000	43.5	7 MB IVa (260)
LZ 115	–	–	–	–	–	–	–	–	–	–
LZ 116	–	–	–	–	–	–	–	–	–	–
LZ 117	–	–	–	–	–	–	–	–	–	–
LZ 118	–	–	–	–	–	–	–	–	–	–
LZ 119	–	–	–	–	–	–	–	–	–	–
LZ 120	D I	DELAG	120.8	18.7	20,000	36.8	–	2,000	10.0	3 Maybach (260)
	D I (rebuilt)	DELAG	130.8	18.7	22,500	35.4	–	2,200	11.2	–
LZ 121	(D II)	DELAG	130.0	18.7	22,500	35.4	–	2,200	11.2	–
LZ 122	–	–	–	–	–	–	–	–	–	–
LZ 123	–	–	–	–	–	–	–	–	–	–
LZ 124	–	–	235.0	29.0	100,000	41.7	–	–	–	12 MB IVa (240)
LZ 125	–	–	–	–	–	–	–	–	–	–
LZ 126	ZR III	USA	200.0	27.65	70,000	34.5	–	8,400	46.0	5 MB VL I (400)
LZ 127	*Graf Zeppelin*	DZR	236.6	30.5	105,000	30.6	–	10,000	60.0	5 MB II (550)
LZ 128	–	–	–	–	–	–	–	–	–	–
LZ 129	*Hindenburg*	DZR	245.0	46.8	200,000	30.6	–	–	60.0	4 DB LOF (900)
LZ 130	*Graf Zeppelin* (II)	DZR	245.0	46.8	200,000	30.6	–	–	60.0	4 DB LOF (900)
LZ 131	–	–	–	–	223,000	–	–	–	–	–

Note: Z = Designation for early Army airships (Z I to Z XII); LZ = Designation for Army airships (LZ 34 onwards); L = Designation for Navy airships (LZ 14 onwards).

APPENDIX IV: SPECIFICATIONS OF SCHÜTTE-LANZ AIRSHIPS

Production no.	Official designation	Type	Where built	Operator	Length (m)	Diameter (m)	Gas capacity (m^3)	Performance (m/sec)	Payload (tonnes)	No/type of engines (hp)
1	SL 1	*A*	Rheinau	SL/Army	131.0	18.4	19,000	19.7	4.5	2 Daimler (250)
2	SL 2	*B*	Rheinau	Army	144.0	18.2	25,000	24.5	8.0	4 Maybach (180)
	SL 2	–	Rheinau	Army	156.0	18.2	27,500	24.8	10.4	4 Maybach (210)
3	SL 3	*C1*	Rheinau	Navy	153.1	19.75	32,390	23.5	13.2	4 Maybach (210)
4	SL 4	*C2*	Sandhofen	Navy	153.1	19.75	32,470	23.6	13.4	4 Maybach (210)
5	SL 5	*C3*	Darmstadt	Army	153.1	19.75	32,470	23.1	14.3	4 Daimler (210)
6	SL 6	*D1*	Leipzig	Navy	162.1	19.75	35,130	25.8	15.8	4 Maybach (210)
7	SL 7	*D2*	Rheinau	Army	162.1	19.75	35,130	25.8	15.6	4 Maybach (210)
8	SL 8	*E1*	Leipzig	Navy	174.0	20.1	38,780	26.9	18.7	4 Maybach (240)
9	SL 9	*E2*	Leipzig	Navy	174.0	20.1	38,780	25.8	19.8	4 Maybach (240)
10	SL 10	*E3*	Rheinau	Army	174.0	20.1	38,800	25.0	21.5	4 Maybach (240)
11	SL 11	*E4*	Leipzig	Army	174.0	20.1	38,780	25.5	21.0	4 Maybach (240)
12	SL 12	*E5*	Zeesen	Navy	174.0	20.1	38,780	24.0	21.0	4 Maybach (240)
13	SL 13	*E6*	Leipzig	Army	174.0	20.1	38,780	25.0	20.5	4 Maybach (240)
14	SL 14	*E7*	Rheinau	Navy	174.0	20.1	38,800	26.0	20.5	4 Maybach (240)
15	SL 15	*E8*	Rheinau	Army	174.0	20.1	38,780	26.5	21.5	4 Maybach (240)
16	–	*E9*	Leipzig	Army	174.0	20.1	38,800	26.5	21.5	4 Maybach (240)
17	–	*E10*	Zeesen	Army	174.0	20.1	38,780	26.5	21.5	4 Maybach (240)
18	–	*E11*	Leipzig	Army	174.0	20.1	38,800	–	21.5	4 Maybach (240)
19	–	*E12*	Leipzig	Army	174.0	20.1	38,800	–	21.5	4 Maybach (240)
20	SL 20	*F1*	Rheinau	Navy	198.3	22.96	56,000	28.5	35.5	5 Maybach (240)
21	–	*F2*	Zeesen	Army	198.3	22.96	56,350	28.5	36.0	5 Maybach (240)
22	SL 22	*F3*	Rheinau	Navy	198.3	22.96	56,350	26.5	37.5	5 Maybach (240)
23	SL 23	*G*	Zeesen	Navy	202.0	25.4	63,800	34.0	46.0	8 Maybach (280)
24	SL 24	*H*	Rheinau	Navy	232.0	25.4	78,000	32.5	59.5	8 Maybach (280)

Photograph Credits
Archiv Bekker; Berlinger Flughafenges. mbH; Sammlung Charles; Clouth AG Archiv; Archiv Dressel; Deutsches Museum; FL e.V. Archiv; Flughafen AG Frankfurt/Main; Flughafen AG Hamburg; Luftfahrtarchiv Griehl; Sammlung Lange; Lichtbildstelle Berlin; Museum für Technik und Arbeit; MTU Archiv; Sammlung Nowarra; Sammlung Prowan; Archib Radinger; Sammlung Riediger; Sammlung Schliephake; Sammlung Schreiber; Sammlung Selinger; Siemens Werksarchiv; Stadtarchiv Düsseldorf; Stadtarchiv Frankfurt/Main; Stadtarchiv Konstanz; Stadtarchiv Kronberg/Ts; Stadtarchiv Mainz; Stadtarchiv Worms; Sammlung Stapfer; Zeppelin Museum; Zeppelin Werke Archiv; Sammlung Zobel.

SELECT BIBLIOGRAPHY

Clausberg, K. *Zeppelin*. Weltbild Verlag (Munich, 1989)

Dieckerhoff, O. *Deutsche Luftschiffe 1914–1918*. Selbstverlag (Wallau, 1973).

Dominik, H. *Die Eroberung der Luft*. Union Deutsche Verlagsges (Stuttgart, 1909).

FAG Berlin, *Gelandet in Berlin*. Berliner Flughafengesellschaft (Berlin, 1985).

Bröckelmann, K. *Wir Luftschiffer*. Ullstein & Co. (Berlin & Vienna, 1909).

Botting, D. *Die Luftschiffe*. Time-Life (Amsterdam, 1982).

Burda, F. *Fünfzig Jahre Motorflug*. Burda Verlag (Offenburg, Baden, 1953).

von Eberhardt, W. *Unsere Luftstreitkräfte 1914–1918*. Verlag C. A. Weller (Berlin, 1930).

Geisenheyner, M. *E. A. Lehmann – Zeppelin-Kapitän*. Societäts-Verlag (Frankfurt, 1937).

Goote, Th. *Peter Strasser, der F.d.L.* Breidenstein Verlag (Frankfurt, 1938).

Gütschow, F. *Das Luftschiff, Geschichte-Technik-Zukunft*. Motorbuch Verlag (Stuttgart, 1985).

Gutt, P. R. *Zeppelin, Unvergängliche Dokumente*. Selbstverlag (Hamelin, 1955).

Italiaander, R. *Ein Deutscher namens Eckener*. Verlag Friedr. Stadler (Constance, 1981).

Kleinheins, P. *Die Grossen Zeppeline*. VDI-Verlag (Düsseldorf, 1985).

Knäusel, H. G. *LZ 1, der Erste Zeppelin*. Kirschbaum Verlag (Bonn, 1985).

Lehmann, E. A. *Auf Luftpatruille und Weltfahrt*. Wegweiser Verlag GmbH (Berlin, 1936).

Meyer, P. *Das Grosse Luftschiffbuch*. E. Rütten Verlag (Mönchengladbach, 1976).

Moedebeck, H. *Die Luftschiffahrt und der Neusten Entwicklung*. Verlag Mittler und Sohn (Berlin, 1887).

von Parseval, A. *Graf Zeppelin und die Deutsche Luftfahrt*. Verlagsanstalt H. Klemm AG (Berlin, 1926).

Robinson, D. H. *The Zeppelin in Combat 1912–1918*. University of Washington Press (Seattle, 1971).

von Schiller, H. *Zeppelin, Aufbruch ins 20. Jahrhundert*. Kirschbaum Verlag (Bonn, 1988).

Stoffregen-B., M. *Himmelfahrten, Die Anfänge der Aeronautik*. Physik-Verlag (Weinheim, 1983).

Wittemann, A. *Die Amerikafahrt des Z.R. III*. Amsel-Verlag (Wiesbaden, 1925).

GLOSSARY

a.D. *ausser Dienst* (= retired)
Ballontrupps Combat section which consisted of 1 balloon
Ballonzüge Unit consisting of two or three *Ballontrupps*
Bespannungsabteilung Supply unit of a *Luftschiffer-Bataillon*
DB Daimler-Benz
DELAG Deutsche Luftschiffahrts Aktien Gesellschaft
d.R. *der Reserve*
DZR Deutsche Zeppelin Reederei
EM Rebuilt Gross-Basenach airship
FdL *Führer der Liftschiffe* (= Leader of Airships)
Feld-Luftschiffer-Abteilung Operational unit consisting of two *Drachenballone*
Feld-Luftschiffer-Trupp Operational section with one *Drachenballon*
Feldluftschifferpark Ordnance establishment comprising several units
Festungs-Luftschiffer-Trupps Operational section inside a fortification
FLA *Feld-Luftschiffer-Abteilung* (q.v.)
Fliegerbataillone Units equipped with aircraft
Fw Focke-Wulf (aircraft company)
Generalkommando Supreme command unit of German Army
Gruppenkommando Command unit of *Gruppennachrichtenstellen* (q.v.)
Gruppennachrichtenstelle *Gruppenkommando* signal section of a *Luftschiffer* unit
ILA *Internationale Luftfahrtausstellung*
Koluft *Kommandeur der Luftschiffertruppe*
L Designation for Navy airships
Luftschiffer-Abteilungsstab Unit consisting of *Ballonzüge*
Luftschiffer-Bataillon Unit consisting of *Luftschiffer-Kompanien*
Luftschiffer-Kompanie Unit consisting of *Luftschiffer-Zügen* (airship platoons)
Luftschiffer-Lehrabteilung Training unit
Luftkreuzer Combat airship
LZ Luftschiff Zeppelin
M Designation for Gross-Basenach airship
Marine-Luftschiff-Abteilung Navy airship detachment
NAG Nationale Automobil Gesellschaft AG
Oberste Heeresleitung German Supreme Headquarters
P Designation for Parseval experimental airships
PL Designation for Parseval production airships
PN Designation for Parseval-Naatz airships
Schutztruppe African forces of Germany during WWI
Sh Siemens-Halske
SS Siemens-Schuckert
Stoluft *Stabsoffizier* (= staff officer) *der Luftschiffertruppe*
SL Schütte-Lanz
SMS Seiner Majestät Schiff
V Designation for Veeh airships
VDI Verein Deutscher Ingenieure e.V.
WDL Westdeutsche Luftwerbung GmbH
Z Designation for Zeppelin Army airship
z.D. *zur Disposition*
ZR Zeppelin (Reparation), e.g. ZR III
z.S. *zur See*

INDEX

Airships are indexed under their military designations (where these apply), production designations being shown in parentheses.

Ae-Ballon, 15–16, 17
Afrikaschiff, *see* L 59 (LZ104)
Arlandes, Marquis d', 8
Ausonia, *see* LZ 120 (LZ 90)

Barth, *Hptm.*, 86, 90
Basenach, *OIng.*, 39–40, 41, 43, 44
Baumgarten, Georg, 18
Berg, Carl, 23
Berlepsch, *OLt* von, 36
Beseler, *General*, 111
Böcker, *Kplt*, 114
Bockholt, *Kplt*, 99, 102
Bodensee, 116, 118–19; *see also* (LZ 120)
Brandt, Rolf, 120
Brinkmann, Otto, 136
Brivonesi, Commandant, 116
Buttlar-Brandenfels, *Kplt* von, 108–10
Charles, Prof. César, 8
Clouth, Franz, 35–7
Clouth, Richard, 36
Clouth I, 36
Colsman, *Direktor*, 69, 70

Daimler, Gottlieb, 18, 19
Degens, Jakob, 17
DELAG, 69–70, 73, 75, 79, 99, 118
Deutschland (1896), 19–21
Deutschland (LZ 7), 69
Deutschland II (LZ 8), 69–70
Dieckerhoff, *Dr*, 113
Dietrich, *Kplt* Max, 107

Dietzius, Alexander, 37
Dietzius, Hans, 37
Dixmude, see (LZ 114)
Dose, *Kplt*, 114
Drachenballon, 9–10, 11–17, 24
Dürr, *Dr* Ludwig, 63, 123

Eckener, Dr Hugo, 26, 70, 71, 93, 102, 104, 109, 110, 113, 116, 118, 123, 129, 132, 141
Ehrlich, *Kplt*, 116
Erbslöh, Oscar, 45–8
Esperia, see Bodensee

Falk, *Hptm.*, 86, 89, 97, 112
Festungs-Ballon, 10
Fliegende Muskitier, Der, 138–9
Fliegende Nippon, Der, 138–9
'Flying Balloon Train', 50–1
Frey, *OLt*, 78
Freyer, *Kplt*, 104
Fritz, *Kplt*, 105

Gaissert, *Hptm.*, 89, 91, 112
Gärtner, *Kplt* Paul, 97
George, *Hptm.*, 104
Giffard, Henry, 9
Goodyear 'L Class', 137
Göring, *Reichsmarschall* Hermann, 128, 135
Götz, *Hptm.*, 82
Graf Zeppelin, 123–8, 136, 141; *see also* (LZ 127)
Graf Zeppelin (II), 132–5, 141; *see also* (LZ 130)
Gross, *Major*, 40, 44
Gross-Basenach airships, 39–45; M I, 41, 43; M Ib, 43; M II, 30, 41, 43; M III, 43–4; M IIIb, 44; M IV, 39, 79, 96; M IVc, 44–5
Grüner, *Hptm.*, 87
Grussendorf, *Fwlt*, 99
'Güldenring', 137–8

Haas, R., 37
Hacker, *Kapt.*, 73
Hänlein, Paul, 17–18
Hanne, *Kplt*, 104
Hansa, 73, 75, 79, 105, 141; *see also* (LZ 13)
Hassl, Hugo, 48
Helmholtz, *Prof.*, 61
'Hensley', *see* (LZ 124)
Hess, Konrad, 138
Hindenburg, 76, 113, 128–32, 141; *see also* (LZ 129)
Hitler, Adolf, 135
Hoeppner, *General* von, 113
Hollender, *Kplt*, 78
Horn, *Hptm.* Alfred, 82, 85

Italia, see (LZ 106)

Jagels, Ernst, 23
Jena, *Hptm.* von, 45, 104
Jungius, Wilhelm, 8

Kaiser, Jakob, 17
K-ballon, see Ae-Ballon
'Kentucky', 136
Kiel I, 50
Kleinschmidt, *Hptm.*, 111
Kleist, *Hptm.* von, 36
Kober, Theodor, 61
Koehler, *Major* Richard von, 9–10
Kranz, Rudolf, 48
Krell, *Prof. Dr-Ing.*, 37
Koreuber, *OLt*, 91
Kugel-Ballon, 9–10

La Quiante, *Hptm.*, 112
Lanz, Karl, 51, 60
Lebaudy, 39
Lehmann, Ernst A., 73, 82, 86, 89, 97, 99, 104, 105, 110–13, 126, 130, 132
Lempertz, *Dr* Eberhard, 73
Lettow-Vorbeck, *General*, 97, 102, 113
Linnarz, *Hptm.*, 82, 86, 89
Lôme, Dupuy de, 17
Los Angeles, 119; *see also* ZR III
Lossnitzer, *Kplt* von, 97, 108, 113

Manger, *Hptm.*, 114
Martial, 8
Masius, *Hptm.*, 81, 104
Mathy, *Kplt* Heinrich, 95, 106, 107, 110
Maybach, Karl, 70
Mediterranée, 116; *see also Nordstern*
Meier, *OLt d. R.*, 34
Messing, *Oberst*, 44
Meusnier, 8, 9
Mirbach, *Hptm.*, 114
Moltke, *General* von, 26, 37
Montgolfier, Joseph, 8
Monheim Corporation, 138
Morveau, Guyton de, 8
Müller, *Steuermann*, 82

Naatz, *Dipl-Ing.*, 35
Nobile, General, 116, 126
Nordstern, 116, 118

Otto, Nicolaus August, 18
Oye, *Général* d', 8

'Pacific', *see* SL 103
'Panamerica', *see* SL 102
Parseval, *Major* von, 9, 10, 24–35, 39, 41
Parseval airships: *A Nr 1*, 25, 26; *A Nr 2*, 26; *B Nr 1*, 27; *P* type, 24, 25; PL 1, 25; PL 2, 27, 30, 43; PL 3, 27, 30; PL 4, 27; PL 6, 27–8, 30–4, 39, 96; PL 8, 30; PL 11, 28; PL 16, 30, 34, 79; PL 19, 30, 34, 96; PL 25, 30, 34–5, 39, 96; PL 26, 35; PL 27, 30, 35; PN 28, 35; PN 29, 35; PN 30, 35
Platen, *Graf* von, 105
Plessis, *Commandant* Jean du, 116
Pochhammer, *Hptm.*, 55

Pruss, Max, 129, 130, 132

Quast, *Hptm.* von, 87

R 100, 123
R 101, 123
Reuter, *Konteradmiral* von, 115
Robert, Nöel, 8
Robinson, Capt. Leefe, 55
Rozier, Pilatre de, 8
Rosendahl, Charles, 130
Ruthenberg, Hermann, 48
Ruthenberg I, 48
Ruthenberg II, 48

Sachsen, 73–5, 79, 91, 104, 110–11, 113, 140, 141
Sammt, *Kapt.* Albert, 129, 130, 132
Samoilowitch, *Prof.*, 127
Schempp-Hirth Sportflugzeugbau, 138
Scherzer, *Hptm.* Ernst, 89, 91
Schramm, *Hptm.*, 82, 86, 107
Schwaben, 70–1, 75, 104, 141
Schwarz, David, 21–3
Schütte, *Prof.* Johann, 51, 60, 136, 137
Schütte-Lanz airships, 51–60, 136–7; SL 1, 51–3; SL II (SL 2), 53–4, 79, 81, 85, 87; SL 3, 55, 96, 110; SL 4, 55, 96; SL 6, 55, 96; SL VII, 54; SL 8, 55–60, 96–7; SL IX (SL 9), 60, 96, 112–13; SL X, 54–5; SL XI, 55; SL 12, 60; SL 13, 60; SL 14, 60, 96; SL 20, 60, 96–7; SL 21, 60; SL 22, 60; SL 23, 60, 136; SL 24, 136; SL 102, 136, 137; SL 103, 136, 137
Siemens, Willi von, 37, 39
Siemens-Schuckert airships, 37–9, 40, 44; SS 1, 38–9
Sigsfeld, *Hptm.* Hans Bartsch von, 9, 10, 24
Sommerfeldt, *Hptm.*, 86
Sperling, *Major*, 39, 104
Stabbert, *Kplt.*, 78
Stahl, *Hptm.* Friedrich, 15–16
Steffen, Bruno, 50
Steffen, Franz, 50
Stelling, *Hptm.*, 34
Strasser, Peter, 60, 78, 93–4, 103, 104–8, 109, 140
Suchard, 39

Tempest, Lt W. J., 95
Tirpitz, *Grossadmiral* von, 105
'Transatlantic', 136
Tschudi, Georg von, 23

Udet, Ernst, 128

Valle, Major, 115
Veeh, *Ing.*, 49–50
Veeh I, 49
Viktoria Luise, 73, 75, 79

Walk, *Lt z. S.*, 99
Warneford, Sub-Lt R., 82, 115
Westdeutsche Luftwerburg airships, 138; WDL 1, 138–9; WDL 1a, 139; WDL 2, 138–9
Wilhelm II, *Kaiser*, 24, 27, 41, 63, 65, 106
Wittemann, Anton, 119, 130
Wobeser, *Hptm.* von, 54, 87
Wölfert, *Dr* Hermann, 18–21
Wölfert I, 19
Wrangel, *Lt* von, 86
Wüllenkemper, Theo, 138–9

Zaeschmar, *Kplt*, 97
Zeppelin, *Graf* Ferdinand von, 27, 39, 60–5, 76, 105, 109–10
Zeppelin airships: L 1 (LZ 14), 93, 94, 104; L2 (LZ 18), 93, 94, 104–5; L 3 (LZ 24), 94, 105–6, 109; L 4 (LZ 27), 104, 105–6, 109; L 5 (LZ 28), 96, 105; L 6 (LZ 31), 104, 109; L 7 (LZ 32), 106; L 9 (LZ 36), 94, 106, 110; L 11 (LZ 41), 106, 109; L 13 (LZ 45), 94, 95, 106, 114; L 14 (LZ 46), 94, 106, 114; L 15 (LZ 48), 106; L 16 (LZ 50), 106; L 22 (LZ 64), 106, 115; L 23 (LZ 66), 99, 115; L 24 (LZ 69), 94; L 25 (LZ 58), 110, 112; L 30 (LZ 62), 97, 109–10; L 31 (LZ 72), 96; L 34 (LZ 78), 96; L 35 (LZ 80), 97; L 36 (LZ 82), 97; L 37 (LZ 75), 97, 115; L 38 (LZ 84), 97, 115; L 39 (LZ 86), 89, 102; L 40 (LZ 88), 106; L 42 (LZ 91), 106; L 43 (LZ 92), 106, 115; L 44 (LZ 93), 77–8, 86, 106–7; L 45 (LZ 85), 106; L 46 (LZ 94), 78; L 48 (LZ 95), 102; L 53 (LZ 100), 108; L 54 (LZ 99), 100, 115; L 57 (LZ 102), 99; L 59 (LZ 104), 97–102, 113; L 60 (LZ 108), 115; L 61 (LZ 106), 115–16; L 63 (LZ 110), 108, 110; L 65 (LZ 111), 108; L 70 (LZ 112), 103, 108, 140–1; L 71 (LZ 113), 115
(LZ 1), 62; (LZ 2), 63; (LZ 4), 51, 63–4; (LZ 6), 65–9, 141; (LZ 7), *see Deutschland*; (LZ 8), *see Deutschland II*; (LZ 9), 70, 104; (LZ 10), *see Schwaben*; (LZ 11), *see Viktoria Luise*; (LZ 13), *see Hansa*; (LZ 17), *see Sachsen*; LZ 34 (LZ 34), 89; LZ 37 (LZ 37), 82; LZ 38 (LZ 38), 82, 113; LZ 39 (LZ 39), 82, 89, 113; LZ 74 (LZ 44), 82–5, 104; LZ 77 (LZ 47), 82, 85, 86, 113; LZ 79 (LZ 49), 82, 86, 89, 91, 113; LZ 81 (LZ 51), 86, 90, 91, 113; LZ 85 (LZ 55), 89, 91, 113; LZ 86 (LZ 56), 89, 91, 113; LZ 87 (LZ 57), 97; LZ 90 (LZ 60), 86, 112, 113, 115; LZ 95 (LZ 65), 86; LZ 97 (LZ 68), 86, 97, 112, 113; LZ 101 (LZ 71), 91, 113; LZ 107 (LZ 77), 86–7; LZ 111 (LZ 81), 97; LZ 113 (LZ 83), 97; (LZ 114), 116; (LZ 115), 119; (LZ 116), 119; (LZ 117), 119; (LZ 118), 119; (LZ 119), 119; LZ 120 (LZ 90), 115; (LZ 120), 97, 113, *see also Bodensee*; (LZ 121), *see Nordstern*; (LZ 122), 119; (LZ 123), 119; (LZ 124), 119, 137; (LZ 125), 119; (LZ 126), *see* ZR III; (LZ 127), 129, 135, *see also Graf Zeppelin*; (LZ 129), 137, *see also Hindenburg*; (LZ 130), *see Graf Zeppelin* (II); (LZ 131), 135–6
Z I (LZ 3), 63, 64–5, 76, 104; Z II (LZ 5), 30, 43, 65, 104; Z III (LZ 12), 73; Z IV (LZ 16), 79, 87, 89, 92–3; Z V (LZ 20), 81, 87; Z VI (LZ 21), 111; Z VIII (LZ 23), 81; Z IX (LZ 25), 79, 81, 115; Z X (LZ 29), 81; Z XI (LZ 30), 89; Z XII (LZ 26), 89, 91, 112, 113; ZR III (LZ 126), 119–22, 132
Zigan, *Vizefeldwebel*, 86
Zorn, Theodor, 50–1
Zorn und Hense, 50–1

FRANK M. KAUFMAN
532 Trippe Avenue
Easton, MD 21601